Starting Out!®

in Community College

Proven Strategies for Academic Success

Editor and Contributor

Dennis H. Congos, M.S.Ed.

Learning Skills Specialist
University of Central Florida

Education

Bothell, WA • Chicago, IL • Columbus, OH • New York, NY

Contributing Editor: Dennis H. Congos, M.S.Ed.

Dennis Congos received his bachelor's degree from Cleveland State University in 1972 and his master's degree from Indiana University in 1974. He has been in the learning skills field since 1978, starting and directing college learning centers and retention programs around the country. He has taught and advised students at a number of universities, and has written more than thirty articles for professional journals on college learning skills. Mr. Congos was also a Supplemental Instruction (SI) program coordinator for 20 years and was the first to take the successful retention program overseas. It is now in over 25 countries around the world. Mr. Congos has frequently presented workshops on learning skills and SI at professional conferences in the US and in England. Currently, he is a college-level learning skills specialist and academic advisor at the University of Central Florida in Orlando, FL.

Image Credits: Front Cover PunchStock; **Introduction** Manchan/Getty Images; **Part I** CORBIS; **CH01** PictureQuest; **Part II** Stockbyte/Getty Images; **CH02** The McGraw-Hill Companies; **Part III** BananaStock/PictureQuest/Jupiterimages; **CH03** CORBIS; **Part IV** Stockbyte/Getty Images; **CH04** Getty Images; **Part V** Stockbyte/PunchStock; **CH05** Getty Images; **Part VI** IT Stock Free/Alamy; **CH06** The McGraw-Hill Companies; **Part VII** Alamy; **CH07** The McGraw-Hill Companies; **Part VIII** CORBIS ; **CH08** Getty Images; **Part IX** Fancy Photography/Veer; **CH09** Getty Images; **Part X** Stockbyte/Getty Images; **CH10** SuperStock; **Part XI** CORBIS; **CH11** Getty Images; **Part XII**; Ingram Publishing/age fotostock; **CH12** Getty Images; **Part XIII** Photodisc/Getty Images; **CH13** Getty Images; **Part XIV** Ingram Publishing/SuperStock; **CH14** Getty Images; **Part XV** Photodisc Red/Getty Images; **CH15** Getty Images; **Part XVI** Comstock/PunchStock; **CH16** CORBIS; **Part XVII** Ingram Publishing/Getty Images; **CH17** The McGraw-Hill Companies; **Part XVIII** Christopher Kerrigan/The McGraw-Hill Companies; **CH18** Getty Images; **Part XIX** Veer; **CH19** The McGraw-Hill Companies; **Part XX** Glen Allison/Getty Images; **CH20 CH21** The McGraw-Hill Companies; **CH22** Getty Images; **CH23** Jupiterimages; **CH24** Mel Curtis/Getty Images; **CH25** Jupiterimages; **CH26** Stockdisc/PunchStock; **CH27** The McGraw-Hill Companies; **CH28** SuperStock; **CH29** Brand X Pictures/PunchStock; **CH30** Alamy; **CH31** Photodisc/Getty Images; **CH32** Siede Preis/Getty Images; **CH33** Comstock/PictureQuest; **CH34** Jupiterimages; **CH35** Fancy Photography/Veer; **CH36** SuperStock; **CH37** Getty Images; **CH38** The McGraw-Hill Companies; **CH39 CH40** Getty Images; **CH41** The McGraw-Hill Companies; **CH42** Photodisc/Getty Images; **CH43** Getty Images; **CH44** PunchStock; **CH45** The McGraw-Hill Companies; **CH46** CORBIS; **CH47** The McGraw-Hill Companies; **CH48** Getty Images; **CH49 CH50** The McGraw-Hill Companies; **CH51** Getty Images; **CH52** Digital Vision/Getty Images; **CH53** The McGraw-Hill Companies; **CH54** PictureQuest; **CH55** Frederick Bass/Getty Images; **CH56** Tomi/PhotoLink/Getty Images; **CH57** The McGraw-Hill Companies; **CH58 CH59 CH60 CH61** Getty Images; **CH62** SuperStock; **CH63** Brand X Pictures/Getty Images; **CH64** Stockbyte; **CH65** Artville/Getty Images; **CH66 CH67** The McGraw-Hill Companies; **CH68 CH69** Getty Images; **CH70** Alamy; **CH71** Getty Images; **CH72** CORBIS; **CH73** Getty Images; **CH74** BananaStock/Alamy; **CH75** The McGraw-Hill Companies; **CH76 CH77 CH78** Getty Images; **CH79** PunchStock; **CH80** Karl Weatherly/Getty Images; **CH81 CH82 CH83** Getty Images; **CH84** Alamy; **CH85** Getty Images; **CH86** CORBIS; **CH87** The McGraw-Hill Companies; **CH88 CH89** Jupiterimages; **CH90** The McGraw-Hill Companies

www.mheonline.com

Education

Send all inquiries to:
McGraw-Hill Education
130 East Randolph Street, Suite 400
Chicago, IL 60601

ISBN: 978-0-07-660765-5
MHID: 0-07-660765-8

Printed in the United States of America.

6 7 8 9 QFR 15 14 13 12 11

Table of Contents

Introduction

Academic success involves hard work over a long period of time, but pays significant dividends after college. Those dividends are not just monetary in nature, but represent our ability to derive the most out of our personal and social lives, solve challenging problems, form strong relationships,  and hopefully contribute to the betterment of our communities and the world at large.

The path toward academic success probably starts with the habits we build in elementary school, such as listening, reading for pleasure, following directions, asking questions, volunteering and participating, and doing homework assignments on time. As we enter high school, academic demands increase considerably, with foreign language requirements, science labs, and many new and challenging courses. Our ability to handle this increasing workload further paves the way for success in the working world.

By the time students are seriously thinking about college, they have already assembled a roster of aptitudes, interests, and accomplishments in many different areas, which may include academic performance; sports proficiency; artistic or musical talent; or possibly design, construction, or repair abilities; social, linguistic, or communication skills. Whatever one's individual interests and talents, they will expand and mature during the college years because of exciting courses, stimulating professors, new ideas, interesting and diverse new friends, and a growing awareness of the problems of the world.

This book has been prepared for college students, to enhance their chances for academic success. It combines the practical wisdom of a learning skills specialist, Dennis Congos, with the advice of dozens of other professors and advisors at more than twenty-five colleges and universities across the country.

The content is extensive, starting with the recommendations for time management and organization, concentration, and motivation. It then delves into the nuts and bolts of academic success, covering listening, note-taking, vocabulary building, reading, writing, library research, memory enhancement, and test-taking. The third section focuses on communication, social adjustment, and stress management, and the final section deals with the different aspects of planning. There are chapters on assessing aptitude and interests, choosing college majors, and thinking about future issues, such as internships and careers.

We hope you will find this book to be a useful guide to the college experience!

Part I

The Transition to College

Chapter 1

How is College Different from High School?

Student Counseling Service,
Texas A&M University, College Station, Texas

High school is a **teach-ing environment** in which you acquire facts and skills. College is a **learning environment** in which you take responsibility for thinking through and applying what you have learned. Understanding

some of the important differences between high school and college may help you achieve a smoother transition.

The following table outlines the differences between high school and college:

Following the Rules in High School	Choosing Responsibly in College
High School is *mandatory* and usually *free*.	College is *voluntary* and *expensive*.
Your time is structure by others.	You manage your own time.
You need permission to participate in extracurricular activities.	You must decide whether to participate in co-curricular activities.
You can count on parents and teachers to remind you of your responsibilities and to guide you in setting priorities.	*You* must balance your responsibilities and set priorities. You will face moral and ethical decisions you have never faced before.

Each day you proceed from one class directly to another, spending 6 hours each day—30 hours a week—in class.	You often have hours between classes; class times vary throughout the day and evening and you spend only 12 to 16 hours each week in class.
Most of your classes are arranged for you.	You arrange your own schedule in consultation with your advisor. Schedules tend to look lighter than they really are.
You are not responsible for knowing what it takes to graduate.	Graduation requirements are complex, and differ from year to year. You are expected to know those that apply to you.
Guiding principle: You will usually be told what to do and corrected if your behavior is out of line.	**Guiding principle:** You are expected to take responsibility for what you do and don't do, as well as for the consequences of your decisions.

High School Teachers	College Professors
Teachers check your completed homework.	Professors may not always check completed homework, but they will assume you can perform the same tasks on tests.
Teachers remind you of your incomplete work.	Professors may not remind you of incomplete work.
Teachers approach you if they believe you need assistance.	Professors are usually open and helpful, but most expect you to initiate contact if you need assistance.
Teachers are often available for conversation before, during, or after class.	Professors have office hours if you have questions.
Teachers present material to help you understand the material in the textbook.	Professors may not follow the textbook. Instead, to amplify the text, they may give illustrations, provide background information, or discuss research about the topic you are studying. Or they may expect you to relate the classes to the textbook readings.
Teachers often write information on the board to be copied in your notes.	Professors may lecture nonstop, expecting you to identify the important points in your notes. When professors write on the board, it may be to amplify the lecture, not to summarize it. Good notes are a must.

Teachers impart knowledge and facts, sometimes drawing direct connections and leading you through the thinking process.	Professors expect you to think about and synthesize seemingly unrelated topics.
Teachers often take time to remind you of assignments and due dates.	Professors expect you to read, save, and consult the course syllabus (outline); the syllabus spells out exactly what is expected of you, when it is due, and how you will be graded.
Teachers carefully monitor class attendance.	Professors may not formally take roll, but they are still likely to know whether or not you attended.
Guiding principle: High school is a teaching environment in which you acquire facts and skills.	**Guiding principle:** College is a learning environment in which you take responsibility for thinking through and applying what you have learned.

Going to High School Classes	Succeeding in College Classes
The school year is 36 weeks long; some classes extend over both semesters and some don't.	The academic year is divided into two separate 15-week semesters, plus a week after each semester for exams.
Classes generally have no more than 35 students.	Classes may have 100 students or more.
You may study outside class as little as 0 to 2 hours a week, and this may be mostly last-minute test preparation.	You need to study at least 2 to 3 hours outside of class for each hour in class each week. *Note: If you are taking 12 credit hours, this is 24-36 hours of study per week.*
You seldom need to read anything more than once, and sometimes listening in class is enough.	You need to review class notes and text material regularly.
You are expected to read short assignments that are then discussed, and often re-taught, in class.	You are assigned substantial amounts of reading and writing which may not be directly addressed in class.
Guiding principle: You will usually be told in class what you need to learn from assigned readings.	**Guiding principle:** It's up to you to read and understand the assigned material; lectures and assignments proceed from the assumption that you've already done so.

Tests in High School	Tests in College
Testing is frequent and covers small amounts of material.	Testing is usually infrequent and may be cumulative, covering large amounts of material. You, not the professor, need to organize the material to prepare for the test. A particular course may have only 2 or 3 tests in a semester.
Makeup tests are often available.	Makeup tests are seldom an option; if they are, you need to request them.
Teachers frequently rearrange test dates to avoid conflict with school events.	Professors in different courses usually schedule tests without regard to the demands of other courses or outside activities.
Teachers frequently conduct review sessions, pointing out the most important concepts.	Professors rarely offer review sessions, and when they do, they expect you to be an active participant, one who comes prepared with questions.
Guiding principle: Mastery is usually seen as the ability to reproduce what you were taught in the form in which it was presented to you, or to solve the kinds of problems you were shown how to solve.	**Guiding principle:** Mastery is often seen as the ability to apply what you've learned to new situations or to solve new kinds of problems.

Grades in High School	Grades in College
Grades are given for most assigned work.	Grades may not be provided for all assigned work.
Consistently good homework grades may raise your overall grade when test grades are low.	Grades on tests and major papers usually provide most of the course grade.
Extra credit projects are often available to help you raise your grade.	Extra credit projects cannot, generally speaking, be used to raise a grade in a college course.

Initial test grades, especially when they are low, may not have an adverse effect on your final grade.	Watch out for your *first* tests. These are usually "wake-up calls" to let you know what is expected—but they also may account for a substantial part of your course grade. You may be shocked when you get your grades.
You may graduate as long as you have passed all required courses with a grade of D or higher.	You may graduate only if your average in classes meets the departmental standard—typically a 2.0 or C.
Guiding principle: Effort counts. Courses are usually structured to reward a good-faith effort.	**Guiding principle:** Results count. Though good-faith effort is important in regard to the professor's willingness to help you achieve good results, it will not substitute for results in the grading process.

Chapter 2

What Does "Study" Mean in College?

Dennis H. Congos, M.S.Ed.,
University of Central Florida, Orlando, Florida

Introduction

In college, the word "study" includes many activities essential to learning and getting good grades. Unfortunately many students do not know what to do beyond re-reading and cramming when studying for college level classes.

Below is a list of important activities for college level study. Some must be done on a regular basis while others are done once or twice per semester. It is important to understand that there are many tasks that must be accomplished to do the job of learning properly in college. Here is a typical list:

☞ Organization and Initiative

» **Set up a study schedule** that includes a minimum of two hours of studying for every hour that you are in the classroom. This will vary depending on courses and majors.

» **Form study groups.** Compare notes, develop potential test questions and answers, quiz one another.

» **Complete homework on time.** Avoid falling behind.

☞ **Reading and Note-Taking**

» **Amplify or re-write lecture notes** after class.

» **Read textbook assignments** and build notes beginning from the first lecture or textbook.

» **Refine note-taking skills** to get the most out of lectures and reading assignments.

☞ **Self-Testing**

» **Quiz yourself** over and over from notes on a regular basis.

» **Self-test on a regular basis.** Discover what you know and what you don't know before you take a test—when you can still do something about it. Do not wait until you get a test back to find out what you have and have not learned. Test yourself until you have committed the material to memory. Discover how many times you have to self-test in order to recall all of the details from memory by looking only at the main idea.

☞ **Projects, Papers, and Labs**

» **Work on assigned projects** on a steady basis. Don't wait until the last-minute.

» **Develop research and writing skills** to produce successful papers and essays.

» **Attend all language and science labs**, since they represent a critical part of your final grade.

☞ **Instructors and Advisors**

» **See instructors during office hours** if you have questions.

» **Meet with a learning skills advisor** to improve study-skills.

» **Find a tutor** if you need supplemental help.

The Pyramid of Efficient Learning

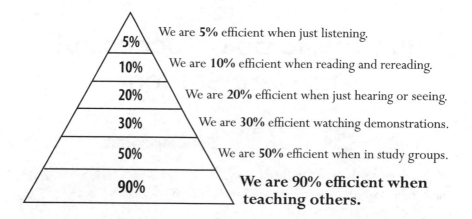

We are **5%** efficient when just listening.

We are **10%** efficient when reading and rereading.

We are **20%** efficient when just hearing or seeing.

We are **30%** efficient watching demonstrations.

We are **50%** efficient when in study groups.

We are 90% efficient when teaching others.

Chapter 3

10 Ways to be a Successful First-Year Student

Dennis H. Congos, M.S.Ed.,
University of Central Florida, Orlando, Florida

Getting a solid start in freshman year will help pave the way for a successful college career. College is a new and challenging environment, but the experiences of thousands of students have shown that you can enhance your success by following a few sensible guidelines:

☞ **1. Make your college education your #1 job.**

It takes time to do the job of learning properly at the college level. Choosing college as a high priority in your life makes it is easier to do the work necessary to succeed and graduate.

☞ **2. Learn how to organize and manage your time.**

The single toughest challenge for college students is to organize and manage the time essential for college success. A very helpful tool is a weekly calendar book where you plan out each week in terms of going to class, studying, appointments, meetings, jobs, free time, etc. Record all due dates for homework papers, projects etc. and record all quiz and test dates.

☞ **3. One of the worst places to study is where you live.**

One's residence is a poor place to study because of distractions and potential disruptions such as roommates, TVs, telephones, stereos, beds, refrigerators, pets, visitors, chores, etc. Many students have found their school's library to be a non-distractive environment for study.

☞ 4. Treat college as if it were your full-time job.

This is an easy model to follow because most college students would be working about 40 hours per week if they weren't in college. Many non-college degree jobs do not pay well and the opportunities for advancement without a college degree are limited. Investing 8 hours per day and 40 hours per week attending class and studying can bring large returns such as graduating on time and a full-time job in your major area of study.

☞ 5. Set up a team for your college success.

Write down a list of people you include on your team for your college success. Include the names of your academic advisor, instructors, teaching assistants, lab assistants, math lab staff, writing lab staff, tutor, Supplemental Instruction leader, personal counselor, learning skills advisor, career counselor, student affairs staff members, resident assistant, housing staff member, etc. Their jobs and expertise exist solely to help you succeed.

☞ 6. Adhere to important university dates and deadlines.

Contrary to popular opinion, university deadlines, policies, and procedures are in place to smooth and speed your progress to graduation. Record important dates and deadlines in your calendar book.

☞ 7. Attend class regularly and don't arrive late.

Class is where you receive at least half of the material that could be on any upcoming exam. It is quite difficult to learn from another's notes. Furthermore, repeatedly arriving late to a class communicates to instructors that you are not that concerned about class. If you give your instructor that opinion, remember it is that same instructor who must give you the grade that you earn.

☞ **8. Dare to be different.**

Up to 60 percent of college freshmen do not graduate from college in the United States Therefore, you increase your chances of **not** graduating by 60 percent if you party, date, socialize, or relax before getting the job of learning done first. Be different. Be successful.

☞ **9. Choose your friends carefully.**

A friend is someone who supports, encourages, and helps you achieve your academic and personal growth goals in college. Beware of those whose social life is out of proportion to academic efforts. Human beings tend to become like the people with whom they spend time.

☞ **10. Balance college to include academic growth and personal growth activities.**

Many students find college life boring if personal growth activities are neglected. Some of these important personal growth activities are belonging to clubs and campus organizations, attending social events, participation in residence hall or campus students government activities, attending athletic events, joining intramural sports, etc. Doing the job of going to class and studying before engaging in personal growth activities is a successful way to balance college life.

Chapter 4

What You Need to Know About Grades

Dennis H. Congos, M.S.Ed.,
University of Central Florida, Orlando, Florida

Part 1: How Learning Skills Affect Grades

Many incoming freshmen earn grades below potential because they *believe* they already have all the learning skills they need. They also believe their academic performance is due to factors outside themselves that they cannot control. Therefore, learning skills courses, workshops, books, or handouts are not utilized. Because of this belief, many learners greatly underestimate the importance of learning skills that can help achieve better grades. This group composes a large portion of the students who never graduate from college. To see how learning skills fit into the learning picture, examine the chart below:

Grade

A +

A +

A +

A +

A +

Learning Skills	Subject Matter	Outcome	Feedback on Learning Skills Effectiveness
Note-Taking, Time Mgmt., Test Prep., Self-Testing, → Memory, Test Taking, Etc.	Economics, History, Sociology, Math, → Chemistry, Biology, Etc.	Knowledge →	Grades

☞ **Notes for the chart on the previous page:**

1. The term **Learning Skills** refers to the skills that are indispensable to college-level learning.

2. The term **Subject Matter** refers to the material to be learned in college.

3. The term **Outcome** refers to the knowledge gained as a result of applying learning skills to subject matter.

4. The term **Feedback** refers to the grades that reflect how well learning skills are working.

To increase knowledge and to earn higher grades, learners must focus on refining the learning skills that are *indispensable* to acquiring the knowledge. If grades are not as desired, then learners must modify their application of skills for learning. It is *ONLY* through the development and application of learning skills that students have control over knowledge and grades.

Part 2: How to Calculate Your Grade Point Average (GPA)

In the Courses column on the next page, list the classes you completed last semester.

» Then, write the number of credit hours assigned to each class in the Credit Hours column. Then total the number of credit hours that you completed last semester at the bottom of that column.

» Assign one of the following point values to the grade you received for each course and place that point value in the Grade Point Value column:
A=4 points   B=3 points   C=2 points   D=1 point   F=0 points

» For each course, multiply the credit hours times the grade point value to get a total for the Quality Points column. Put the total at the bottom of that column.

Grade-Point Calculations:

Courses	Credit Hours	Times	Grade Point Value	Equals	Quality Points
		X		=	
		X		=	
		X		=	
		X		=	
		X		=	
		X		=	
		X		=	

Total credit hours:
Total quality points:

» *Divide the total quality points by the total credit hours completed to get your GPA.*

_____ ÷ _____ = _____

    Quality points   *Credit hours completed*   *GPA*

This chart works for semesters, quarters, or for overall GPA.

Chapter 5

Putting Your Extracurricular Skills to Use in Your Studies

 Harold W. McGraw, Jr. Center for Teaching and Learning, Princeton University, Princeton, New Jersey

Many of the skills and qualities you've developed in your extracurricular activities are useful to you as a college student. If you're facing an academic challenge and can't figure out how to tackle it, you might take a cue from your extracurricular experiences. Whether you play an instrument or a sport, perform in the theater or in an a cappella group, the skills you've learned from these activities can help you succeed in your classes too.

Develop discipline and focus

☞ **Activities:** You know the importance of getting in "the zone" and blocking out all distractions in order to perform at your best.

☞ **Academics:** You can benefit from minimizing distractions and training yourself to study when and where you are productive.

Do something every day

☞ **Activities:** Daily practice is necessary for you to perform and excel—no matter what the activity may be.

☞ **Academics:** Daily attention to each course will keep you on top of assignments and help you retain what you are learning.

Acknowledge your weaknesses and strive to improve

☞ **Activities:** Like everyone else, you achieve success by capitalizing on your strengths. But you also know that you have to work—sometimes quite hard—on overcoming your weaknesses.

☞ **Academics:** College work frequently presents challenges to students who have breezed through high school. You can meet those challenges by honestly assessing how you need to grow and working to develop new skills.

Set goals and work toward them

☞ **Activities:** You did not excel in your field by simply hoping it would happen. You did it by setting out to do it and meeting small goals in order to achieve your ambition.

☞ **Academics:** Resolving to achieve a big goal like "I want to do better in organic chemistry" isn't nearly as effective as setting out smaller, achievable goals like "I'm going to review my notes every day" or "I'll go every Tuesday to the chemistry study group."

Learn from a mentor

☞ **Activities:** All performers benefit from the guidance, support, experience, and rigor that coaches and teachers provide.

☞ **Academics:** Mentors are everywhere: faculty, graduate students, and even fellow students. Make connections with people and not just grades.

Part II

Time Management & Organization

Chapter 6

Effective Time Management

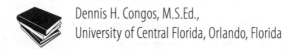

Dennis H. Congos, M.S.Ed.,
University of Central Florida, Orlando, Florida

16 Traits of Effective Time Managers

Many students initially struggle with keeping a schedule, but anyone can become an effective time manager. Just use the following suggestions:

☞ **1. Break projects into steps,** each with a measurable result.

☞ **2. Generate manageable due dates** for the achievement of these steps and schedule specific times to complete each step to meet these due dates.

☞ **3. Use due dates to monitor progress** toward the completion of steps in your project.

☞ **4. Write down daily tasks** and cross them off as they are accomplished.

☞ **5. Use a calendar book** to record appointments and intended dates for completion of tasks.

☞ **6. Have daily objectives** to move them toward the completion of multiple tasks.

☞ **7. Continually review long-term goals** so the sight of long range objectives is not lost.

☞ **8. Begin projects early** to give yourself time and freedom to brainstorm the best ways to accomplish your tasks. Begin early on assignments to create the opportunities to gather information, think over the material, and collaborate with others for assistance and suggestions.

☞ **9. Be honest about how plans are going.** Don't hesitate to modify plans to achieve better results.

☞ **10. Seek advice from others.** Seek and accept input from anyone in a position to assist you or offer helpful information. Review suggested materials, converse and correspond with expert campus sources, and consider their ideas as you plan a course of action.

☞ **11. Use campus resources** and don't try to go it alone.

☞ **12. Inform people involved**, as much in advance as possible, about any role these people may play. This allows time for others to plan ahead as well.

☞ **13. Remain flexible and prepare for the unexpected**. Successful people have plans B and C.

☞ **14. Try to anticipate obstacles** but be ready to adapt plans in cases of the unexpected.

☞ **15. Remain committed in the face of adversity** by considering other avenues of approach when encountering barriers. Effective time managers find ways to be successful.

☞ **16. Realize that a polite "no" is sometimes a proper response.** An effective time manager has the ability to say, "I will get back to you on that. I want to think about it overnight" or "No, I cannot do that now" if the request is disruptive to task completion and progress toward goals.

Part 2: The 8-Hour Day College Time Management Schedule

One of the most important study skills in college is time management. Many students earn grades below potential or flunk out of college because of poor time management skills. One model for organizing time in college centers around the 8-hour workday.

Without a college degree, you will most likely be working at an entry-level job at pay scales near minimum wage. In any case, you will be working 8 hours per day and 40 hours per week if you are not in college. After 4 or 5 years of working in low-skill jobs, where will you be? At what wage level?

The 8-hour per day model for managing time in college has you in class or studying for 8 hours per day. These are the same 8 hours you would be putting in each day if you weren't in college, only in this case, you are self-employed and working toward your personal academic goals.

Most students are in class 2 to 3 hours per day (not counting labs). This leaves 5 to 6 hours per day for studying—reading textbooks, taking notes, revising notes, building and practicing solutions to problems, and reciting and self-testing on existing notes. Students who spend 5 to 6 hours per day studying usually do quite well in college.

Using the chart on the next page, set up an 8-hour per day model for managing your time in college. Remember that only time in class and studying count toward the 8 hours. The steps are:

» *Cross off meal times*

» *Cross off work or activities times*

» *The total should be 8 hours/day and 40 hours/week on the job as a student.*

» *The rest is your free time, to relax and work on personal growth activities.*

Set up your personal 8-hour per day schedule for doing your job as a student on the next page. Use a pencil or erasable ink to allow for changes later.

TIMES	Monday	Tuesday	Wednesday	Thursday	Friday
7:00-7:30 a.m.					
7:30-8:00					
8:00-8:30					
8:30-9:00					
9:00-9:30					
9:30-10:00					
10:00-10:30					
10:30-11:00					
11:00-11:30					
11:30-12:00					
12:00-12:30					
12:30-1:00					
1:00-1:30					
1:30-2:00					
2:00-2:30					
2:30-3:00					
3:00-3:30					
3:30-4:00					
4:00-4:30					
4:30-5:00					
5:00-5:30					
5:30-6:00					
6:00-6:30					

	Monday	Tuesday	Wednesday	Thursday	Friday	Total/ week
Hours in Class						
Hours Studying						
Total Hours as a Student						

Chapter 7

List Your Way to Success

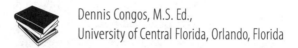

Dennis Congos, M.S. Ed.,
University of Central Florida, Orlando, Florida

Researchers who study the characteristics of successful people have found that well-developed organizational skills are a common characteristic. Successful people keep track of what needs to be done on the way to success. Consider using one of the following techniques for **listing your way to success.**

☞ **Daily To-Do List:** This type of list entails writing down what you need to do day-by-day. For example, you may use a notecard for recording your "to do's, then check off each item as you complete it. This process allows you to see your progress and feel a sense of accomplishment each day.

MONDAY	TUESDAY
1. Ch. 6 Calculus	1. Study Psych. quiz
2. Pgs. 235-276 History	2. Pgs. 276-298 History
3. Wash clothes	3. Chem. Lab, 2 p.m.
4. Appointment w/ Dr. Smith	4. Calc. homework due
5. Work 1 hour on Chem. research paper	5. Begin English essay
6. Date 7 p.m.: Jim	6. Work 1 hr. on Chem. research paper
	7. Basketball 8 p.m.

☞ **Priority List:** This type of list involves recording what needs to be done in order of importance or by due dates. The most important or "first due" item is listed at the top and moves down in rank to the lesser-important items.

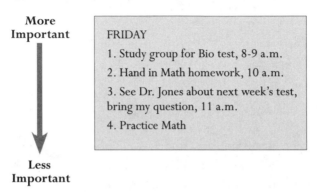

More
Important

FRIDAY

1. Study group for Bio test, 8-9 a.m.

2. Hand in Math homework, 10 a.m.

3. See Dr. Jones about next week's test, bring my question, 11 a.m.

4. Practice Math

Less
Important

Another version of a priority list includes what must be done today, what must be done by a certain date, and upcoming due dates. These tasks could also be listed in order of importance or by deadline.

Must do today	Must be done by ____	Upcoming due dates

☞ **Chronological List:** This third type of list uses time to indicate which tasks need to be completed before others. This list can be kept on notebook paper but is most effective when using a calendar book available at campus bookstores and office supply stores.

> THURSDAY
>
> 1. Study group for Bio test
> 2. Hand in Math homework
> 3. See Dr. Jones about next week's test
> 4. Practice Math problems
> 5. Go over notecards for Bio
> 6. Bio class
> 7. Chem. Lab
> 8. 1 hour for History research paper
> 9. Dinner w/ Photography club

☞ **Assignment List:** Here, assignments are recorded just as you would record tasks on a real job after college. You may prefer to record assignments and due dates for a whole week instead of one day at a time.

> TUESDAY
>
> 1. Read Math pgs. 67-78
> 2. Hand in Soc. paper
> 3. History quiz
>
> WEDNESDAY
>
> 1. English paper due
> 2. Read Soc. chapter 4
> 3. Bio homework due
> 4. Review Math, chapter 7
> 5. Review Soc., chapter 5

☞ **Weekly Calendar Book:** One of the most effective, easy to use, and popular methods of tracking and completing college tasks involves the use of a weekly calendar book. These are available at most college bookstores and office supply stores. When open, a whole week is displayed before you. This way it is easier to see what is coming up a day or more ahead.

Below is an example of one college student's calendar book filled in.

Monday Feb 2, 2010	Tuesday Feb 3, 2010	Wednesday Feb 4, 2010
8a Chem Class	*8a* Study Math	*8a* Chem class
9a Redo Chem notes	*9a* " "	*9a* Redo Chem notes
10a English class	*10a* Wash clothes	*10a* English class
11a Read Literature	*11a* Bio class	*11a* Read Literature
Noon Lunch	*Noon* " "	*Noon* Lunch
1p Photo club	*1p* Lunch	*1p* Review Chem
2p Review Chem	*2p* Review Math	*2p* " "
3p " "	*3p* " "	*3p* Read Lit. notes
4p Read Lit. notes	*4p* Bio class	*4p* Work Study
5p Supper	*5p* " "	*5p* " "
6p Relax	*6p* Supper	*6p* Supper
7p Review Bio notes	*7p* Relax	*7p* Relax
8p Relax	*8p* Review Chem notes	*8p* Review Math notes
9p " "	*9p* Relax	*9p* Relax
10p " "	*10p* " "	*10p* " "
11p To Bed	*11p* To Bed	*11p* To Bed
12a	*12a*	*12a*
To Do	**To Do**	**To Do**
Oil & Lube car	Clean the room	Take the dog to the Vet
Form study group in Bio	Molly's Birthday	E-mail to Tommy
Drop off photos	Pick up photos	
Call Mom about tuition		

Myths About Lists and Schedules

Time schedules restrict you.
Ridiculous! How can something restrict you that you control 100 percent?

I can't do what I need to do if I schedule everything.
Absurd! You decide what to include in your schedules and lists. A schedule contains only what you put there. It is a tool for keeping track of what you need to do instead of leaving important tasks to memory, mood, or chance. Schedules are tools that increase chances for success.

I don't like to schedule my life.
Silly! You can choose to schedule your life every day or leave it to chance. Which way will help you reach your goals quicker? A list only helps you keep better track of what needs to be done, helps you get it done, and moves you toward your goals much faster and more successfully.

Chapter 8

Ten Steps to Organization at College

Reprinted with permission from The University of Kansas
Counseling and Psychological Services (CAPS)

Organization: Putting First Things First

Time pressure is a major source of stress for many people. Organization doesn't make more hours in the day, but it can reduce time pressure by making it easier to get done what needs to be done and freeing up time for other things. In addition, chances are good you'll feel better as you accomplish things and increase your sense of personal control. Listed below are some tips to improve your organizational skills:

1. **Start by uncluttering your work area.** Clear your work surface of files, books, and loose papers since they can distract you from what needs to be done. Staying tidy takes a fraction of the time you will waste if distracted.

2. **Allow enough desk space** to work comfortably on one assignment or project at a time without distractions.

3. **Use one calendar** to track all important reminders, notes, tasks, tests, assignments, and even social events. An effective tracking system can help reduce the stress of trying not to forget, and also the stress of dealing with the consequences of not getting something done.

4. **Create a master list on paper or a computer file** that prioritizes

and updates every pending assignment or project; use whatever method holds your attention.

5. **Avoid interruptions that can rob you of time and momentum.** When a project or assignment requires special attention, escape to a quiet area to work more effectively.

6. **Delegate tasks when you can**, since trying to do everything can be overwhelming.

7. **Think before you keep a piece of paper** since most of what you keep for later use won't be needed again. The "OHIO Rule" reduces clutter and makes organization easier. "Only Handle It Once"

8. **Stop collecting so much stuff**—the more you have, the more time you need to manage it. If it hasn't been used in a reasonable period of time, get rid of it.

9. **Know your personal limits** and say "no" when you need to.

10. **Take a few minutes at the end of each day** to clear your work area and plan for the next day. Planning what really must get done—and how and when to do it—can help you know how to spend your time and energy, as well as minimize anxiety about deadlines.

Keep in Mind...

☞ Review your schedule at the start of each week to make sure you have allocated enough time to do what needs to be done that week.

☞ List what you need to do each day, balancing work and fun.

☞ Allocate time for each subject. Cramming is stressful and usually produces poorer performance and results.

☞ Break large tasks into small steps, scheduling each step into your planner. This strategy makes those difficult tasks less overwhelming.

☞ Prioritize your tasks by what is most important to do. Rank tasks from "necessary to do" to "can wait until later."

☞ Schedule in breaks so you don't burn out or work inefficiently because you are too fatigued to do your best.

☞ Use time between classes to study so your evenings will be free for fun.

☞ Spread your work out, doing a little each day. You'll get more accomplished as well as avoiding last-minute crunches.

☞ Avoid time-wasters during your work time. (You know what yours are—we all have them.)

☞ Procrastination usually takes more energy in the long run than just doing the task.

☞ Recognize your limits. There are only 24 hours in a day and we cannot do everything, so pick what matters most and spend your time doing it.

☞ Remember your life goals. They can provide motivation and can help prioritize.

☞ Reward yourself for accomplishments (buy yourself something, catch a movie, tell a friend who will pat you on your back).

Other Tips

☞ Don't wait until you are "in the mood." There is no perfect time, so stop waiting for it.

☞ Be realistic and don't aim for perfection. Write down the basic information needed for the task. Plan to revise and fine-tune it later.

☞ Schedule regular down time for recreation, exercise, and socializing with friends.

☞ Keep reminding yourself that you CAN do it! You've done it before successfully and you can again. Think of strategies that have worked before when you were successful and use them again.

☞ Eat healthy foods and get enough sleep. Most adults function best on 7–8 hours of sleep nightly. Getting less than 6.5 hours nightly impairs your memory and ability to concentrate.

☞ If an assignment doesn't seem relevant to you, remember your life goals. They can provide motivation and help us prioritize.

Pay continual attention to your balance of work and fun; doing so will pay off substantially in the long run.

Part III

Concentration and Motivation

Chapter 9

Combating Distraction and Building Concentration

Dennis H. Congos, M.S.Ed.,
University of Central Florida, Orlando, Florida

Learning to concentrate and tackle a task in an efficient way is a skill that can be learned. Students usually have a very busy schedule of activities, so it is especially important to learn some useful techniques to improve personal focus. Make your study time as productive as possible.

Part 1: Causes of Distraction and How to Fight Them

There are many kinds of distraction that cause us to lose focus and stop concentrating. Use the following table to help you discover what is distracting you, and how you can control the distraction to get back on track and concentrate.

Internal Causes of Poor Concentration	What You Can Do to Control Them
Hunger	• Eat fruit or high-protein snacks and regular, balanced meals.
Drowsiness	• Plan to study when you are most alert. • Get adequate nighttime sleep. • Do five minutes of light exercise to wake up.

Boredom, dislike, or disinterest in a class	• Identify something you like about the subject. • Join a study group. • Ask instructors for other recommended reading on the topic.
Anxiety about a class	• Talk with students/instructors about the class. • Make sure you know how to study effectively. • Make sure anxiety about your studies is not something personal. See a counselor. • Learn the material well.
Intimidating assignments	• Break up large assignments into smaller pieces and do a little each day. • Do the most difficult part first. • Give yourself rewards for progress. • Work with one or more other students.
Personal worries	• Identify the problem and tell yourself mentally that you will set aside time, when finished with studying, to develop a concrete, specific plan to resolve it. • Talk with someone who can help: a friend, relative, or a college counselor.
Daydreaming	• When your mind wanders, write down the interrupting thought and go back to studying. • Deliberately stop trying to study and intentionally daydream. When you're ready to read again, do so. Don't try to read and daydream at the same time.

External Causes of Poor Concentration	What You Can Do to Control Them
• TV in background • Overly comfortable chairs • Food nearby • Friends and family • Computer or video games • Pets • Cell phone	• Leave or rearrange a distracting environment. • Go to the library or an empty classroom when you seriously intend to study. • Train yourself to study away from others and to study in silence.

Part 2: Nine Tips to Improve Concentration

Here are some suggestions to improve your focus and concentration.

1. **Intend to Concentrate**
   Humans tend to do what they tell themselves to do. Therefore, it's easier to concentrate if you set a specific length of time to study and consciously tell yourself that "I will concentrate" for that length of time.

2. **Prepare to Concentrate**
   Have everything you will need before you begin to study: pencils, pens, paper, notes, textbooks, reference books, etc.

3. **Vary Your Study Activities**
   If your study style is not to focus on one subject for long periods of time, then vary what you do. Read and take notes for awhile, formulate questions and answers for a time, recite and review to break the monotony. Another example is to do math problems for awhile, then read about another subject, rewrite and organize lecture notes, and then go back to math.

4. **Find a Non-Distracting Study Environment**
   Study in the same place and use that place only for studying. Remove potential sources of visual and auditory distractions or remove yourself to a less distracting study environment.

5. **Set Up a Specific System for Studying and Learning**
   An effective step-by-step plan for studying and learning makes concentration easier. For example, take ideas, facts, or concepts and place them on one side of a notecard. On the other side, formulate a question that requires recalling all of the details. Use the cards to practice answering the questions from memory. Go back to these study aids on a regular basis so that you master the material and can handle it on a test.

6. **Eat Regular and Well-Balanced Meals**
   Research shows that those with healthy diets earn higher grades. Avoid quick uppers such as sugary snacks and drinks because quickly rising and falling blood sugar levels negatively affect concentration. Oily and high fat foods cause sluggishness and drowsiness. Snack on fresh fruits and vegetables.

7. **Get Plenty of Nighttime Sleep**
   Sleepiness lowers concentration. College students need 7 to 9 hours of nighttime sleep to maximize learning.

8. **Set Daily, Weekly, Monthly, and Semester Academic Goals**
   It is easier to concentrate and feel motivation when you have goals and can see yourself progressing towards those goals. Make a list of what you have to study and learn, and check off items as you master them. Plan ahead for more than just the day. Look at the entire week's assignments and set aside enough time to get everything done.

9. **Take Regular Study Breaks**
   It is normal for concentration time to vary individually from five minutes on up. Judge your own attention span and divide your work into small units of time, interspersed with short breaks to refresh yourself. Take a short five-minute break when concentration becomes difficult.

Chapter 10

Improving Motivation

Dennis H. Congos, M.S.Ed.,
University of Central Florida, Orlando, Florida

When Motivation is a Problem

To be a successful student you need to set concrete and realistic educational goals and then apply the necessary energy and commitment to realize those goals. Motivation is the force that will move you along your college path. Although other people may try to motivate you to perform, it is your internal drive that will ultimately determine your level of success.

☞ **Who you are is more valuable than what you do.**
Your worth as a person is not based only on your intelligence, your grades, or how hard you work. It is the summation of all your personal attributes.

☞ **Practice impulse control by contemplating the consequences of your actions.**
How will you feel afterwards? Is this what you really want to do?

☞ **Write out a plan for yourself.**
Jot down personal and academic goals and priorities, and reread them when you're in a slump. Try to keep the big picture in mind.

☞ **Don't worry about or dwell on things that go wrong.**
Concentrate on your successes. Remember that little successes build up just as quickly as little failures.

☞ **Give yourself time to change.**
Forgive yourself for backsliding and making mistakes. Mistakes are a normal part of the learning process. Without them, learning is difficult to impossible. Most mistakes are mislabeled when they are really good attempts that didn't work.

☞ **Don't choose to be a perfectionist.**
Make approaching and the process of achieving your goals the basis of your self-respect, rather than reaching your goals.

☞ **Don't allow feelings of inadequacy to get you down.**
Think about all the things you have going for you. Choose to believe in yourself.

☞ **Imagine the worst that could happen if you're feeling down or hopeless.**
Exaggerate your fantasies and then smile at them. This puts your current situation in perspective.

☞ **When you're down, go to someone whom you know cares for you and ask for a "pep talk"** that reminds you of your good qualities, talents, and abilities.

☞ **Be willing to risk failure for something you really care about.**
If you are willing to risk failure, you are also willing to risk success!

☞ **Learn to recognize when events are not turning out as you expect and act early to redirect your efforts to achieve satisfaction.**

☞ **No one else is forcing you to do your work.**
You've decided to take it on. Don't waste your energy on activities that don't move you toward your goals. Periodic rest and relaxation are also important goals.

☞ **Start early.**
The sooner you start, the more time you'll have to learn from non-

productive attempts and the sooner you'll be free to do other activities.

☞ **Expect a degree of tension.**
Use that tension as energy to motivate yourself.

☞ **Different people have different styles of working.**
For example, some people need competition to do their best, while others work better independently.

☞ **Make long and harder tasks as comfortable for yourself as possible.**
One way is to do them in short bits (but stay with it), do them in comfortable clothes, among friends, in familiar surroundings, with whatever you need to keep moving forward.

☞ **Pause every now and then, as needed, to remind yourself why you have chosen to take on certain work and what you expect to get out of it.**
Give yourself a pep talk.

☞ **Reward yourself with a treat when you've done something you feel good about.**
You did it so you deserve the rewards.

☞ **Completed tasks keep interest and motivation higher.** If a large task is not completed, be sure to complete one or more small tasks before you quit for the day.

☞ **Pure motivation is rare.**
Most of the time we mortals must keep plugging away before we can enjoy success. Sometimes the plugging can even be enjoyable.

Chapter 11

Procrastination and How to Beat It

Dennis H. Congos, M.S.Ed.,
University of Central Florida, Orlando, Florida

Many students suffer needlessly from procrastination. As a result, these students learn and earn grades far below their potential. Staying on track with necessary tasks will make it easier to earn a degree, find a job, or gain acceptance to graduate or professional school.

Ways to Overcome Procrastination

☞ **Log Your "Procrastinatables"**

Keep a log for one week, jotting down whatever it is you put off. After one week of **logging "procrastinatables,"** you may begin to see certain patterns about what kinds of tasks you put off. You may see that you regularly avoid certain kinds of work or certain types of situations. Maybe you will notice that "putting off" has to do with particular people, teaching styles, environments, moods, or attitudes. Finding the reasons for procrastination will help you tackle this problem.

☞ **Look for Common Delaying Tactics**

If you choose to create a log, you may want to look for **common "delaying tactics."** Many procrastinators discover an "inner voice" telling them what to do just before something is put off. This inner voice, called "self-talk," is normal and exists in all of us. Try to listen consciously for negative or delaying self-talk when you find yourself putting off a task.

We may also find ourselves using delaying tactics due to our hesitation to start something new or tackle a large or intimidating task.

☞ Positive Self-Talk

If you find yourself repeatedly using delaying or negative self-talk, you might want to experiment to see what happens to you if you consciously employ **positive self-talk** that says the opposite of your habitual self-talk.

Some ex-procrastinators jot down positive self-talk phrases on note-cards that they carry with them. If you feel this may be a good idea, you might use notecards for reminders of what to say to yourself when facing commonly put-off tasks.

Some examples of positive self-talk that you could put on a notecard are:

» *I will do it now.*

» *I may not want to do it, but I will for half an hour.*

» *I'd rather swim, but it won't help me graduate so I will study first.*

» *I'll feel better when it's done, so I'll do it at 2 p.m.*

» *I'll do this for one hour and then go out.*

» *I'm a good student and good students do this, so I will do it now.*

» *I may hate this, but I will finish it before I watch TV.*

» *I haven't liked this in the past, but maybe I can learn to like it.*

» *I haven't done well on this in the past, but I can learn to do it well.*

You may come to agree that most positive self-talk involves saying the opposite of what you used to tell yourself just before you procrastinated.

☞ Break Down a Job Into Parts

Just as most people can't eat a whole cake in one bite, some jobs cannot be done all at once. Some people come to realize that it is harder to put something off if they slice a job up into manageable pieces and **do the task piece by piece**, little by little. This process might mean breaking down the time into smaller chunks to do a task that is spaced over several days or weeks. Some people don't like large doses of something distasteful. They find that smaller doses spaced over time makes things easier to do and less subject to procrastination.

☞ Begin With the Easiest Piece

Another way some people have reduced procrastination is to begin with **an easy, enjoyable, or the least distasteful piece** of a job to get started.

☞ Work with Someone Else

Many ex-procrastinators have realized that **working with someone else** makes it less likely that they will put something off. Perhaps this would work for you.

☞ Set a Deadline

It could be that you will come to realize that making a commitment to someone or **setting a deadline** for completing a task is one way to make procrastination more difficult. It is known that for many people, setting a goal within a time frame results in motivation. For this to work, ex-procrastinators have found that the goal must be something they want to achieve.

☞ Find a Quiet Workplace

Maybe you will discover that doing a job in the **least distracting environment** makes putting off work more difficult. For many college students, homes, dorm rooms, or apartments have many actual and potential distractions. Try finding a place like the library to study where it is quiet and is going to stay quiet until you are ready to leave.

☞ Reward Yourself

Many people find that having a reward system helps them start and complete tasks they would normally put off. Choose a self-reward system that makes sense to you and helps increase your motivation.

Major characteristics of a self-rewarding system:

» *Rewards need not be "big" as long as they are rewarding to you.*

» *The rewards must be immediate after performing the desired activity.*

» *The amount of work needed to get rewards should be small in the beginning, but may increase as progress is made.*

» *It is important that rewards only be earned IF you do the required work. If you cheat on the system, you are less likely to obtain your goal.*

» *You are the one in charge. If your system begins to break down, it is the result of your choices. Make adjustments accordingly.*

Don't Be Too Critical of Yourself

Sometimes people are unaware of a degree of self-criticism or self-anger which is a common cause of procrastination. Through no fault of their own, procrastinators in this escapable trap lapse into a cycle of negative critical thinking, feeling, and behaving that promotes procrastination. Examine the cycle below and on the following page to see if any part of it reflects your thinking. If so, you may choose to enlist the help of a college counselor to eliminate this possible cause of your procrastination.

When some people procrastinate, they become critical of themselves and that causes them to become angry with themselves. This leads to low self-esteem and discouragement. The self-talk language may go something like this:

Part 1:   "I'll do that later."

Part 2:   "Now it's too late and I screwed up again!" "Why do I do this? It makes me so angry when I get into this situation."

Part 3:   "I just don't have what it takes to succeed, I guess."

Part 4:   "Maybe I'll quit."

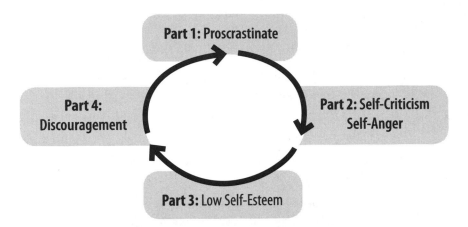

The sinister part of this cycle is that you may inadvertently enter into it at any point and continue circling not realizing what is happening. To exit this cycle, many ex-procrastinators have chosen to practice one or more of the possible solutions listed in this chapter.

Conclusion

By using some of these solutions to procrastination, you may realize that you are not stuck with your present degree of procrastination, if you don't want to be. You may also begin to realize as others have, that you are not powerless to modify and eventually control this behavior. You may even find that reading this chapter several times could possibly give you more ideas to try in order to reduce your procrastinating behavior. You may come to believe, as many ex-procrastinators have, that you may choose to control and even eliminate procrastination by making habits out of one or more of the suggestions listed in this chapter, when you are ready.

Part IV

Classes and Lectures

Chapter 12

The Importance of Attending Classes and Lectures

Starting Out!® Research Group

There are students who sleep late and miss classes and then use the lecture notes of other more conscientious students to catch up. They find many excuses for not attending early morning classes, and then rationalize that it doesn't really matter as long as they read the textbook or reserve readings. Such practices are a big mistake for many reasons as this article will explain.

Much more can and often does happen in a class or lecture than a review of a textbook chapter, since a face-to-face session between instructors and students is a far better and more dynamic way to learn than simply memorizing facts and dates in a book.

Instructors and professors put serious time into the preparation of their student sessions, often employing different teaching techniques and coloring their presentations with personal experiences, useful contextual material, and personal research and knowledge that is not available in a textbook. These techniques may include any of the following:

1. PowerPoint presentations which boil concepts down into smaller units

2. Visual material, such as charts, graphs, and illustrations that make the subject come alive.

3. Videos that enhance the learning process

4. Question-and-answer sessions to focus on the topics that students are finding difficult to understand

5. Field trips to gain first-hand views of subjects

6. Guest speakers and experts whose knowledge adds new points of views and perspectives

7. Lively class discussions that can affect a student's grade by showcasing knowledge he or she has gained

Each of us learns in different ways. Some people need visual reinforcement of information, which can be provided with visual aids and videos, while others need to ask pointed questions to clarify material and hear others talk about the topic so they absorb the concepts.

If you are solely relying upon readings and notes, you lose all the benefits of the instructor's personal knowledge and teaching methods, and you especially lose the opportunity to place new material in an understandable context.

One of the most practical and compelling reasons to attend class is to have a sense of what the instructor is likely to include on an exam, and what he or she thinks are the most important points to learn about the topic. If you're absent, you lose this automatic advantage that other students will have if they attend class.

Common Reasons for Missing Class

Here are some of the most frequent reasons given for missing class and ways to avoid them.

Excuse	What You Can Do to Address It
I was too tired to get up, or I had to finish another assignment.	Organizing your time and getting enough sleep are basic requirements for being a successful student. Don't look for excuses to avoid learning. Learning is why you're in college.
I had a direct conflict with an away game that I could not miss.	This is understandable. Direct conflicts that involve other college commitments cannot be entirely avoided. Try to schedule classes so they don't interfere with athletic practices or games or other commitments you make ahead of time.
I didn't finish the reading or preparation for the class.	This is one of the worst reasons for not attending class, because you lose the opportunity to learn from the class or lecture even if you are not well-prepared. It is your responsibility to be prepared, but if you just could not finish the homework, you can still benefit greatly from the class experience.
The class is boring or not challenging, and I can get more out of the readings on my own.	Again, you lose the learning opportunities outside the readings that can arise in a class or lecture. And, not every class is going to be boring, so try to get the most out of each one. Some will be more stimulating than others.
I have a part-time job, and my boss urgently needed me.	This may be an acceptable reason to miss a class, but then be sure to contact the instructor to catch up on what you missed.
I'm taking the course pass-fail, so I don't need to attend the classes.	There are many benefits you may get from a course regardless of how you are graded. Don't fail to take advantage of these opportunities.
The class is huge, so nobody will miss me.	This is another big mistake. Even if you are not noticed, you will lose the opportunity to learn from the instructor or professor, and that is why you are paying serious money to attend college.

Chapter 13

Class Discussion and Participation

 Reprinted with permission from the Russell Conwell Center, Office of the Senior Vice Provost for Undergraduate Studies, Temple University, Philadelphia, Pennsylvania

Participation is often an important evaluative measure in a class. Many professors include class participation when calculating final grades. When a student participates in class, he/she demonstrates to the professor the sincere desire to learn and understand the class material and conveys a positive overall impression.

☞ **Why it is important to contribute to class discussions:**

» *It demonstrates that you are interested in learning the material, not just getting a grade.*

» *It demonstrates that you are up-to-date on the assignments.*

» *It allows the professor to get an impression of you as a person apart from your exams and papers.*

» *It gives you the opportunity to express your opinions and ideas in a safe environment.*

» *It will help you learn more by participating.*

» *It will make the class more stimulating and challenging to all (including the professor).*

☞ **How to contribute positively to class discussions:** Be prepared—this means completing the reading, homework, or other assignments before class (answering questions from the assignments gives the professor the impression that you value the class and work hard— quite the contrary when you do not know answers that are clearly answered in the assignments).

> » *Be careful to avoid stereotyping groups and individuals.*

> » *Think about and relate concepts learned in class to your personal life and the "real world."*

> » *Articulate your perspective in an organized fashion - do not ramble.*

> » *Make comments relative to the readings/assignments/topics - do not go on tangents off the topic.*

> » *Be able to support your viewpoint with fact and/or research.*

> » *Be respectful of others' points of view.*

> » *Be open and honest.*

> » *Control your emotions and nerves (see the public speaking and anxiety topics).*

> » *Do not interrupt others or argue from an emotional standpoint.*

☞ **Other faculty expectations of students:**

> » *Come for help if needed.*

> » *Complete intensive reading.*

> » *Be prepared.*

> » *E-mail the professors with questions.*

> » *Be ready to discuss the materials or address a question.*

> » *Study with classmates - work together.*

> » *Ask questions when you are unclear of something.*

Contrast the expectations to those of the most common negative behaviors that professors observe in their classes. Do you
notice yourself in any of these?

☞ **Common negative academic behaviors :**

» *Being unprepared (not having read the material, cannot participate in
class discussions).*

» *Not handing in homework or assignments.*

» *Having poor note-taking skills.*

» *Trying to hand in work late.*

» *Failing to ask questions or seeking help.*

» *Not taking responsibility to follow or understand the syllabus.*

» *Not taking the course seriously.*

☞ **Common negative social behaviors:**

» *Leaving class early without notifying the instructor of another commitment.*

» *Being unable to discuss material that runs counter to personal beliefs.*

» *Maintaining no contact with the professor.*

» *Having a lack of respect of others' opinions.*

» *Showing general rudeness and lack of civility (inappropriate speech).*

» *Being inattentive.*

» *Sleeping.*

» *Eating.*

» *Talking to others, not paying attention.*

» *Missing class.*

» *Using cell phones.*

Chapter 14

Lecture Clues

Dennis H. Congos, M.S.Ed.,
University of Central Florida, Orlando, Florida

Many words and phrases provide clues to important ideas while listening or reading. Recognizing these clues will increase your ability to spot main points in lectures and in text-books, too.

Additive Words and Phrases

Additive words and phrases communicate that additional information is forthcoming.

- » *also*
- » *besides*
- » *furthermore*
- » *moreover*
- » *another*
- » *and*
- » *further*
- » *in addition*

Alternative Words and Phrases

These words and phrases indicate choices or differences or lack thereof.

- » *either*
- » *or*
- » *neither*
- » *nor*
- » *otherwise*
- » *the difference*
- » *similarly*
- » *other than*

Repetitive Words and Phrases

Repetitive words and phrases emphasize ideas that are so important that they are repeated directly or paraphrased.

- » *again*
- » *in other words*
- » *that is (i.e.)*
- » *to repeat*

Cause and Effect Words and Phrases

Cause and effect words and phrases indicate relationships between events or ideas.

- » *accordingly*
- » *because*
- » *consequently*
- » *since*
- » *so*
- » *thus*

» *for this reason*

» *then*

» *as a result*

» *therefore*

» *the outcome is*

Contrast/Change Words and Phrases

These words and phrases suggest similar or opposing circumstances.

» *but*

» *in spite of*

» *notwithstanding*

» *conversely*

» *still*

» *despite*

» *in contrast*

» *instead of*

» *though*

» *however*

» *whereas*

» *even though*

» *rather than*

» *yet*

» *nevertheless*

» *regardless*

» *similarly*

Qualifying Words and Phrases

Qualifying words and phrases modify the conditions which affect important ideas or situations. There are two kinds: absolutes and sometimes words. Absolutes mean 100 percent of the time and sometimes words mean undefined portions or numbers of times.

☞ **Absolute words and phrases:**

>   *no*
>   *all*
>   *never*
>   *always*
>   *only*
>   *ever*
>   *none*
>   *no one*
>   *forever*
>   *every time*

☞ **Sometimes words and phrases:**

>   *few*
>   *many*
>   *occasionally*
>   *some*
>   *most*
>   *somewhat*
>   *sometimes*
>   *usually*
>   *nearly always*

Emphasis Words and Phrases

These clues indicate a degree of importance of ideas and events in relation to each other:

- » *above all*
- » *less importantly*
- » *most importantly*
- » *key idea*
- » *more importantly*
- » *the crux*
- » *main point*
- » *less so*
- » *a central fact*
- » *of significance*

Time and Order Words and Phrases

Time and order words and phrases indicate specific organization patterns of ideas. Many times, order is crucial to an accurate understanding of ideas or events:

- » *finally*
- » *first*
- » *then*
- » *next*
- » *last*
- » *afterwards*
- » *before*
- » *formerly*
- » *later*
- » *now*
- » *finally*

» *meanwhile*

» *ultimately*

» *presently*

» *previously*

Summarizing Phrases

Summarizing phrases indicate that important ideas will be reviewed:

» *in brief*

» *to sum up*

» *for these reasons*

» *to review*

» *in conclusion*

Becoming an Attentive Listener

Now that you are aware of some of the lecture cues that call special attention to key ideas, time frames, orders of events, and special emphasis, listen more carefully when you attend your next lecture. Learn to take notes based upon the importance of the information you are hearing. Add your own emphasis in your notes with underlining, stars, or other visual cues.

Chapter 15

Listening and Learning in Class

 Starting Out!® Research Group

Listening is one of our most powerful learning tools. We are taught to listen from the time we start speaking and then again as soon as we enter school. Well before we know how to read or write we are learning from the people around us and from the voices on radio, television, and in videos and movies. And, as we grow older, we depend even more upon building strong listening and learning skills, not just to master growing amounts of knowledge, but to function effectively on the job and within interpersonal and social settings.

Listening is a key cognitive act, requiring us to focus, to be receptive to ideas, and then to store and process them and ultimately learn from them.

Become a Good Listener

To become a successful classroom student and listener, consider the following steps to good listening and learning:

1. **Be ready and willing to listen.** Put aside other thoughts, concerns, and competing activities and be prepared to focus on the

instructor and his or her ideas. Try to prepare for the class and do your assignments along the way so you get the most out of the class or lecture.

2. **Take the lecture or class seriously.** Your job as a student is to listen and learn. Don't let anything else get in the way of this importance responsibility.

3. **Listen with a goal in mind and focus.** Be prepared to listen to a particular topic and master the knowledge that is being presented. Focus on the lecture with your complete attention.

4. **Be open minded.** Listen with an open mind and a willingness to entertain new and different ideas and concepts.

5. **Be engaged in the process.** Listen to make sure you understand questions, and be prepared to give answers or express your own opinion. Don't let your mind wander.

6. **Be an active listener.** Try to process the information being presented, and follow the direction of the presentation. Take quick, short notes of key points that will remind you of the lecture later.

7. **Focus on difficult concepts.** Increase your attention when difficult concepts are being presented. If you don't understand something, raise your hand and ask for a further explanation.

8. **Ignore distractions.** In focusing on the speaker, try to disregard background noise or interference. If you are in a large lecture hall, sit up front where you will hear better and have fewer distractions between the speaker and yourself.

9. **Avoid multi-tasking.** Don't look at text messages during the lecture, or you will lose your focus and miss important information or ideas. When in class, your job is to listen, take notes, ask questions, and focus on the subject being presented.

10. **Do not interrupt the speaker until you have permission.** Instructors will ask for questions periodically or at the end of a lecture. Let the speaker complete his or her thought on a specific point.

11. **Learn to take good notes.** A good listener can jot down ideas without missing the continuing points being made. This takes practice, however.

12. **Listen for the main ideas and concepts.** Through language or repetition, a speaker will let you know what is important. Listen for these clues.

Learn to Take Useful Notes:

➤ Practice your note-taking skills, and learn to jot down short notes or reminders of ideas.

➤ Develop your own abbreviations.

➤ Look over your notes after the class or lecture and make additions or add details before you forget them.

➤ Save your notes to review before future classes or exams.

Avoid These Bad Listening Habits:

☞ **Deciding ahead of time that a class or lecture will be boring.** Don't go into a classroom, lecture, or meeting convinced that you are not interested. Be receptive and willing to get as much out of the presentation as you can. There is always something to learn, even if the topic is not exciting.

☞ **Being critical of the speaker beforehand.** Don't look for reasons to be negative about a speaker, or judge the content based upon the speaker's appearance or personal style.

☞ **Not letting the speaker make his or her points.** Don't interfere with the speaker or lecture while he or she is trying to make points, even if you don't agree with them. Be patient, and let the speaker finish a thought.

☞ **Trying to write down everything.** Don't get so engaged in taking notes that you lose many of the points that continue to be made. Write short notations and expand them after the class or lecture if they are not sufficient.

☞ **Trying to do something else while listening.** Set aside other tasks and distractions, and only focus on the speaker.

☞ **Whispering or talking during a lecture.** Don't create your own distractions or side conversations, or you will miss important ideas and information you need to know. You will also disturb the speaker, and this is not fair or polite.

☞ **Being disrespectful or judgmental.** Even if you don't agree with what you are hearing, you should not be disrespectful or pre-judge the value or importance of what you are hearing. Hearing a very different point of view is not a waste of time.

Part V

Note-Taking

Chapter 16

Note-Taking Time Savers

Dennis H. Congos, M.S.Ed.,
University of Central Florida, Orlando, Florida

Keeping up with a lecture while taking notes in class is difficult to impossible for learners who try to write down *every word*. Note-taking is more effective if learners practice a few simple Time Savers designed to make taking notes faster and easier.

Time Saver #1: Don't Try to Record Every Word

Students can keep up better with lectures by writing down key points and eliminating unnecessary words. Below is a paragraph, which is followed by a way that it could be condensed, organized, and recorded in short notes:

> "One theory of learning based on behavior is Pavlovian Conditioning or Classical Conditioning. This theory involves a reflexive response associated with a new stimulus. For example, a reflexive response of a dog when he sees food is to salivate. In Classical Pavlovian Conditioning, we can teach a dog to salivate with a new and unrelated stimulus, such as a ringing bell, by teaching a dog to associate a ringing bell with food."

Notes:

Behav. Lrng Thry: Pavlovian/Classical—assoc. reflexive resp. w/new stim.
Ex: dog salivates when hears bell = assoc. bell w/food

It is easier and faster to write a short series of words using abbreviations and short phrases than it is to write down whole words in complete sentences. When there is less note-taking involved, learners have more time to listen and focus on understanding lectures or absorb additional textbook content.

Time Saver #2: Record Words as They Sound Using as Few Letters as Possible

Record the words below *as they sound*. Omit unneeded vowels and consonants. Look at the examples below.

Word	Abbreviation
Ready	rdy
Enough	enuf
Because	bcz
Height	ht
Weight	wt

Time Saver #3: Use Common Shorter Forms

Another way to save time is to use a *common shorter form*.

Word	Abbreviation
Difference	dif.
Telephone	tel.
System	sys.
Example	ex.
General	gen.

Time Saver #4: Substitute Letters or Numbers for Syllables

The words listed below use letters or numbers in place of syllables instead of writing out the whole word.

Word	Abbreviation
Before	B4
Forget	4get
Create	CR8
Foreign	4N

Time Saver #5: Use Standard Abbreviations

These words are shortened using abbreviations considered standard in business/industry/education.

Word	Abbreviation
Company	co.
Department	dept.
Without	w/o
Information	info.
Amount	amt.

Time Saver #6: Use Common Symbols to Replace Words

Using common symbols, instead of writing out whole words, saves time and effort in note-taking.

Word	Abbreviation
Money, cost, price	$
Number	#
Percent	%
And	&
With	w/

Time Saver #7: Use the First Letter or First Few Letters Only

For specialized terms repeated frequently in lectures and textbooks, spell them out the first time you record them. Thereafter, use only an abbreviation or even a letter to save time.

Word	Abbreviation
Democracy	dem. *or just* D
Capitalism	cap. *or just* C
Government	govt. *or just* G
Legislature	leg. *or just* L
Technology	tech. *or just* T

Time Saver #8: Take or Re-write Notes Using as Few Words as Possible

Many words add little or nothing to notes if included. These words can be safely eliminated without losing the meaning of ideas when re-writing and reorganizing notes.

Conclusion

Use these **Note-taking Time Savers** as you take notes from textbooks and lectures. As you use abbreviations more and more, you will spend less and less time writing notes and more time listening or reading for important ideas. Since abbreviations condense notes, there will be less written material to learn and remember.

Notes are personal in that only *you* need to understand them. Many students fear they will forget the meaning of abbreviations they use. While this is an understandable fear, it rarely happens. One reason is that the context surrounding each abbreviation gives clues to its meaning.

Chapter 17

Using Patterns as Aids in Note-Taking

Dennis H. Congos, M.S.Ed.,
University of Central Florida, Orlando, Florida

Lecturers and text authors organize ideas in predictable patterns in order to present material more clearly and understandably. Once you recognize these patterns, they can help you organize notes and speed up learning. Below are seven basic patterns for presenting text or lecture information:

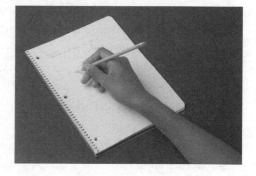

☞ **1. Chronological:** This pattern is **based on time** periods such as seconds, minutes, hours, days, weeks, months, years, etc. Examples: "the next day…", "4 hours later…", "previously…", "over the next 3 years…"

☞ **2. Process or Sequence:** In this pattern, information is presented according to **stages, steps, or logical development** of an idea. These may be numbered or lettered to help you understand the progression. *Examples:"the first step…", "the next stage…", "finally", "1), 2), 3), etc.*

☞ **3. Cause and Effect:** Something happens because **something else happened first.** *Examples:"When this event took place, the impact was…", "The fallout from this was…"*

☞ **4. Problem and Solution:** A **situation is presented** and one or more **alternatives for resolution** are identified, proposed, attempted, or demonstrated. *Example: "The problem is how to distribute the wealth. Several proposals were made in the legislature."*

☞ **5. Inductive:** This logical pattern goes from **general to specific.** A general statement is made and then details are presented to explain or support it. *Example: "Sometimes, the hardest part of writing is seeing the different styles. There are five basic kinds of writing."*

☞ **6. Deductive:** This logical pattern goes from **specific to general.** Specifics are presented and then a general statement is made from these. *Example: "The five kinds of exposition are classification, compare/ contrast, definition, narrative, and process. Learning to write in these formats is sometimes difficult."*

☞ **7. Compare/Contrast:** This pattern focuses upon **similarities and/ or differences** when comparing and differences only when contrasting. *Example: "Memorizing and understanding are alike and different in the following ways."*

Watch for these patterns as you read textbook material, listen to lectures, and take notes. Recognizing these patterns will help you organize, learn, and recall notes for exams.

Chapter 18

Cornell Note Organization Format

Dennis H. Congos, M.S.Ed.,
University of Central Florida, Orlando, Florida

To succeed in college, important ideas from lectures and textbooks must be *identified, organized, recorded, practiced, and stored in long term memory* for recall when needed. The **Cornell Format** helps learners do these important tasks required for learning. Using the Cornell Format has helped many learners uncover a previously hidden ability to learn and remember better than ever before and earn higher grades.

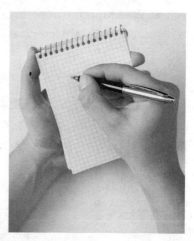

One immediate benefit from the Cornell Format is that it offers an easy way to gather and organize information to be learned. A second benefit is that it saves time. A third benefit of using the Cornell Format is the ability to self-test to discover what has and has not been learned <u>before</u> a test is taken when something can still be done about it.

Setting up the Cornell Format

☞ **The Cornell Format is set up by:**

(1) Drawing a vertical line the length of the page about one-third of the way from the left margin.

(2) Turning main points from lectures and textbooks into questions and placing them to the left of the line.

(3) Forming answers to explain these main ideas and placing them on the right side of the line.

This process should be completed as soon as possible after attending lectures to reinforce memory. According to individual style, questions may be formulated before, during, or after reading text assignments.

The Cornell Format encourages reading for the purpose of finding specific information to include as answers to possible test questions. This technique directly attacks the problems of poor concentration and weak memory. For lectures, the Cornell Format is a simple way to reorganize notes into a format from which it is easy to learn and retain knowledge.

How the Cornell Format Looks

Here is An Example of Notes Using the Cornell Format:

What are 4 good reasons for good notes?	1. Provides material to study and review for exams.
	2. Helps focus attention in class.
	3. Writing what I learn is a first step in learning.
	4. Provides material on which to self-test to see what has not been learned before an exam when I can still catch up on learning.
What are 5 tips for taking notes?	1. Focus on a main ideas first, and then the details.
	2. Leave space between one main idea and its details and another main idea and its details.
	3. Use abbreviations, short phrases, symbols, diagram, sketches, etc.
	4. Number the details.
	5. Use a specific format such as the Cornell Format or outlines, etc.

What are 4 things to do after taking lecture notes?	1. Always rewrite and reorganize notes. 2. Compare notes with other students in the class. 3. Make questions out of main ideas and use details for answers. 4. Add diagrams, sketches, charts, and mnemonics to enhance recall.
What are the 4 steps in reviewing notes?	1. Cover up the details. 2. Looking only at the main idea, recite the details aloud from memory without looking. 3. Uncover the details to see if you have learned the material or not. 4. Discover how many times you have to quiz your self in this matter to get all the answers correct using this method of self-testing.

After the important points have been placed in this format, the next step is to recite the information. *Regular and repeated recitation of notes is the most important step to reinforce memory!*

How to Recite Information in the Cornell Format

☞ **Step 1.** Read a question aloud with the answer covered.

☞ **Step 2.** Recite the answer aloud as completely as possible from memory, as if lecturing a class. Some learners prefer to write an answer from memory as if taking a test. The best way is to alternate these methods.

☞ **Step 3.** Check the accuracy of the answer.

☞ **Step 4.** If *recited* correctly, move on to the next main idea.

☞ **Step 5.** If an answer is not recalled or is recalled incorrectly, look at it and read it aloud. Then, reread the question and recite aloud as much of the answer as possible from memory before checking. Do this step as many times as needed until the answer is recited or written cor-rectly *from memory.* Place a check mark in pencil next to the question to until you have learned the answer.

☞ **Step 6.** Review the "I don't know it" material *at least*, every other day. Review "learned" material about every two to three days to keep the information fresh and to prevent forgetting. As the number of times the information is reviewed increases, the ability to recall is increased and with greater accuracy.

Why the Cornell Format Works

A human's memory works much like a computer. There is immediate recall, short-term memory, and long-term memory. Items must be stored in long-term memory to be available for later recall whether for exams or on the job. Your task is to move knowledge from immediate recall, to short-term memory, and then into long-term memory.

Information must be held in the short-term memory for about five seconds in order to move that information from short-term toward long-term memory. When the **Cornell Format** is used properly, the learner holds information in short-term memory for three to five seconds, beginning the process of long-term information storage.

Chapter 19

Notecard Question-and-Answer Technique

Dennis H. Congos, M.S.Ed.,
University of Central Florida, Orlando, Florida

Another note-taking technique that works well for some students is the **Notecard Question-and-Answer Technique (NQAT)**.

How the Notecards Are Set Up

Notecards are set up by (1) recording details from a lecture or textbook and placing them on one side of a notecard, and (2) creating a question that requires all the details from the flip side as the answer.

This process should be followed as soon as possible after attending lectures in order to reinforce memory. According to individual style, questions may be formulated before, during, or after reading text assignments.

The **NQAT** notetaking format *encourages reading for the purpose of finding specific information* and using it as answers to related questions you have created. This technique helps to increase focus and attention and reduce poor concentration. For lectures, **NQAT** is a *simple way to reorganize notes* into a format from which it is easy to learn and one that promotes learning.

Advantages of NQAT

☞ Notecards are **portable**, making them convenient to review during short periods of time, such as traveling to and from school, between classes, etc.

☞ Notecards are a fast way to review that **reduces study time**.

☞ **Material to be learned is recalled and recited in the same manner as it is on exams.** That is, learners see questions and practice recalling answers from memory just as they would on exams. It is said that we become better at that which we practice. If learners practice seeing questions and recalling answers from memory, they become better at doing this at exam time as well.

☞ **It's easier to recognize correct answers to exam questions.** When instructors compose exams, they find important details in the text or lecture and make a question for the exam that requires all or a portion of the details. Learners must read questions and then recall answers from memory. Learners who formulate questions from the main ideas in notes are doing what instructors do when exams are made. If learners have learned the answers ahead of time, they have the knowledge needed for earning higher grades on exams.

☞ Notecards are **easily rearranged and re-categorized** which provides a variety of ways to respond to a question no matter how it is asked on an exam.

☞ **Students find out what they have and have not learned before an exam or quiz,** while there is still time for further study. Material is readily visible and can be easily separated into two stacks of notecards: the "learned" and the "not yet learned." This way, it is easy to focus one's time and energy on the "not yet learned" material.

☞ Learners can **better recall the material**. Reading for details and making questions that match makes it easier to remember what was just read.

Below are examples of well-organized notecards. The topic used is the Frontier Vocabulary System from How To Study In College (3rd ed.) by Walter Pauk, pp. 292-300.

How Notecards Look

Question on front   *Answer on back*

text p. 292 What is the Frontier Vocab Sys. (FVS)?	Sys. to master new vocab.

text p. 293-294 How does FVS work?	1. Look for somewhat familiar words. 2. Learn meanings.

For easiest review, there should be one main idea per notecard, that is, one notecard for each question and answer. After the important points have been placed on notecards in question-and-answer form, the next step is to recite.

How to Recite Notecards

The cards are used to review information in a similar way to the Cornell Format. The major difference is that you are able to create two piles of cards: "Learned" and "Not Yet Learned."

☞ **Step 1.** Read a question aloud from a notecard.

☞ **Step 2.** Recite the answer aloud as completely as possible from memory. Some learners prefer to write an answer from memory as if taking a test. The best way is to do both but at different times.

☞ **Step 3.** Turn the card over and check the accuracy of the answer.

☞ **Step 4.** If stated correctly, place the card in the "I know it" pile.

☞ **Step 5.** If an answer is not recalled or is recalled incorrectly, look at it and read it aloud. Then, reread the question and recite as much of the answer as possible from memory before checking. Do this step as many times as needed until the answer is recited or written correctly *from memory*. Then, place this notecard in the "not yet learned" pile and go to the next notecard.

☞ **Step 6.** Review the "not yet learned" pile AT LEAST, every other day. Review "known" notecards about every 2-3 days to prevent forgetting. As the number of times increases that notecards are reviewed, the ability to recall is faster and more accurate.

General Suggestions

☞ Place only **one question and its answer per notecard.** This makes it easier to organize and reorganize the ideas into meaningful groups, categories, or sequences, if needed.

☞ **Indicate where the information on each notecard is from** by jotting down page numbers (if from the text), or dates (if from lecture). This permits quick reference should there be confusion or uncertainty.

☞ **Avoid complete sentences** or spelling out every word. This results in summarization of material and, therefore, less total substance to recall.

☞ **After a test, complete a Post-Test Survey** and look for the causes of incorrect answers.

Conduct a Post-Test Survey

☞ If information for correct answers is not on notecards but appears in the text or was given in lecture, this suggests that more attention is needed to spot the indicators of main points in lectures and text-books.

☞ If information for correct answers is on notecards but missed on the exam, this suggests that a greater number of recitations and reviews are needed, a distractive study environment needs changing, or there may be personal concerns which need resolution before more effective learning can take place.

☞ Any incorrect information on notecards should be corrected immediately. Missing information should be added to notecards and learned in preparation for subsequent exams and for more knowledge. This is especially valuable if there is a comprehensive final exam.

Chapter 20

Notecard Problem-and-Solution Technique

Dennis H. Congos, M.S.Ed.,
University of Central Florida, Orlando, Florida

The Notecard Problem-and-Solution Technique (NPST) is similar to NQAT, but is especially suited to math and science classes.

How to use the NPST

This problem-and-solution organization format involves setting up problems and solutions in a manner that promotes the understanding and learning of solutions. This format minimizes the risk of memorizing problems and solutions without understanding *how to solve* the various kinds of problems. In textbooks or lectures, **NPST** is a simple way to organize notes into a format that speeds understanding, learning, and recall of problem solutions.

☞ **The 1st step involves purchasing notecards on which problems and solutions will be recorded.** These cards may be 3 x 5, 4 x 6, or 5 x 8 inches in size depending on the amount of material to be recorded and the size of one's handwriting.

☞ **The second step entails placing problems on one side of a notecard. On the other side, solutions are built, step-by-step.** Having step-by-step solutions speeds understanding and learning.

☞ **In step three, a narrative or verbal description of what is done in each step is included in solutions.** Learners with dominant verbal learning ability, as opposed to dominant quantitative learning ability, can use their verbal learning strengths to determine solutions.

☞ **The fourth step involves practicing solutions by looking at problems and attempting solutions on scrap paper.** This method promotes faster understanding of solutions and speeds accurate recall. It also acts as a check of what has and has not been learned before an exam is taken while there is time for further study. The more often notecards are practiced, the more likely information is to move from short-term memory toward long-term memory; that is, become learned.

The Secret to Success in Math and Physics Classes: Unless learners practice doing problems repeatedly and regularly, it is difficult or impossible to learn and remember solutions (and this is normal!).

How to Practice Solutions on Notecards

☞ Look at a problem on a notecard.

☞ Attempt the solution on scrap paper as completely as possible, from memory, and step-by-step.

☞ Turn the card over and check the accuracy of the solution.

☞ Place the card in the "I know it" pile if solved correctly.

☞ If solutions are partially or completely incorrect, read the solution aloud while you correct your attempt. Attempt a solution again from memory. Place this notecard in the "I don't know it, yet" pile because the solution was missed on the first attempt.

☞ Practice the "I don't know it, yet" pile, at least, every other day. Practice "known" notecards about every 2 to 3 days to keep the information fresh in the memory and to prevent forgetting. The more often notecards are reviewed, the speed of learning increases and the ability to recall is faster and more accurate.

Using the Cornell Format for Problems and Solutions

The Cornell Format can also be used to take notes for math and science classes. Problems and questions are placed to the left of the verticle line and solutions and answers to the right. You can self-test by covering up the solutions and working them out on paper and then checking.

Part VI

Vocabulary

Chapter 21

The Value of Vocabulary

Reprinted with permission from the Cuesta College
Academic Support Center, San Luis Obispo, California

Words are unique and interesting. A limited vocabulary
keeps you from fully expressing your
thoughts and feelings. A strong vocabulary gives you the right words to use at
the right time.

Vocabulary building takes patience
and continued effort. Your vocabulary can and should be a reflection of you.
Your vocabulary reflects who you are. Your vocabulary should be alive and
should change and grow to meet your needs.

The Purpose of Vocabulary

Words are great subjects to investigate. When you become a student of
language and delight in discovering word relationships, you become aware
of how you can make words work for you. You are also more likely to stop
when you encounter an unfamiliar word to consider its meaning. If you do
this, you will become a master of words and your vocabulary will grow.
You must develop strategies to conquer unfamiliar words when you find
them in your college textbooks and in your learning to make words work
for you.

Why Vocabulary Development Counts

☞ **Vocabulary is a basic part of reading comprehension.** If you don't know enough words, you are going to have trouble understanding what you read. An occasional word may not stop you, but if there are too many words you don't know, comprehension will suffer. The content of textbooks is often challenging enough; you don't want to have to work as well on understanding the words that express that content.

☞ **Vocabulary is a major part of almost every standardized test,** including reading achievement tests, college entrance exams, and armed forces and vocational placement tests. Vocabulary is a key measure of both one's learning and one's ability to learn. The more words you know, then, the better you are likely to do on such important tests.

☞ **Studies have indicated that students with strong vocabularies are more successful in school** and that a good vocabulary is an influential factor for people who enjoy successful careers. Words are the tools not just for better reading comprehension, but for better writing, speaking, listening, and thinking as well. The more words you have at your command, the more effective your communication can be, and the more influence you can have on the people around you.

☞ **In today's world, a good vocabulary counts more than ever.** Many jobs provide services or process information, and the skills of reading, writing, listening, and speaking are essential. The keys to survival and success in the workplace are the abilities to communicate skillfully and learn quickly. A solid vocabulary is essential for both of these skills.

Improving Your Vocabulary

Throughout your college years, new words will be flooding into your consciousness. Many of them are the keys to ideas and information that will be new to you. When students have trouble in a course, the trouble can often be traced back to their imperfect comprehension of terms that are essential to understanding a subject matter. A first-year science or social science course may introduce you to almost as many new words as a first course in a foreign language. Then there are also words which may not literally be new to you, but which have specific meanings within the context of a specific course and therefore must be learned as if they were new words.

For a college student, a large, wide-ranging vocabulary is a necessary tool for grasping fundamental ideas and facts. Words are the tools of communication, learning, and thinking, and a student with an inadequate vocabulary cannot function effectively and efficiently.

Chapter 22

Building a Stronger Vocabulary

Dennis H. Congos, M.S.Ed.,
University of Central Florida, Orlando, Florida

Building Vocabulary One Word at a Time

With anything in life, you get better with practice. If one of your goals is to speak well and increase your chances of success in your profession, use the techniques that follow.

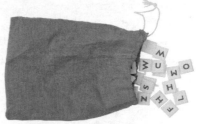

Each time you encounter a word that you don't know, look up the meaning in a dictionary or online glossary and record that word on one side of a notecard. On the other side include the definitions and, if needed, a sentence in which the word is used correctly.

Quiz yourself several times on the new words you have learned until you feel they are a part of your core vocabulary.

Try to use your new words in speaking and writing. There is an adage that says if you use a new vocabulary word three times in one day, it becomes yours. There are many chances per day to use your new words such as in conversations, essays, homework, and e-mails.

Here is an example of a note card you might use:

Front: · Back:

mesmerize	**absorb somebody's attention:** to fascinate somebody or absorb all of somebody's attention
	The speaker mesmerized the audience with his dramatic tale.

Building Vocabulary by Learning Roots, Prefixes, and Suffixes

There are numerous lists of roots, prefixes, and suffixes that pave the way for understanding hundreds of related words. Search for these lists on-line, and you will have the key to ramping up your vocabulary in a hurry.

For example, if you understand that the root "itis" means inflammation, then you will understand many medical terms, such as appendicitis or tonsillitis. Similarly, if you know that "ego" is a root that means "self," you will remember the meaning of words such as egotist, or egomania.

There are more examples of roots, prefixes, and suffixes in Chapters 23, 24, and 25.

Understanding Word Derivations: Etymology

Words, like facts, are difficult to remember out of context. Remembering is greatly facilitated when you have a body of information with which to associate either a word or a fact. For words, interesting origins or histories will help provide a context.

Etymology is the study of the origins of words. The English language is living and growing. Although many of our words have been part of our language for hundreds of years, new words are added all the time. Following are some of the ways that words enter into our language:

1. Words or phrases derived from foreign words, such as buffet, hors d'oeuvres, and cliché (French), siesta, rodeo, and chocolate (Spanish), tattoo and ukulele (Polynesian), typhoon and ketchup (Cantonese), and kayak, chipmunk, toboggan, and squash (Native American).

2. Words with a Latin origin, such as "ad infinitum" instead of infinity.

3. Words derived from commercial product names, such as "Kleenex" for tissue, or "Xerox" instead of copy.

4. Words arising through new technology, including computer terms like bytes, disk, or mouse.

5. Words coined from people's names, such as "sideburns" from the Union General, Ambrose Burnside.

6. Words or expressions associated with acronyms, such as DWI (driving while intoxicated), COD (cash or collect on delivery), or SCUBA (self-contained underwater breathing apparatus).

Chapter 23

Understanding Roots

Starting Out!® Research Group

Expand your vocabulary by memorizing one root per day.

Make a conscious attempt to use words with this root several times during that day.

ROOT	MEANING	EXAMPLE	DEFINITION
-ann, enn	year	biennial	twice per year
-bene	well, good	benevolence	an inclination to do good
-bio	life	biology	the study of living organisms
-cede	go	precede	go before
-cogni	know	recognize	to perceive as something previously known
-dict	say, tell	dictum	an authoritative pronouncement
-duct	take, lead	deduct	to take away or subtract
-dyna(m)	power	dynamic	energetic or lively
-fac	make, do	manufacture	to make a product from raw materials
-fer	carry	transfer	to carry or send from one place to another

ROOT	MEANING	EXAMPLE	DEFINITION
-fin	end, limit	finale	the closing part of a performance
-fort	strong	fortify	strengthen
-graph	write	monograph	a written treatise on a narrow academic topic
-jur, jus	law	jurist	one who has a thorough knowledge of the law
-manu	hand	manual	done by hand
-mit, mis	send, throw	missle	an object projected to strike at a distance
-path	feeling	sympathy	inclination to feel the same as another
-pel	drive	impel	to urge or drive forward
-pend	hang	impend	to hover threateningly
-spect	see	inspect	to examine closely
-temp, tempor	time	contemporary	existing in the same time period
-vac	empty	vacant	unoccupied
-vert	turn	avert	to turn aside or avoid

Chapter 24

Understanding Prefixes

Starting Out!® Research Group

Expand your vocabulary by memorizing one prefix per day.

Make a conscious attempt to use words with this prefix several times during that day.

Prefix	Meaning	Example	Definition
a-	not	amoral	without moral sensibility
ab-	away from	abduct	to take away by force
ad-	to, toward	advance	move ahead
ambi-	both	ambidextrous	able to use both hands equally well
ante-	before	antemortem	before death
anti-	against, opposite	antidote	remedy to counteract a poison
arch-	chief, principal	archrival	main competitor
auto-	self, self-acting	automaton	machine that is self-operating

Prefix	Meaning	Example	Definition
be-	make, cause to be	befriend	become friends with
bi-	two	bilateral	having or concerning two sides
circum-	around	circumvent	go around or avoid
co-	together	cooperate	to work together
com-	together	commiserate	to share feelings
con-	together	conspire	to join in secret agreement
contra-	against	contradict	to express a competing truth or belief
counter-	opposite	counterfactual	not consistent with fact
de-	remove, reduce	devalue	to lessen or eliminate the value of
di-	two	dimorphic	occurring in two different forms
dis-	not, apart	disproportionate	not proportionate
en-	put into or onto	enslave	to put into slavery
epi-	over, attached to	epidermis	outer layer of skin
equi-	equal	equidistant	being the same distance
ex-	former	ex-president	former president
exo-	outside	exoskeleton	exterior supportive structure of an organism
extra-	beyond	extraordinary	beyond what is normal
hemi-	half	hemisphere	half of a sphere
hetero-	different	heterogeneous	made up of different elements

Prefix	Meaning	Example	Definition
homo-	same	homogeneous	made up of a single substance or element
hyper	above, excessive	hyperactive	excessively active
hypo-	below, less than normal	homogeneous	made up of a single substance or element
il-	not	illegal	not legal
im-	not	immaterial	not material or relevant
in-	not	ineffective	not effective
infra-	below	infrastructure	underlying foundation
inter-	between, among	interstate	connecting or existing between two states
intra-	within	intrastate	within a single state
ir-	not	irrelevant	not relevant
macro-	large	macroscopic	large enough to be seen by the naked eye
mal-	bad, abnormal	malfunction	to fail to function normally
meta-	after, outside	metaphysical	beyond the physical world
micro-	small	microscopic	too small to be seen by the naked eye
mis-	bad, wrong	misnomer	an incorrect name
mono-	one	monoplane	a plane with a single wing
multi-	many	multistage	consisting of many stages
new-	new, different	neologism	a new word
non-	not	nonconformist	one who does not conform
omni-	all	omnipotent	all powerful

Prefix	Meaning	Example	Definition
out-	surpass	outperform	to perform better than another
over-	excessive	overuse	to use more than is desirable
para-	subsidiary	paraprofessional	trained aide who assists a professional
peri-	around	perimeter	boundary
post-	after	post-war	following a war
pre-	before	precede	go before
pro-	forward	proceed	to go forward
re-	again, back	retell	to tell again
retro-	backward	retrospect	a review of past events
semi-	half, partial	semicircle	half of a circle
sub-	under	subterranean	under the ground
super-	above, excessive	superimpose	to place above or over something
syn-	with, together	synchronous	happening at the same time
tele-	far	telescope	instrument used to see distant objects
trans-	across	transmit	to send across
tri-	three	tricolor	three colors
ultra-	beyond	ultrasonic	beyond the range of human hearing
un-	not	unhappy	not happy
uni-	single	unilateral	concerning one side

Chapter 25

Understanding Suffixes

 Starting Out!® Research Group

Expand your vocabulary by memorizing one suffix per day.

Make a conscious attempt to use words with this suffix several times during that day.

Suffix	Meaning	Example	Definition
-able, -ible	able, suitable	collectible	worth collecting
-acy	quality, state	normalcy	the state of being normal
-age	state, process	breakage	the process of breaking
-al	relating to	causal	relating to a cause
-ance, -ence	process, state	attendance	the process of attending
-ant	quality, person	servant	person who serves
-arium, -orium	place for	auditorium	a large room for public gathering
-ary	pertaining to	pulmonary	pertaining to the lungs
-ate	cause to be	activate	cause to be active
-ation, -ition	action, state	domination	the act of dominating
-dom	state of being	freedom	state of being free
-er, -or	perform	singer	person who sings
-esque	in the manner of	picturesque	resembling a composed picture

Suffix	Meaning	Example	Definition
-ferous	bearing, producing	carboniferous	producing or containing carbon
-ful	abounding in	colorful	abounding in color
-hood	state, quality	childhood	the state of being a child
-ic	relate to	acidic	being or relating to acid
-ify, -fy	make, cause	magnify	make larger
-ile	similar to	juvenile	similar to a youth
-ion	state, process	dehydration	the state of being dehydrated
-ish	like, inclined toward	childish	being like a child
-ist	performer or expert	bicyclist	person who rides a bike
-ive	inclined toward	creative	inclined to create
-ize	cause to become	minimize	make as small as possible
-less	lacking	guiltless	lacking guilt
-let	diminutive	droplet	a small drop
-ling	diminutive	duckling	a young duck
-ly	like, in the manner of	queenly	being or acting like a queen
-ment	quality, state	enlightenment	the state of being enlightened
-mony	condition or state of	matrimony	the state of being married
-ness	condition or state of	happiness	the state of being happy
-ory	relating to	illusory	relating to an illusion
-ous, -ose	full of	glamorous	full of glamour
-ship	quality or state of	friendship	the state of being friends

Part VII

Reading

Chapter 26

Textbook Reading Skills

Dennis H. Congos, M.S.Ed.,
University of Central Florida, Orlando, Florida

What you do before and after reading is as important as what you do during reading when learning from textbooks. The ultimate objective of all textbook reading should be to understand what is read and add it to your general store of knowledge. The goal should be to make the information your personal possession. You may need this information in the future.

Things to Do Before Reading

➤ Set aside a specific time to read assignments for each course. Mentally commit yourself to these time periods to read about these subjects. This makes concentration easier.

➤ Recall what you already know about the topic.

➤ Bring an open mind to what you read. You don't have to agree in order to understand what an author says.

➤ Intentionally state a reason to read (e.g. "I want to find out about ......") or create questions out of titles, subheads, and key words, and then read to find the answers. Concentration and memory improve when there is a specific purpose for reading beyond the fact that something has been assigned.

➤ Divide a long chapter or assignment into pieces. It is easier to tackle new material if you focus on one piece at a time, instead of trying to digest the entire chapter or assignment at once.

➤ Take a few minutes to skim through a chapter before reading to see how it is structured and where the subject matter leads. Look at the title, introduction, subheads, and summary.

Things to Do While Reading

✓ Read only when you are able to concentrate. Monitor yourself by putting a check mark on a piece of paper whenever concentration wanders. This technique will help return your mind to the reading assignment. If you cannot concentrate, do something else for five or ten minutes or study a different subject for a little while.

✓ As you read, take notes from the text. Condense ideas using abbreviations, symbols, short phrases, and sketches. Avoid complete sentences.

✓ Use a specific format for organizing notes from textbooks. A note-taking system developed at Cornell University is popular among many students. It involves drawing a line one-third from the left margin of your notebook page. Then, list major ideas, concepts, or facts on the left side and further details you want to remember on the right side. See Chapter 18 got more information on this format.

✓ Another convenient note format is to list and number details on one side of a note card. Create a question that can be answered with the details and place it on the other side. This procedure will help you remember what was just read and provide a fast and easy way to have organized notes that speed learning. We always learn faster when we write information on paper.

✓ When you take notes, use your own words to record ideas. This approach will aid in learning and in later recall on tests. Whenever you repeat information in your own words, you are speeding the learning process.

✓ Change reading speed according to the difficulty of the material and the purpose for reading. No single reading speed is effective for all types of reading material. Textbook reading should be done fairly slowly and deliberately when compared to reading newspaper articles or novels. If you take good notes, you should not have to read a textbook chapter more than once.

✓ Read and study in locations free of visual and auditory distractions. All sound interferes with learning, but certain kinds of music may help perform repetitive tasks.

✓ When you have difficulty concentrating and absorbing textbook material, read aloud as if explaining material to someone else.

Things to Do After Reading

☞ In your spare time, discuss what you have read with others, such as in a study group.

☞ Relate what you read to the ideas presented in class.

☞ Look at main ideas, concepts, or facts and recite them aloud, or write down the facts you wish to memorize and practice recalling them without looking, as if you are taking a test. If you can recall answers completely and accurately from memory, you know that you have mastered the material. If you cannot, you know immediately where you need to focus your study efforts.

Things that Improve Your Reading and Comprehension

➤ A slower reading speed increases understanding. Textbooks require slower reading speeds than novels, journals, or newspapers. If text material is difficult, reread it several times by emphasizing each word aloud or in your mind.

➤ Find meanings of vague or unknown terms. Look up the meaning of key words before reading further when a word or term isn't understood the first time it is encountered. It only takes a few unknown words before a chapter becomes difficult or impossible to understand. Look for definitions in the text, lecture notes, glossaries, and dictionaries.

➤ Discuss unclear material with your teacher. Have specific questions ready when you go to class. This preparation makes it easier for your teacher to help because he or she can see more quickly what it is that you do not understand.

Chapter 27

Problems That Lead to Slow Reading

Dennis H. Congos, M.S.Ed.,
University of Central Florida, Orlando, Florida

This chapter is designed to help identify and eliminate problems that lead to slow reading. To get the most out of this exercise, take a sheet of paper and draw a vertical line down the middle. As common causes of slow reading are covered, list those reasons you believe may be slowing your reading on the left side of the line. On the right side of the line, list some of the suggested remedies you are willing to try.

When finished reading this chapter and making your list of problems and remedies, you will have a self-diagnosis of some of the factors that affect your reading speed and some definite steps you can take to increase it. Whatever you discover, it's a good idea to discuss your results with a staff member in your campus learning center and set up a plan for further refinement of college reading skills.

Keep in mind that campus learning centers have many kinds of written materials and exercises to help with faster reading and better memory. Also, there are easy-to-use-computerized exercises available for increasing reading speed and comprehension. As long as you are willing to work on remedies, there are no good reasons why you should not be able to improve reading speed and comprehension.

How Fast Should I Read?

The average person reads at about 250 words per minute (wpm). Some of the faster readers can cover 500 to 600 wpm with comprehension. Good reading is a combination of reading speed and comprehension adjusted to the material being read. For example, reading at 700 wpm with the ability to remember 20–30 percent of what was just read is not very useful unless you are reading for entertainment. If you are looking up a phone number, you are probably "reading" at about 25,000 wpm! Other than a phone number you looked up, there is no comprehension, and you are likely to forget that number in less than a minute.

For textbook learning, **reading faster than 250 wpm increases the risk that important ideas and clarifying details will be missed.** Most problems with reading speed come from the lack of practice and from trying to read and commit the information to memory at the same time.

For information that must be remembered, humans learn faster and remember better when they keep reading and learning separate. Most humans can be in the information-gathering mode **or** in the learning mode, *but not in both modes at the same time.*

Learning is promoted when reading material is mentally manipulated in some form. Mental manipulation speeds learning. Simply stroking words with your eyes involves little mental manipulation, consequently, little learning results.

Problem #1: Poor Concentration

Having to reread frequently may be caused by a lack of concentration. Here are some typical symptoms of and remedies for ineffective concentration:

☞ **Lack of Interest in the Subject:** You have to focus harder with material that you may not enjoy reading or which seems dull. Artificial interest may be created by actively finding reasons for reading and learning.

☞ **Daydreaming:** If you catch yourself daydreaming while you read and don't know what to do to stop it, try "The Mark Technique." Put a checkmark, an "X", or a star on a piece of paper each time you catch yourself daydreaming. By doing this one simple task, many students find that they daydream less and concentrate more.

☞ **Worrying About Problems:** This impediment to reading is common to college students but can be controlled by "The Worry List Technique." Each time you catch yourself thinking about something not related to what you are reading, write that thought down with the intention of doing something about it later. *Then DO something about it later.*

☞ **Can't Remember What Is Read:** Check the distraction level in your study environment. Auditory and visual distractions interfere with concentration. Eliminate TV, radio, stereo, and other sources of sound or remove yourself from the environment in which they are contained. In other words, study where it is quiet and where it is going to stay quiet. The potential for noise can be just as distracting as the actual noise itself.

Remove pictures, souvenirs, and objects from easy view. They can attract visual attention and interrupt concentration. Don't try to study in front of a window. While it is a good idea to rest the eyes by looking up from the page periodically, if the view is more appealing than the reading assignment, there will be trouble returning to the reading.

A remedy for visual distractions may entail moving to a less visually attractive study environment where an open textbook is the most stimulating thing to see.

Problem #2: Underdeveloped Vocabulary

A second cause of slow reading involves a vocabulary in need of further development. A large part of a college education entails learning new terminology with which to grasp new ideas and concepts. Without new terminology, understanding new ideas and concepts in college courses is difficult for most and impossible for the rest.

Therefore, successful college students must be willing to do what's necessary to acquire and expand vocabularies and refine techniques for doing so. You may want to read Part VI of this book about vocabulary.

Problem #3: Poor Reading Techniques

To become good at anything, you must practice. Reading is no exception.

A third cause of slow reading for college students stems from insufficiently refined reading techniques for handling college level reading material. The good news is that students can improve reading speed and comprehension by practicing effective reading techniques used by successful college students.

In response to the poor reading technique problems listed below, there are suggestions you can implement to overcome each of them.

☞ **Stuck in One Gear:** The cure for this problem is to **vary reading speed.** Understanding what you read depends on the type of material you are reading and the reading speed you apply.

☞ **Focusing on Words, not Phrases:** The **"Phrase Technique"** is an excellent way to increase reading speed. One characteristic of college students who read more rapidly is the ability to read words in groups instead of one by one.

☞ **Cannot Find Main Points and Important Details** The **"May I Introduce Technique"** is one way to spot main ideas and important details. Virtually every author uses cue words, phrases, and location in the text to attract attention and introduce important ideas and facts. Textbooks, being instructional in nature, are especially noted for this. The reader's job involves learning to recognize the special words and phrases that typically introduce major points and important facts.

Once this ability is mastered, main points and valuable facts literally *"jump out"* at you as you read.

Without the ability to recognize cues that introduce main points, college reading is difficult to master. Below are examples of introductory cue words and phrases to important information:

First...	One important...
This means...	Several factors...
For example...	Clearly...
Next...	Another development...
Finally...	Still another point...
The first thing...	An important reason...
An illustration...	In other words...
Note that...	The evidence is...

There are many kinds of introductory cue words and phrases which authors use to draw attention to important material. The above list includes a few of many examples of how authors try to attract attention to important information in college textbooks.

Another way that helps spot main ideas and important details is the **"Neon Arrow Technique."** Authors of college textbooks really do want students to learn what is contained in their books. If flashing neon arrows could be included in textbooks that point to important ideas, many authors would include them. Until that is possible, there are things just as useful that indicate the location of major points and valuable details and, in a way, point to the key ideas just as bright, flashing "neon arrows" would.

Once you are able to recognize "neon arrows" in textbooks, reading speed and comprehension will improve. Examples of "neon arrows" authors use to indicate the location of important material are listed below:

• TITLES
• HEADERS
• SUB-HEADS
• Bold print

- *Italics*
- CAPITAL LETTERS
- Indented material
- Numbers...1, 2, 3
- Letters...A,B,C
- Highlighted text
- Summaries
- Terms in margins
- Diagrams, charts, pictures, graphs
- End of chapter questions
- Glossaries at the end of a chapter or the book

Learn to recognize the "neon arrows" and enjoy the benefits of greater understanding in textbook reading.

☞ **How Fast Should You Read?** Effective readers have different reading speeds for different material. In other words, reading speed should be flexible depending on what is read. Following is a chart containing five common reading speeds and the kinds of material for which to use each of them.

Reading Rate Chart

Type of Material	Type of Reading	Purpose	Speed
Dictionaries, thesauri, telephone books, material where material is clearly presented (lists, numbered items, etc.)	Scanning	Locating specific information	About 1500 words per minute or more
Newspapers, journals, research	Skimming	Reading for general topics and main ideas	About 1000 words per minute or more
Easy textbooks, newspapers, stories, magazines, any material where only main ideas are to be learned; generally lighter study	Exploratory Reading	General understanding of main ideas and details or relating new information to what is already known; creating interest in reading material; reading what you will be tested on	About 400-600 words per minute
Most textbooks, journals, and technical materials	Reading for Learning	Reading with maximum understanding of main ideas and their relationships to each other; making questions from main ideas; taking notes; recalling material	About 250 words per minute
Detailed textbooks in math, science, poetry, novels; material to be studied intensively or read aloud such as drama, philosophy, religion; any material that requires or stimulates deep thinking	Analytical and Critical Reading	Evaluating and reflecting on content; following directions as in performing an experiment; extracting precise meanings; reading aloud; reading for emotional stimulation	Less than 250 words per minute

Chapter 28

Understanding Scholarly Material

Patrick Rael, *Reading, Writing, and Researching for History: A Guide for College Students,* Bowdoin College, Brunswick, Maine

Reading scholarly material requires a new set of skills. You simply cannot read scholarly material as if it were pleasure reading and expect to comprehend it satisfactorily. Yet neither do you have the time to read every sentence over and over again. Instead, you must become what one author calls a "predatory" reader. That is, you must learn to determine quickly the important parts of the scholarly material you read. The most important thing to understand about a piece of scholarly writing is its argument. Arguments have three components: the problem, the solution, and the evidence. Understanding the structure of an essay is key to understanding these things. Here are some hints on how to determine structure when reading scholarly material:

☞ **1. Think pragmatically.** Each part of a well-crafted argument serves a purpose for the larger argument. When reading, try to determine why the author has spent time writing each paragraph. What does it "do" for the author's argument?

☞ **2. Identify "signposts."** Signposts are the basic structural cues in a piece of writing. Is the reading divided into chapters or sections? Are there subheads within the reading? Subheads under subheads? Are the titles clearly descriptive of the contents, or do they need to be figured out (as in titles formulated from quotations)? Are there words or concepts in the titles (of the piece, and of subheads) that need to be figured out (such as novel words, or metaphors)?

☞ **3. Topic sentences.** Topic sentences (usually the first sentences of each paragraph) are miniature arguments. Important topic sentences function as subpoints in the larger argument. They also tell you what the paragraph that follows will be about. When reading, try to identify how topic sentences support the larger argument. You can also use them to decide if a paragraph seems important enough to read closely.

☞ **4. Evidence.** Pieces of evidence—in the form of primary and secondary sources—are the building blocks of historical arguments. When you see evidence being used, try to identity the part of the argument it is being used to support.

☞ **5. Identify internal structures.** Within paragraphs, authors create structures to help the reader understand their points. Identify pairings or groups of points and how they are telegraphed. Where are they in the hierarchy of the argument? Hierarchy of major points is very important, and the most difficult to determine. Is the point a major or a minor one? How can you tell?

☞ **6. Examine transitions.** Sometimes transitions are throwaways, offered merely to get from one point to another. At other times, they can be vital pieces of argument, explaining the relationship between points, or suggesting the hierarchy of points in the argument.

☞ **7. Identify key distinctions.** Scholars often make important conceptual distinctions in their work.

☞ **8. Identify explicit references to rival scholarly positions.** Moments when a scholar refers directly to the work of another scholar are important in understanding the central questions at stake.

☞ **9. Stay attuned to strategic concessions.** Often authors seem to be backtracking, or giving ground, only to try to strengthen their cases. Examine such instances in your readings closely. Often, these signal moments where authors are in direct conversation with other scholars. Such moments may also help steer you toward the thesis.

☞ **10. Remember that incoherence is also a possibility.** Sometimes it is very difficult to determine how a section of a piece is structured or what its purpose in the argument is. Authors do not always write effectively or clearly, and there may be incoherent or unstructured portions of essays. But be careful to distinguish between writing that is complex and writing that is simply incoherent.

☞ **11. Finally, remember that you cannot read each piece of scholarship closely from start to finish and hope to understand its structure.** You must examine it (or sections of it) several times. It is much better to work over an article several times quickly—each time seeking to discern argument and structure—than it is to read it once very closely.

Part VIII

Research and Library Skills

Chapter 29

Introduction to Research

Patrick Rael, *Reading, Writing, and Researching for History: A Guide for College Students*, Bowdoin College, Brunswick, Maine

For all who have taken courses in college, the experience of writing a research paper is etched indelibly in memory: late nights before the paper is due, sitting in pale light in front of a computer monitor or typewriter, a huge stack of books (most of them all-too-recently acquired) propped next to the desk, drinking endless cups of coffee or bottles of cola. Most of all, we remember the endless, panicked wondering: how on earth was something coherent going to wind up on the page—let alone fill eight, or ten, or twelve of them? After wrestling with material for days, the pressure of the deadline and level of caffeine in the body are high enough to finally put the pen to paper. Many hours later, a paper is born - all too often something students are not proud to hand in, and something professors dread grading.

"Whatever does not kill us makes us stronger." While Nietzsche may have been right in some cases, he likely did not have writing papers in mind. On the contrary, I sometimes wonder if students' bad experiences writing papers does not drive some them away from academics. How can we make this process less traumatic, more educational, and ultimately more rewarding for all concerned?

The assignment of preparing a research paper for a college-level course is an important one which should not be neglected. In no other endeavor are so many research-related skills required of students. Just think of the steps required:

1. **First, students must find a problem or subject worth addressing.** This is done most often by reading and comparing secondary sources, such as monographs and journal articles. Simply finding relevant secondary materials requires its own particular set of skills in using the library: searching catalogs, accessing on-line databases, using interlibrary loan systems, and even knowing how to pose questions to reference librarians. Reading these sources, determining their arguments, and putting them in conversation with each other constitute another broad set of skills which are enormously difficult to master.

2. **Secondly, having developed a subject, students must find a set of primary sources which can actually address the question they have formulated.** Once again, this is no easy task. It requires another array of skills in using the library. Students must know how to message the online library catalog, and perhaps even (gasp!) use the card catalog. They must be willing to explore the stacks, learn to use special collections, travel off-campus to other libraries, or interview experts. This kind of primary source research demands a diligence and persistence rare in these days of easy Internet access.

3. **Finally, students must put all this information together and actually produce knowledge.** They must craft a paper wherein they pose a clear problem and then offer a thesis addressing it. In a well-structured, grammatically correct essay, they must work their way through an argument without falling into common fallacies. They must match evidence to argument, subordinate little ideas to big ones, and anticipate and preempt challenges to their argument.

Phew! It is little wonder that college students, especially first-year students, can find the research paper assignment so traumatic. It doesn't help that professors often have trouble teaching the essay-preparation process. This is understandable. Professors often represent that portion of the under-graduate population that "got it"; we are the students who somehow, often in spite of our professors, learned how to write papers. Having received the information virtually through osmosis, we often do not un-derstand how we think about the writing process, let alone how to teach it. By and large, we follow the advice of a shoe company and "just do it."

Most students do not have it so easy. Many do not have the innate passion for the subject which propelled teachers over their steep learning curve. Many do not have learning styles which make them likely candidates for the "osmosis" technique many of us used. These students deserve every op-portunity to succeed, and it is important that they do. Even those with little apparent interest need to approach what they read with a critical, analytical eye. In this age of information overload, they need to know how to pose critical questions, uncover the data which can answer their queries, and present their findings to themselves, their profes-sors, and to the world at large.

Chapter 30

Critically Analyzing Books

Reproduced and adapted with permission from
Olin Library Reference, Research and Learning Services,
Cornell University Library, Ithaca, New York

Y ou can begin evaluating a physical information source (a book or an article for
instance) even before you have the physical item
in hand. Appraise a source by first examining the
bibliographic citation. The bibliographic citation is the written description of a book, journal
article, essay, or some other published material
that appears in a catalog or index. Bibliographic
citations characteristically have three main components: author, title, and publication information. These components can help you determine

the usefulness of this source for your paper. (In the same way, you can
appraise a website by examining the home page carefully.)

Initial Appraisal

☞ Author

> » What are the author's credentials—institutional affiliation
> (where he or she works), educational background, past writings,
> or experience? Is the book or article written on a topic in the
> author's area of expertise? You can use the various Who's Who
> publications for the U.S. and other countries and for specific sub-
> jects and the biographical information located in the publication
> itself to help determine the author's affiliation and credentials.

» Has your instructor mentioned this author? Have you seen the author's name cited in other sources or bibliographies? Respected authors are cited frequently by other scholars. For this reason, always note those names that appear in many different sources.

» Is the author associated with a reputable institution or organization? What are the basic values or goals of the organization or institution?

☞ Date of Publication

» When was the source published? This date is often located on the face of the title page below the name of the publisher. If it is not there, look for the copyright date on the reverse of the title page. On webpages, the date of the last revision is usually at the bottom of the home page, sometimes every page.

» Is the source current or out-of-date for your topic? Topic areas of continuing and rapid development, such as the sciences, demand more current information. On the other hand, topics in the humanities often require material that was written many years ago. At the other extreme, some news sources on the Web now note the hour and minute that articles are posted on their site.

☞ Edition or Revision

» Is this a first edition of this publication or not? Further editions indicate a source has been revised and updated to reflect changes in knowledge, include omissions, and harmonize with its intended reader's needs. Also, many printings or editions may indicate that the work has become a standard source in the area and is reliable. If you are using a web source, do the pages indicate revision dates?

☞ Publisher

» Note the publisher. If the source is published by a university press, it is likely to be scholarly. Although the fact that the publisher is reputable does not necessarily guarantee quality, it does show that the publisher may have high regard for the source being published.

☞ Title of Journal

» Is this a scholarly or a popular journal? This distinction is important because it indicates different levels of complexity in conveying ideas. One way to tell is to check your journal title in the latest edition of Katz's Magazines for Libraries for a brief evaluative description.

Content Analysis

Having made an initial appraisal, you should now examine the body of the source. Read the preface to determine the author's intentions for the book. Scan the table of contents and the index to get a broad overview of the material it covers. Note whether bibliographies are included. Read the chapters that specifically address your topic. Scanning the table of contents of a journal or magazine issue is also useful. As with books, the presence and quality of a bibliography at the end of the article may reflect the care with which the authors have prepared their work.

☞ Intended Audience

Ask yourself:

» *What type of audience is the author addressing?*

» *Is the publication aimed at a specialized or a general audience?*

» *Is this source too elementary, too technical, too advanced, or just right for your needs?*

☞ Objective Reasoning

» Is the information covered fact or opinion? It is not always easy to separate fact from opinion. Facts can usually be verified; opinions, however may be based on factual information, evolve from the interpretation of facts. Skilled writers can make you think their interpretations are facts.

» Does the information appear to be valid and well-researched, or is it questionable and unsupported by evidence? Assumptions should be reasonable. Note errors or omissions.

» Are the ideas and arguments advanced more or less in line with other works you have read on the same topic? The more radically an author departs from the views of others in the same field, the more carefully and critically you should scrutinize his or her ideas.

» Is the author's point of view objective and impartial? Is the language free of emotion-arousing words and bias?

☞ Coverage

» Does the work update other sources, substantiate other materials you have read, or add new information? Does it extensively or marginally cover your topic? You should explore enough sources to obtain a variety of viewpoints.

» Is the material primary or secondary in nature? Primary sources are the raw material of the research process. Secondary sources are based on primary sources. For example, if you were researching Konrad Adenauer's role in rebuilding West Germany after World War II, Adenauer's own writings would be one of many primary sources available on this topic. Others might include relevant government documents and contemporary German newspaper articles. Scholars use this primary material to help generate historical interpretations—a secondary source. Books, encyclopedia articles, and scholarly journal articles about Adenauer's role are considered secondary sources. In the sciences, journal articles and conference proceedings written by experimenters reporting the results of their research are primary documents. Choose both primary and secondary sources when you have the opportunity.

☞ Writing Style

» Is the publication organized logically?

» Are the main points clearly presented?

» Do you find the text easy to read, or is it stilted or choppy?

» Is the author's argument repetitive?

☞ Evaluative Reviews

» Locate critical reviews of books in a reviewing source, such as Book Review Index, Book Review Digest, OR Periodical Abstracts. Is the review positive? Is the book under review considered a valuable contribution to the field? Does the reviewer mention other books that might be better? If so, locate these sources for more information on your topic.

» Do the various reviewers agree on the value or attributes of the book or has it aroused controversy among the critics?

» For websites, consider consulting one of the evaluation and reviewing sources on the internet.

Chapter 31

Evaluating Web Pages

University of California, Berkeley Library, Berkeley, California
www.lib.berkeley.edu/TeachingLib/Guides/Internet/Evaluate.html, 11/25/09

Evaluating web pages skillfully requires you to do two things at once. First, you must train your eye and your fingers to employ a series of techniques that help you quickly find what you need to know about web pages. Second, you must train your mind to think critically, even suspiciously, by asking a series of questions that will help you decide how much a web page is to be trusted.

The process begins with looking at your search results from a search engine or other source, progresses to investigating the content of the page, and extends beyond the page to what others may say about the page or its author(s).

What can the URL tell you?

☞ **Techniques for Web Evaluation:**

» Before you leave the list of search results—before you click and get interested in anything written on the page—glean all you can from the URLs of each page.

» Then choose pages most likely to be reliable and authentic.

Questions to Ask	What are the Implications?
Is it somebody's personal page? • Read the URL carefully • Look for a personal name (e.g. jbarker or barker) following a tilde (~), a percent sign (%), or the words "users", "members", or "people". • Is the server a commercial ISP or other provider of web hosting (*like aol.com or geocities.com*)	Personal pages are not necessarily "bad," but you need to investigate the author carefully. For personal pages, there is no publisher or domain owner vouching for the information in the page.
What type of domain does it come from? (educational, non-profit, commercial, government, etc.) • Is the domain extension appropriate for the content? • <u>Government sites</u>: look for .gov or .mil • <u>Educational sites</u>: look for .edu • <u>Nonprofit organizations</u>: look for .org (though this is no longer restricted to nonprofits) • Many country codes, such as .us, .uk. and .de, are no longer tightly controlled and may be misused. Look at the country code, but also use the techniques in this chapter to see who published the web page.	Look for appropriateness. What kind of information source do you think is most reliable for your topic?
Is it published by an entity that makes sense? (Who "published" the page?) • In general, the publisher is the agency or person operating the "server" computer from which the document is issued. • <u>The server</u> is usually named in first portion of the URL (between http:// and the first /) • Have you heard of this entity before? • Does it correspond to the name of the site? Should it?	You can rely more on information that is published by the source: • Look for New York Times news from *www.nytimes.com* • Look for health information from any of the agencies of the National Institute of Health on sites with "nih" somewhere in the domain name.

Scan the perimeter of the page, looking for answers to these questions:

☞ **Techniques for Web Evaluation :**

» Look for links that say "About us," "Philosophy," "Background," "Biography", etc.

» If you cannot find any links like these, you can often find this kind of information if you truncate back the URL.

Instructions for Truncating back a URL: In the top Location Box, delete the end characters of the URL stopping just before each / (leave the slash). Press enter to see if you can see more about the author or the origins/nature of the site providing the page.

Continue this process, one slash (/) at a time, until you reach the first single / which is preceded by the domain name portion. This is the page's server or "publisher."

Look for the date "last updated," usually at the bottom of a web page. Check the date on all the pages on the site.

☞ **Questions to Ask:**

The following charts raise important questions to ask as you assess a web source.

1. Who wrote the page?

2. Is the content dated and current?

3. What are the author's credentials?

4. How can you assess quality?

5. What do others say about this web page or source?

6. Does it all add up?

Questions to Ask	**What are the Implications?**
Who wrote the page? • Look for the name of the author, or the name of the organization, institution, agency, or whomever is responsible for the page; an e-mail contact is not enough! • If there is no personal author, look for an agency or organization that claims responsibility for the page. • <u>If you cannot find this, locate the publisher by truncating back the URL</u> (see technique above). Does this publisher claim responsibility for the content? Does it explain why the page exists in any way?	Web pages are all created with a purpose in mind by some person or agency or entity. They do not simply "grow" on the web. You are looking for someone who claims accountability and responsibility for the content. An e-mail address with no additional information about the author is not sufficient for assessing the author's credentials. If this is all you have, try e-mailing the author and asking politely for more information about him/her.
Is the page dated? Is it current enough? • CAUTION: Undated factual or statistical information is no better than anonymous information. Don't use it.	How recent the date needs to be depends on your needs. For some topics you want current information. For others, you want information put on the web near the time it became known. In some cases, the importance of the date is to tell you whether the page author is still maintaining an interest in the page, or has abandoned it.

What are the author's credentials on this subject?

- Does the purported background or education look like someone who is qualified to write on this topic?
- Might the page be by a hobbyist, self-proclaimed expert, or enthusiast?

Is the page merely an opinion? Is there any reason you should believe its content more than any other page?

Is the page a rant, an extreme view, possibly distorted or exaggerated?

- If you cannot find strong, relevant credentials, look very closely at documentation of sources (next section).

Anyone can put anything on the web for pennies in just a few minutes. Your task is to distinguish between the reliable and questionable.

Many web pages are opinion pieces offered in a vast public forum.

You should expect from the author the same degree of credentials, authority, and documentation that you would expect from something published in a reputable print resource (book, journal article, good newspaper).

Look for indicators of quality information:

☞ **Techniques for Web Evaluation:**

» Look for a link called "links," "additional sites," "related links," etc.

» In the text, if you see little footnote numbers or links that might refer to documentation, take the time to explore them.

» What kinds of publications or sites are the references? Reputable? Scholarly? Are they real? On the web (where no publisher is editing most pages), it is possible to create totally fake references.

» Look at the publisher of the page (first part of the URL).

» Expect a journal article, newspaper article, and some other publications that are recent to come from the original publisher if the publication is available on the web. Look at the bottom of such articles for copyright information or permissions to reproduce.

Questions to Ask	What are the Implications?
Are sources documented with footnotes or links? • Where did the author get the information? • As in published scholarly/academic journals and books, you should expect documentation. • If there are links to other pages as sources, are they to reliable sources? • Do the links work?	In scholarly/research work, the credibility of most writings is proven through footnote documentation or other means of revealing the sources of information. Making a statement without documentation is not much better than just expressing an opinion or a point of view. An exception can be journalism from highly reputable newspapers. But these are not scholarly. Check with your instructor before using this type of material. Links to other weak or fringe pages do not help strengthen the credibility of your research.
If information is reproduced (from another source), is it complete, not altered, not fake or forged? • Is it retyped? If so, it could easily be altered. • Is it reproduced from another publication? • Are permissions to reproduce and copyright information provided? • Is there a reason there are not links to the original source if it is online (instead of reproducing it)?	You may have to find the original to be sure a copy of something is not altered and is complete. Look at the URL: is it from the original source? If you find a legitimate article from a reputable journal or other publication, it should be accompanied by the copyright statement and/or permission to reprint. If it is not, be suspicious. Try to find the source. If the URL of the document is not to the original source, it is likely that it is illegally reproduced, and the text could be altered, even with the copyright information present.

Are there links to other resources on the topic? • Are the links well chosen, well organized, and/or evaluated/annotated? • Do the links work? • Do the links represent other viewpoints? • Do the links (or absence of other viewpoints) indicate a bias?	Many well developed pages offer links to other pages on the same topic that they consider worthwhile. They are inviting you to compare their information with other pages. Links that offer opposing viewpoints as well as their own are more likely to be balanced and unbiased than pages that offer only one point of view. Is anything not said that could be said and perhaps would be said if all points of view were represented? Always look for bias. Especially when you agree with something, check for bias.

What do others say?

☞ **Techniques for Web Evaluation:**

» *Find out what other web pages link to this page.*

1. Use alexa.com:
Type or paste the URL into alexa.com's search box.
Click on the link marked "Get site info for:"

You will see, depending on the volume of traffic to the page:
• Traffic details.
• Contact/ownership info for the domain name.
• "Related links" to other sites visited by people who visited the page.
• Sites that link to the page.
• A link to the "Wayback Machine," an archive showing what the page looked like in the past.

2. Do a link search in a search engine where this can be done:
• Copy the URL of the page you are investigating (Ctrl+C in Windows).

• Go to the search engine site, and type link: in the search box.

• Paste the URL into the search box immediately following link: (no space after the colon).

• The pages listed all contain one or more links to the page you are looking for. If you find no links, try a shorter portion of the URL, stopping after each / .

» Look up the title or publisher of the page in a reputable directory that evaluates its contents (Librarians' Index, Infomine, About.com, or a specialized directory you trust).

» Look up the author's name in a search engine!

Instructions in Google to search the name three ways:

1. without quotes - Joe Webauthor

2. enclosed in quotes as a phrase - "Joe Webauthor"

3. enclosed in quotes with * between the first and last name - "Joe * Webauthor" (The * can stand for any middle initial or name in Google only).

Questions to Ask	What are the Implications?
Who links to the page? • Are there many links? • What kinds of sites link to it? • What do they say?	Sometimes a page is linked only to other parts of its own site (not much of a recommendation). Sometimes a page is linked to by its fan club, and by detractors. Read both points of view.
Is the page listed in one or more reputable directories or pages?	Good directories include a tiny fraction of the web, so inclusion in a directory is therefore noteworthy. But read what the directory says! It may not be 100 percent positive.

What do others say about the author or responsible authoring body?	Researching someone through a search engine can be revealing. Be sure to consider the source. If the viewpoint is radical or controversial, expect to find detractors. Also see which blogs refer to the site, and what they say about it. Google Blog Search is a good way to do this; search the site's name, author, or URL.

Does it all add up?

☞ **Techniques for Web Evaluation:**

» Step back and think about all you have learned about the page. Listen to your gut reaction. Think about why the page was created, the intentions of its author(s). If you have doubts, ask your instructor or go to a library reference desk and ask for advice.

» Be sensitive to the possibility that you are the recipient of irony, spoof, fraud, or other falsehood.

» Ask yourself if the web is truly the best place to find resources for the research you are doing.

Questions to Ask	What are the Implications?
Why was the page created? • To inform, give facts, give data? • To explain, persuade? • To sell, entice? • To share? • To disclose?	These are some of the reasons to consider. The web is a public place, open to all. You need to be aware of the entire range of intentions behind web pages.

Might it be ironic? Satire or parody? • Think about the "tone" of the page. • Is it humorous? A parody? Exaggerated? An overblown argument? • Does it have outrageous photographs or juxtapositions of unlikely images? • Does it argue a viewpoint with examples that suggest that what is argued is ultimately not possible?	It is easy to be fooled, and this can make you look foolish in turn.
Is this web page as credible and useful as the resources (books, journal articles, etc.) available in print or online through the library? • Are you being completely fair? Too harsh? Totally objective? • Do you require the same degree of "proof" as you would from a print publication? • Is the site good for some things and not for others? • Are your hopes biasing your interpretation?	What is your requirement (or your instructor's requirement) for the quality of reliability of your information? In general, published information is considered more reliable than what is on the web. But many, many reputable agencies and publishers make great content available by "publishing" it on the web. This applies to most governments, most institutions and societies, many publishing houses, and news sources. But take the time to check it out.

WHY? Rationale for Evaluating What You Find on the Web

The World Wide Web can be a great place to accomplish research on many topics. But putting documents or pages on the web is easy, cheap or free, unregulated, and unmonitored (at least in the USA). There is a famous Steiner cartoon published in the New Yorker (July 5, 1993) with two dogs sitting before a terminal looking at a computer screen; one says to the other "On the Internet, nobody knows you're a dog." The great wealth that the Internet has brought to so much of society is the ability for people to express themselves, find one another, exchange ideas, discover possible peers worldwide they never would have otherwise met, and, through hypertext links in web pages, suggest so many other people's ideas and personalities to anyone who comes and clicks. There are some real "dogs" out there, but there's also great treasure.

Therein lies the rationale for evaluating carefully whatever you find on the web. The burden is on you—the reader—to establish the validity, authorship, timeliness, and integrity of what you find. Documents can easily be copied and falsified or copied with omissions and errors—intentional or accidental. In general, the World Wide Web has no editors (unlike most print publications) to proofread and "send it back" or "reject it" until it meets the standards of a publishing house's reputation. Most pages found in general search engines for the web are self-published or published by businesses small and large with motives to get you to buy something or believe a point of view. Even within university and library websites, there can be many pages that the institution does not try to oversee.

The web needs to be free like that! But, if you want to use it for serious research, you need to cultivate the habit of healthy skepticism, of questioning everything you find with critical thinking.

Chapter 32

Plagiarism

Susan Thompson and Bruce Thompson,
California State University San Marcos,
San Marcos, California

Plagiarism seems like such an easy concept to understand: the dishonest practice of claiming credit for something you didn't do. Avoiding plagiarism seems equally simple: giving credit where credit is due. And it is that simple — sort of.

While some instances of plagiarism are well understood by most people, other types are not as obvious. Students know that putting their name on a paper written by someone else is plagiarism, but they are less clear about when to give credit to others for ideas included in their papers. This chapter attempts to clarify what actions are considered plagiarism and provide techniques for avoiding them.

Part 1: What is Plagiarism?

"Plagiarism is using others' ideas and words without clearly acknowledging the source of that information" (Writing Tutorial Services, 2004). Notice that it does not matter whether or not the failure to give credit is intentional. Any lack of credit, even accidental, is considered plagiarism.

Any form of information requires acknowledgement. A common perception is that only the exact copying of words from a printed publication constitutes plagiarism. The requirement to acknowledge sources is much broader. In particular, it is important to understand that the source of ideas—opinions, theories, facts, etc.—as well as words must be credited.

This chapter focuses on plagiarism as it appears in student papers using written sources, but the concepts can be applied to any type of source material. Information sources can include:

» *spoken words such as conversations and interviews;*

» *written words including e-mail and web pages as well as published print materials;*

» *multimedia sources such as movies, music, and photographs; and*

» *any other expression of an idea including statistics, drawings, maps, etc.*

Exact Copy Plagiarism

There are two types of exact copy plagiarism—**whole source** and **partial copy**.

Whole source plagiarism is claiming an entire work as your own. The most common example is when a student puts his or her name on a paper written by another person. Whole source plagiarism also includes claiming to be the creator of such things as a work of art, an entire song, or a scientific theorem.

Partial copy plagiarism occurs when the exact words or content from a source are inserted as part of your paper *without giving proper attribution*. Examples include:

» *cutting and pasting from an electronic source*

» *copying from a printed source*

» *repeating a conversation, interview remarks, etc. verbatim*

» *inserting a photo, audio clip, or other multimedia element*

Paraphrase

Many people believe that putting a piece of text or an idea into "their own words" avoids the issue of plagiarism. This is called **paraphrasing**. The purpose of paraphrase is often to summarize or simplify the author's ideas, making them easier to understand, more approachable, or to add more emphasis. Paraphrasing is acceptable, but it is important to acknowledge the original author's ideas, even if it is has been substantially re-expressed.

Close paraphrase, where trivial changes are made such as substituting similar words or changing the sentence order, is essentially the same as copying the author's words directly and so is still considered a form of exact copy plagiarism.

Common Knowledge

Not all ideas require attribution; specifically, facts that are common knowledge. Common knowledge exists when a fact can be found in numerous places or is likely to be known by a lot of people. For example, you do not need to document the fact that *Abraham Lincoln was the 16th president of the United States* since this information is widely known. On the other hand, you must credit your source for facts that are not generally known or ideas that interpret facts. For example, *Lincoln's tall and gangly stature is consistent with symptoms of Marfan syndrome* (Davidson, 2004).

Whether a reference source needs to be cited depends more on the nature of the information than the type of source. It also depends on the student's reason for citing the information. For example, if you wish to establish authority for the information, then you need to cite the source: However, if you are merely trying to inform your reader of something that is common knowledge in a field, then it is not necessary to cite the source.

Other issues

☞ **Information from the Internet:**

A common mistake is thinking that, because Internet information is free and often appears to have no "owner," it can be used without giving credit. In fact, the source makes no difference what-so-ever. The important point is that when you use ideas or words that are not your own, no matter what the source, you must give credit.

☞ **Informal and non-fixed sources:**

A similar issue is using ideas and words from informal and non-fixed sources. Information from a conversation or a telephone call, unless you should happen to record it, can never be revisited by another person. Letters and e-mail are another source of information that, while fixed, are generally not available to other people. Other transient sources might be information heard on the radio, television or at a lecture or seen in a museum or art gallery. In all these cases, you are required to give attribution for ideas and words you take from those sources.

☞ **Relationship of plagiarism with copyright:**

People sometimes confuse plagiarism with copyright. Copyright is concerned with whether you have the right to access and use a work. Plagiarism is about whether credit has been given for ideas or words taken from that work. For instance, it may be perfectly fine, as far as copyright goes, to copy a few paragraphs from a book but, if you put these words in your paper without crediting the source, you will have committed plagiarism. The bottom line is that plagiarism has nothing to do with copyright. You are obligated to acknowledge your sources whether or not their work is copyrighted.

☞ **Self plagiarism:**

Self plagiarism refers to the use of your own work, or a substantial portion of it, in another course than the one for which it was originally written. While you are not stealing an idea from someone else, it is still considered dishonest unless you have obtained permission from your instructor to reuse the material.

☞ **No author:**

Sometimes people assume credit only needs to be given when there is someone, an identifiable author, to credit. However, giving credit simply acknowledges that the source of the ideas, words, etc. that you used came from somewhere outside your own thoughts. You need to cite even if the source doesn't have an author you can identify.

Part 2: How to Avoid Plagiarism

We often assume that all people who plagiarize are deliberately dishonest. In fact, intentionally planned plagiarism is fairly rare. Much of plagiarism is simply due to carelessness, or to not understanding what plagiarism means. The following chart, taken from a website at Purdue University, represents plagiarism as a spectrum.

SPECTRUM OF ACTIONS THAT MIGHT BE SEEN AS PLAGIARISM

Buying, stealing, or borrowing a paper	Using the source too closely when paraphrasing
Hiring someone to write your paper	Building on someone's ideas without citation
Copying from another source without citing (on purpose or by accident)	

Deliberate Plagiarism   **Possibly Accidental Plagiarism**

Since most plagiarism is unintentional, the best way to avoid plagiarism is to develop good habits of scholarship and writing, and to be familiar with the concepts related to plagiarism. Some of the necessary habits of scholarship are simple common sense.

When writing a paper:

» *Give yourself enough time to do a good job. Students who procrastinate are more likely to plagiarize because rushing makes them sloppy. (Being out of time is also the primary incentive for deliberate dishonesty.)*

> » *Revise your paper. Significant re-writing can eliminate plagiarized passages.*

> » *Proofread for errors. Proofreading can help you find missing citations and quotation marks, as well as other errors.*

Using other people's ideas is a recognized and important part of being a good scholar. It becomes plagiarism only if credit is not given appropriately to the original source.

Note Taking

Accidental plagiarism is often a result of how you take notes. When we research a topic, most of us are delighted to find any information on a topic. The focus of our notes is recording any and all information that might be useful for our final paper.

By the time we use our notes, however, we've usually forgotten exactly where they came from and whether we had copied the author's exact words, paraphrased her, or written our own interpretation of the information. If the source of the information is not clearly indicated on your notes, it is easy to overlook direct quotes, paraphrase, and common knowledge when you use these notes in writing your paper. Any of these oversights might result in unintentional plagiarism.
The following strategies can help you avoid these problems when you are taking notes.

> » *Always include information about your source with the notes from that source.*

> » *Highlight or put quotation marks around direct quotes, the information that you have copied word-for-word from the source.*

> » *It is better to copy your source's exact words than closely paraphrase or slightly alter the author's words. You run the risk of plagiarizing if you don't remember which words were the author's and which were yours.*

> » *Many sources recommend the best way to take notes is to close the book and not look at your source, to ensure you are writing your own interpretation of*

the ideas in your own words. Once you've written your version, you can check the original source for accuracy and to make sure you didn't accidentally use the author's original wording. The result is a true paraphrase or summary.

» *In some manner highlight true paraphrases you have written in your notes (underline, highlighter pen, etc.) so you remember to properly acknowledge the original author's ideas if you include the information in your final paper.*

» *If your professor accepts as common knowledge information that appears in a number of sources, it is worth noting the sources where potential common knowledge items appear so you can objectively determine if they meet the criteria.*

Direct Quotation

Knowing how to quote correctly is key to avoiding plagiarism. Words that are an exact copy of the original should always be identified by quotation marks or, for longer quotes, set-off in an indented paragraph. The requirement to put quotation marks around material that has been exactly copied is the form of acknowledgement with which most people are familiar. However, while proper quotation will avoid plagiarism, it does not necessarily result in a good paper.

Students are often told to use direct quotes when they feel the original author's phrasing expresses the idea so well that no better expression can be found. However, be careful not to create a "Frankenstein" paper that is little more than a string of quotes sewn together by a few transition sentences.

Each field of study has specific guidelines about direct quotation. Students can check with their professor on the preferred style in their discipline. Most quotes should be very short, under two lines in length with the fewer the words the better. Even longer quotes should be as brief as possible. In general, the use of quotes should be kept to a minimum.

Short quote example:

"Hoemann says that there is very little absolutely new knowledge. The process of learning is, in fact, a long tradition passed on from generation to generation."

Hoemann, George. Electronic Style—Why Cite? 14 September 1998. University of Tennessee. Retrieved October 3, 2000 from, <http://web.utk.edu/~hoemann/why.html>

This use of short quotation is acceptable because:

- ✓ it's brief;
- ✓ the phrase quoted is genuinely unusual and apt; and
- ✓ it cites the original source of the information.

Remember that using quotes does not relieve you of the responsibility of expressing the ideas for yourself. Usually, a longer direct quote—one set off in an indented paragraph—should be accompanied by your own paraphrase of the quoted passage. This shows your reader how you interpret the passage and draws out the points that you think are worth emphasizing. Shorter direct quotes—those under two lines in length—do not usually need to be paraphrased, but may be used effectively as part of a paraphrase. Since you need to paraphrase anyway, there is no point using long direct quotes unless:

» the point is so important that it is worth saying twice (once by you and once by the original author);

» you need to document that the original author really does say what you claim she says, (for instance, it is a surprising or out of character thing for this author to say); or

» the original author's turn of phrase is so clever or so apt at expressing the idea in question that you cannot resist sharing it with your reader.

Long quote example:

Intellectual honesty is the admission that humanity is linked together in a kind of collective learning process. Very little is discovered "de novo," that is, without a solid foundation in other researchers' previous exploration and understanding. Citation is an act of humility and an act of appreciation for what other scholars have pieced together about the nature of a particular problem or an aspect of some phenomenon (Hoemann).

Hoemann, George. *Electronic Style—Why Cite?* 14 September 1998. University of Tennessee. Retrieved October 3, 2000 from, <http://web.utk.edu/~hoemann/why.html>

What Hoemann is saying here is that most of our discoveries take advantage of work done by those who have gone before us. The process of learning is, in fact, a long tradition passed on from generation to generation. New ideas are important, but Hoemann wants to emphasize the extent to which we ought to appreciate the contributions of past scholars.

This use of a long quotation is acceptable because:

- ✓ the passage quoted includes some uniquely stated ideas;
- ✓ we have included a paraphrase pointing out the ideas which should be emphasized; and
- ✓ it cites the original source of the information.

Paraphrase

Paraphrase is a re-expression of someone else's ideas in your own words. While it is true that you do not have to enclose paraphrased information in quotes, you are still responsible for giving proper attribution to the original source of the information and for making sufficiently substantial changes to create a paraphrase that is a genuinely new expression of the idea, not merely a trivial rewording of the original passage. Incorrect paraphrase is perhaps the most common type of "accidental" plagiarism.

☞ **Key points:**

✓ First, it is important to recognize that paraphrased material must be credited.

✓ Second, how you paraphrase can determine whether the material is considered plagiarized.

Original text:

Intellectual honesty is the admission that humanity is linked together in a kind of collective learning process. Very little is discovered "de novo," that is, without a solid foundation in other researchers' previous exploration and understanding. Citation is an act of humility and an act of appreciation for what other scholars have pieced together about the nature of a particular problem or an aspect of some phenomenon.

☞ **The Unacceptable Paraphrase**
Unacceptable paraphrase is usually caused by making only superficial changes to the original text such as replacing some of the words with synonyms or changing the sentence order. The paraphrase is so close to the original that it is considered essentially a direct quote without attribution.

Unacceptable paraphrase:

Intellectual honesty is the admission that humanity is linked together in a kind of joint learning process. Not very much is discovered new without really understanding other scholars' previous research and knowledge. Citing shows you are grateful and appreciate what other researchers have figured out about a particular issue.

This paraphrase is considered plagiarism because it only makes trivial changes such as:

Original text	Paraphrase
collective learning process	joint learning process
de novo	new
researchers previous exploration	scholars' previous research
other scholars have pieced together	other researchers have figured out

✓   it doesn't indicate where words are copied directly from the source;

✓   it doesn't cite the source for either the paraphrased or the directly copied information; and

✓   it doesn't accurately convey the meaning of the original source.

☞ **The Acceptable Paraphrase**

When you have achieved an acceptable paraphrase, it feels dramatically different. It sounds like an entirely new way of expressing the idea even though every effort has been made to capture the original meaning.

Acceptable paraphrase example

Hoemann says that there is very little absolutely new knowledge. Most of our discoveries take advantage of work done by those who have gone before us. The process of learning is, in fact, a long tradition passed on from generation to generation. Acknowledging the source of ideas gives recognition to the contributions of others in this tradition and is, as Hoemann says, an "act of humility."

Hoemann, George. *Electronic Style—Why Cite? 14 September 1998.* University of Tennessee. Retrieved October 3, 2000 from, <http://web.utk.edu/~hoemann/why.html>

This paraphrase is acceptable because it:

✓   accurately conveys the information;

✓   re-expresses it in substantially different words and phrases;

✓   identifies where words are exactly copied from the original;

✓   cites the original source of the information; and

✓ the author is mentioned in the text. This is not necessary, but is often considered good form to identify your source in the paraphrase itself.

Common Knowledge

There is no clear boundary on what is considered common knowledge. Even experts on plagiarism disagree on what counts as common knowledge. For instance, many sources only consider facts—current and historical events, famous people, geographic areas, etc.—to be potentially common knowledge. Others also include nonfactual material such as folklore and common sayings. Some sources limit common knowledge to only information likely to be known by others in your class; other sources look at what is common knowledge for the broader subject area.

The two criteria that are most commonly used in deciding whether or not something is common knowledge relate to quantity—the fact can be found in numerous places; and ubiquity—it is likely to be known by a lot of people. Ideally both conditions are true. A third criterion that is sometimes used is whether the information can be easily found in a general reference source.

If you are not sure, assume that an idea is not common knowledge and cite the source. It is much easier to remove a citation than it is to hunt down a citation and try to add it later. Finally, when in doubt, check with your professor.

Online sources

Online sources primarily include Internet web pages, electronic books, and full-text journal articles (usually available from a library databases). Any material you use in a paper from an online source, including information from the web, should be acknowledged just as it would be if it came from a traditional print publication. Being in the electronic environment does not change the rules.

Cutting and pasting information from online sources into your paper can make it particularly vulnerable to plagiarism. Careful documentation is required to avoid losing the information you need to properly acknowledge your source. It is also difficult to tell where you have copied information word-for-word when it is inserted directly into a document containing your own original text unless you use some method to identify copied material.

Cutting and pasting can also lead to "Frankenstein" papers. With proper attribution, "Frankenstein" papers can avoid accusations of plagiarism. However, they usually receive low grades since it is difficult to create a cohesive, well-thought-out paper from bits and pieces of other people's words. Good writing practice recommends reading the source material, then 'closing the book' and writing notes in your own words to ensure you have understood the material and have begun the process of creating an original paper. Cut and paste can short circuit this process.

A problem unique to the Internet is that web page sources may change over time. A web page used as a source for your paper may move or cease to exist. Your professor may not be able to find it to confirm your research. Information on a web page may also be deleted or changed affecting the conclusions you drew from it in your paper or passages you have quoted.

You have several options to protect your research in this unpredictable environment:

- ✓ Include the date you visited the web page as part of your citation.

- ✓ Make a copy of pages from which you have quoted or used significant information.

- ✓ Locate the original version of the site you used. Several search engines can help you track down an older version of a website. Google's cached link, included with each listing, has a snapshot of the site from the date it was last crawled. The Wayback Machine, *web.archive.org/collections/web.html*, is a more complete archive of older versions of websites. However, you need to know the URL of the site you are looking for so it is still important to document your sources in the first place.

References

California State University San Marcos 2008-2010 catalog. (2008). California State University San Marcos: San Marcos, CA.

Davidson, Glen W. (2004) Abraham Lincoln and the DNA controversy. Retrieved February 5, 2008, from *http://www.historycooperative.org/journals/jala/17.1/davidson.html*

Merriam Webster's medical dictionary. (2007-2008). Retrieved February 5, 2008, from *http://medical.merriam-webster.com/medical/marfan*

Purdue University Online Writing Lab (OWL). (2002). Avoiding Plagiarism. Retrieved August 14, 2002 from *http://owl.english.purdue.edu/handouts/research/r_plagiar.htm*. [Note: chart from old version of site.]

Writing Tutorial Services, Indiana University. (2004, April 27). Plagiarism: What it is and how to recognize and avoid it. Retrieved February 5, 2008, from *http://www.indiana.edu/~wts/pamphlets/plagiarism.shtml*

Chapter 33

How to Credit Sources

Susan Thompson, Systems Coordinator,
California State University San Marcos,
San Marcos, California

An Overview of Citation in Research Papers

T he growth of human knowledge is, in many ways, like a great conversation. Each new generation of scholars critiques the opinions of older scholars, sometimes defending and sometimes offering objections, much as people do who are having a polite but serious  conversation on important matters. In a normal conversation it is easy to know who is talking, and it is easy to keep track of who has offered which opinions. In the Great Conversation of human knowledge this is more difficult, since the conversation takes place over many centuries, and in many languages.

Citation could be thought of as a set of conventions that have been adopted to help the Great Conversation proceed more smoothly. Any conversation has such conventions. For instance, it is impolite to walk up to a conversation and start speaking before you know what the conversation is about. In the Great Conversation, a new speaker is also expected to know what the conversation is about before offering his or her own opinion. To show that you know what has been said by others, you need to explain how your own opinion has been influenced by previous "speakers" in the Great Conversation. To do this, you need to refer to those speakers, i.e. you need to cite their work.

When to Give Credit

Need to cite when:	No need to cite when:
• referring to someone else's ideas, opinions, or theories, such as by paraphrasing • copying exact words • reprinting or copying graphical elements such as diagrams, illustrations, maps, charts, and pictures • using ideas from others given in conversation, interviews, correspondence (letters or e-mail) or heard during lectures, speeches, and from media such as television and radio	• using ideas, opinions, or theories that are genuinely original to you • writing up your own experiment results including your own artwork or other original creation • recording anecdotes about other people, in which those people remain anonymous • using common knowledge according to accepted criteria

Why Cite?

Citing your sources has several specific benefits for you the student. Of course, a primary benefit is that it shows you are crediting your sources and so avoiding the possibility of plagiarizing. Even more important though is that it gives you credibility. It is concrete documentation of the hard work you have done in researching the background of your topic including the ideas other people have had on the subject. Professors generally respect and reward well-researched papers.

☞ **Citations accomplish several purposes:** Identify the source of an idea, specific words, or other material in order to acknowledge its contribution to your paper. It is the existence of these acknowledgments, or lack there of, that is the determiner of whether material has been plagiarized.

☞ **Enable the reader to locate the original source:**

» so that they may verify the accuracy of your information; and

» so that they may use it in their own research. In fact, a highly successful research strategy is to locate one good source and then use the citations in its bibliography and notes to identify additional relevant sources.

Provide the reader with a sense of the **relevance and quality** of the sources used in researching the paper and, hence, a sense of the quality of the paper. Indicators of quality include:

✓ the variety of sources from different viewpoints and mediums (print and online);

✓ the source's appropriateness to the topic as inferred from the title;

✓ the source's objectivity as implied by the type of site (.edu vs. com) and sponsoring organization; and

✓ the authority or expertise on this topic of the author or sponsoring organization of the website.

Overview of Attribution

Attribution, at its most basic level, requires that you include a bibliographic citation for each source that you use. These citations usually appear in a list at the end of the paper in a section titled variously bibliography, endnotes, references, and works cited. Footnotes, which provide the full citation on the same page as the information cited, may also be used. The type of list you use depends on whether you also refer to, or cite, the source in the text of your document. Bibliographies and references usually list all the sources you used in the course of your research whether or not you end up citing them in your paper. Endnotes, footnotes, and works cited only include citations for those sources you directly cite in the body of your text. Endnotes and footnotes are formatted such that a direct tie is established to the location in the text where the source is cited. The citation style you use and your professor's preferences usually determine the type of citation list you should use.

Citing a particular source within the text of your paper involves an additional format—a brief mention of the source at the point it is used. This mention of the source cited in the body of the paper is usually tied to the full citation located in either a footnote or an endnote. There are two common ways you can identify or 'cite' a source in the body of your paper. One is to provide a signal phrase, usually the author's name, as a lead-in to the quote or other information from the source. Another method uses an identifier, such as a number or the author's last name in parentheses, after the quote or reference.

Typical elements in bibliographic citations from the print publication world include:

- ✓ **author**, editor, translator, organization (corporate author) or other creator of the content
- ✓ **title** and subtitle
- ✓ indication of which **edition** or version
- ✓ name of journal, series, encyclopedia, or other **parent publication** in which the work appears
- ✓ **publication information**
  - place of publication
  - name of publishing body
  - date of publication

A comment about quotation marks. Quotation marks typically are used to indicate the beginning and ending of directly quoted material—words copied exactly from the original source. However, quotation marks can also be used for other purposes, in particular, as scare quotes. Scare quotes are used to emphasize particular words, often to indicate irony or a special or a typical use of language such as slang. They can either use double quotation marks, " ", or single, ' '. The following excerpt from Hoemann (1998) illustrates the use of scare quotes: "Very little is discovered "de novo," that is, without a solid foundation in other researchers' previous exploration and understanding."

Citation Styles

Rules for citing sources and citation formats can get complicated. A number of style guides have been developed that provide consistency in how information is cited. Some of the most common styles are APA, Chicago, and MLA. Citation styles are often associated with certain professional groups and disciplines. For instance, APA, American Psychological Association, is often used in the sciences while MLA, Modern Language Association, is popular in the literature and humanities area. Some professors don't care which citation style you use as long as you are consistent.

The following lists the major style guides and an Internet site which outlines the style. Note that while the Internet sites are convenient they usually only have the most basic information. For all the rules and exceptions, look at the official manual published by the style's sponsor. Rules for citation styles change over time, particularly recently with the Internet, so it is important to use the latest edition. Any library will have some, if not all, of these style guides.

☞ **APA**

Publication Manual of the American Psychological Association, 6th ed. (2009). Washington, DC: American Psychological Association.

http://www.apastyle.org/

☞ **Chicago Manual of Style**

University of Chicago Press, The Chicago Manual of Style, 16th ed. Chicago : University of Chicago Press, 2010.

http://www.chicagomanualofstyle.org/home.html

☞ MLA

MLA Handbook for Writers of Research Papers, 7th ed. New York, Modern Language Association of America, 2009.

http://mlahandbook.org/

For More Information

More information on citing online sources (including web pages, full-text articles in journal databases, e-mail, live chat, etc.) for these styles and others can be found in these guides:

Diana Hacker. Research and Documentation Online. Retrieved Dec. 3, 2009 from, *http://www.dianahacker.com/resdoc/*.

California State University San Marcos. (Sept. 11, 2009). Citation Style Guides. Retrieved from, *http://lib2.csusm.edu/subject-guide/94-Citation-Style-Guides*.

Citing Online Sources

The rules for citation styles were developed for print sources—long before online documents were available. So not too surprisingly, it can be difficult to locate identifying information equivalent to that available in print publications in an online source and fit it into a traditional citation format. Sometimes you have to do some investigation, or even be a little creative, to get the necessary information. Understanding the basic purposes of citation can help you determine what information you really need.

The three basic purposes of citation are to:

1. identify your source;

2. enable others to locate the source; and

3. provide brief criteria to evaluate the source's relevance and quality.

Web Sources

Electronic forms of publications, especially web pages, turn many of the traditional citation elements on their ear. This is mainly due to a sea change in how the information is created. In traditional print publications, determination of which writing is accepted and how it will appear is highly controlled, resulting in high quality, easy-to-document sources. In the web environment, anyone can publish in any style they wish. There are often no editors to make sure the author puts his or her name and date on the page, provides meaningful content, or even makes sure the facts are straight. As a result, the burden is put on the reader, including you, the researcher, to locate the citation identifying the source and to judge if the web page's content is accurate and of an appropriate quality. The following list takes a look at traditional citation elements in the web environment:

☞ **Author:** Often lacking altogether, or at other times a name is present on the page without explaining the status—is this the creator of the information or the webmaster maintaining the computer? Frequently the author's name appears somewhere on the website but not on the page you are looking at. The following examples illustrate two strategies for hunting down the author's name:

Example: looking for author in "About"
Many websites have an "About this site" page that has basic information such as the author, date of creation, and purpose of the site. The About page concept seems to come from the Microsoft Windows protocol in which information describing the software is described in an About section in the Help menu.

The trick is **locating** the About information, assuming it is present. Most commonly a link is provided at the home page level of the site. A link may also appear in the footer at the bottom of individual web pages or in some part of the navigation structure. About information may be a part of the help section of the site. It may not be named "About" so look for likely names in the navigation structure such as "overview," "summary," "purpose," etc.

Example: finding the author using the URL

The URL or address of a web page may have a link to information about the author. The URL consists of two main parts:

1. the address of the sponsoring organization's web server, e.g., *www2.csusm. edu;*

2. the directory structure, with each directory separated by a slash, in which this particular page is located, e.g., *http://www2.csusm.edu/sthompsn/presentation_frame.htm*

Sometimes authors are provided with their own directory within this structure. If they treat it as their personal home page, the author will usually provide their name and information about themselves, such as their credentials and affiliations, which can help you judge their expertise. Often, but not always, these personal directories are identified with a tilde "~" in front of the directory name (usually a form of the author's name). Deconstructing the URL, by deleting the trailing directories, will reveal the author's personal page if it is present, e.g., *http://www2. csusm.edu/sthompsn/.*

☞ **Corporate author:** Often an organizational entity rather than an individual is responsible for creating the content. The line between corporate author and sponsoring organization is somewhat slippery in the web environment but basically an organization acting as a corporate author has a planned, deliberate relationship with the website and is responsible for its content. For example:

Purdue University Online Writing Lab (OWL). (August 14, 2002). *Avoiding Plagiarism.* Retrieved from, *http://owl.english.purdue.edu/handouts/research/r_plagiar.html.*

☞ **Title, subtitle:** This most basic of citation elements is often very difficult to pick out on a web page—is it the words in the biggest type on the page, words in the banner, the filename in the top bar of the browser, …? When trying to decide between competing elements for title on a web page, choose the one that is most descriptive of the page's content. Some web pages have no title at all. Because the title is so important in conveying a sense of the relevance of the source to the reader, it is imperative that you supply one. You should check with your professor, but it is often considered OK to construct an appropriate title yourself rather than not have any title in the citation or one irrelevant to the page's content. You might also include an annotation, providing a brief description of the content, after the citation if the web page's title is missing or irrelevant.

☞ **Edition:** Changes to publications in the print world are usually infrequent so it is important to indicate new versions. Edition information appears most frequently in reference works such as *Merriam-Webster's Collegiate Dictionary, Eleventh Edition.* The very nature of the Web is such that information is constantly being updated making the idea of 'editions' seem arcane. However, it is more important than ever for your reader to know which version of the source you used. Otherwise, how do you explain to your professor why the information you quoted last month isn't on the website when she checks your paper today? Including the date when you viewed the site acts as a kind of 'edition' indicator. It is so important, that most style guides specify that you include some sort of date-visited information in your citation.

☞ **Parent publication:** Typical print publications which have parents are magazines and journals, for which you include both the article title and title of the magazine/journal, and edited books, for which you include the section title and the title of the book. The relationship of a web page to its overall website can fall into this parent/child category of publication. While you always want to use the URL of the actual page you are citing, sometimes it can provide a helpful context to include information about the parent or overall website in the citation for an individual page.

Sometimes it is difficult tell if a web page is part of a larger site if you didn't navigate to it through the site's home page. Usually it is clear from the navigation structure that the page is part of a larger site. You can also use the URL deconstruction technique described in the author example to see if the next directory up contains the parent website. In the citation, the home page or overall site name is italicized as the parent work and the title of the page itself is surrounded by quotes as you would an article title. Whether or not you choose to include the parent site information can also affect how you write your title for the page:

Harnack, A. and Kleppinger, E. (2001). "Chapter 5: Using MLA Style to Cite and Document Sources." *ONLINE! a Reference Guide to Using Internet Sources*. Accessed Sept. 12, 2002, *http://www.bedfordstmartins.com/online/cite5.html*.

vs.

Harnack, A. and Kleppinger, E. (2001). *Using MLA Style to Cite and Document Sources*. Retrieved Sept. 12, 2002 from *http://www.bedfordstmartins.com/online/cite5.html*.

☞ **Publication information:** Traditionally, these attributes include the name and location of the publisher and the date of publication. Information about the publisher is important for locating print sources but is usually not relevant to many websites. However, when there is a clear intentional publisher relationship to a site, that information should be included in the citation. Note that the organization sponsoring the website is not necessarily the same as the publisher. Less clear is whether you need to include the publisher's location in a web citation.

☞ **Date:** This is every bit as important in the web environment as it is in the print world but all too often this critical information is missing. Some websites include a "last updated" or "last modified" date. More and more sites are providing a copyright date. Date information is usually provided in the footer at the bottom of the page. You might also look at a website's home page and their "About" page for date information.

If more than one date is given, such as both copyright and last-updated dates, you should use the one most specific to the actual page you are citing. For instance, the copyright may be for the year 2002, but the site may have been updated several times during the year. On the other hand, the whole site may have a copyright date of 2002 but the page you are using was last modified in 2001. A recent date for a website does not necessarily indicate that information on a particular web page has been updated.

☞ **Date visited:** Most online citation styles now ask that you include the date that you viewed the page. Often this will serve as the only date information in the citation. The date visited also tells the reader which version or 'edition' of the page you based your research on.

☞ **Sponsoring organization:** Not part of citations in the print world unless the organization is the corporate author or the publisher. However, for web sources, the organization sponsoring or associated with the website may be the only 'author' information available. In addition, even if the author is known, the sponsoring organization can provide important context by which the quality of the information may be judged. Some style guides, like MLA, recommend including sponsoring organization information whenever possible.

☞ **Page numbers:** Pages, as such, do not exist in HTML, the document form most web pages use. (Web pages that are in PDF format can be broken into individual pages and may have page numbers.) Page numbers are normally required when citing direct quotations. If the web page has some kind of logical divisions, such as subheads, you can use these in place of page numbers. Some citation styles recommend counting the number of paragraphs from the last division or from the top of the page and including that information in the citation. Still other styles say page numbers are not needed or are optional for web pages.

☞ **DOI:** The Digital Object Identifier. This unique string of number is assigned to online periodicals to identify their content and provide a consistent link to their location on the Internet. Where a DOI is present, you may no longer have to include the URL in your citation.

☞ **URL:** The universal resource locator, or web page address, is a critical component of web page citations since it is required to find the exact same page again. For this reason, it is important that you make sure the URL works. If you have a very long URL, don't use hyphens as a break between lines—people will assume they are part of the address. Instead, break the URL after a slash (the start of a new directory). Finally, the URL for the specific page is generally preferred, rather than the address for the larger website, in order to connect readers directly to the information cited.

In general, the more information you can include in your web page citation, the better. The MLA section of the Research and Documentation Online Website (www.dianahacker.com/resdoc/) provides a good list of suggestions on the types of information to include in your citation.

Online Full-Text Sources

Electronic full-text journal articles can present some unique problems in citation. Full-text sources are almost always generated from a print version of the same information. Unlike Internet sources, all the source information is usually present but it may not appear the way it would in the print version of the article. Most notable are page numbers, which may be missing from some online formats. Full-text in PDF format is usually an exact copy of the original print version and includes all illustrations in their original location in the document and the original text formatting such as headers and footers, where pagination and other source information typically appears. It is possible to cite the information displayed in this format just as if you held the print version in your hand.

Full-text in HTML, or other computer formats, may include all the text from the print version, but it has been input separately into the online content management system. As a result, the original text formatting is lost and illustrations and other incidental material may not appear at all or may be in a different location. The source information may be included as part of the full-text file or it may only be complete in the original citation that linked you to the full-text. You may want to get in the habit of printing out the citation results page of your search as well as the full-text itself to be sure you have all the source information.

Page numbers are a more complicated issue. The continuous file structure of HTML eliminates any kind of pagination. The source information may or may not include the page number range of the print version of the article. For direct quotes, where you need the exact page number, either find a print copy to use or treat the article like a web source and use natural divisions in the text, such as section heads and indicate how many paragraphs after that your quotation appears.

Because HTML versions of full-text articles do not look exactly like the print version, it is important to include the library database information in your citation. This allows your professor to look at the same version that you used so there is no question on page numbers or other differences from the original print version. Typically, database information for the citation includes the name of the database, the name of the database provider, and any relevant retrieval information. The date you accessed the site is also advised since the database's journal holdings may change over time. Herbert Coutts (see "References"), University of Alberta, explains how to include database information for each of the major citation styles. For example:

Fitzgerald, Mark, (July 2002) "A plague of plagiarism," *Writer*, 115 (7): p. 16. Retrieved from Academic Search Elite, *http://library.csusm.edu/databases*.

References

Coutts, Herbert T. (Sept. 24, 2007). "Citation Style Guides for Internet and Electronic Sources," *Libraries — Learning Services*, University of Alberta. Retrieved Feb. 5, 2008 from *http://www.library.ualberta.ca/guides/citation/*.

Diana Hacker. Research and Documentation Online. Retrieved Dec. 3, 2009 from, *http://www.dianahacker.com/resdoc/*.

Hoemann, George. Electronic Style—*Why Cite?* (September 1998). University of Tennessee. Retrieved September 18, 2002 from, <*http://web.utk.edu/~hoemann/why.html*>

Purdue University Online Writing Lab. (Sept. 18, 2007) *Avoiding Plagiarism: Safe Practices.* Retrieved Feb. 5, 2008, from, *http://owl.english.purdue.edu/owl/resource/589/03/* .

Part IX

Writing

Chapter 34

The Mechanics of Good Writing

 Reprinted with permission from Susan Snively, former Director of the Amherst College Writing Center, Amherst, Massachusetts

Many students believe that a good writer is simply born that way, or has lucked into a procedure for getting words on paper quickly and easily. This mythological "good writer" simply sits down at the keyboard or yellow legal pad and lets the ideas flow neatly onto the page, then prints the pages, stacks them together, does a quick proofread, turns the paper in and gets an A. The writer never rethinks (all his ideas have cooked perfectly in his head into a gourmet masterpiece), never rereads, never rewrites. He never struggles and he feels no pain.

Believing this myth can interfere with the facts that a good writer learns from experience and turns the learning into habits of mind. Writing is like living. Because it is alive, it grows, and just as living things do not evolve in smooth graceful leaps, writing does not either. The writer struggles for form and voice to make the writing comprehensible. Recognizing this fact can help you turn the wayward, awkward moments into meaningful connections.

☞ **First, a good writer knows writing is a process.**

A good writer thinks of writing as a process and not just as a product. From this belief come other good habits which the writer learns from writing. But keep in mind that these are habits, not character traits. You can learn them if you want to; they aren't imprinted on people from birth like finger prints or awarded to the lucky few like blue ribbons at a cattle show.

☞ **Second, a good writer thinks, and thinks about thinking.**

But thinking is not the same thing as filling your head with facts, names, and dates. It means noticing relationships, raising questions, testing feelings and opinions, and asking how something can be proved true.

A good writer tries to balance thinking about a subject with thinking about the approach to the subject. "Have I got the evidence I need to prove that World War I began in 1914?" (a seemingly easy question) might turn into an interesting problem if the writer asks, "What do I mean by 'began'?" "How far can I trace the war's origins?" A good writer seeks **definitions of the terms** he uses or is asked to use, and looks for **many meanings** instead of just one.

A good writer also asks about his or her own biases and conditioning, about the influence of popular opinion, TV, films, journalism, on these opinions.

☞ **Third, a good writer takes time.**

Franz Kafka kept a sign above his desk that read WAIT. This sign told him to let a story mature in his head before writing it down. At college you may think that you don't have time for such a luxury: deadlines don't let you WAIT but tell you to GET GOING. Thinking of writing as a process will help you with the problem of time.

1. First, think about the **how** as well as the **what.** Thinking about the process from beginning to end may help you see where you can find more time to think, write, and rewrite. Evaluating your habits of composing can help you see where you bogged down.

2. Second, try to balance WAIT with GET GOING as you plan your paper: reserve time for reflection and imaginative thinking, as well as time for writing and rewriting.

   Many students wait until the last minute to write papers, hoping that the pressure of deadlines will force out profundities directly onto the page, like icing from a decorator tube. If you can write good papers at the last minute and feel good about doing so, then read no further. But if you find yourself feeling uneasy with that game of brinkmanship, or if the papers turn out to be not as good as they might be, then consider a change of habit:

» *Turn the One Big Deadline into a series of smaller deadlines set by yourself, for the first draft, second draft, etc. This will give you a sense of control and help you feel that you are moving towards completion. That sense of control may make your thinking clearer and your writing stronger.*

» *Give yourself air. Take breaks between bouts of writing so that you can relax and come back refreshed. The writing will go better, you'll feel less martyred, and you may think more creatively.*

» *Talk positively, even if you don't feel positive. During exams you may hear fellow students uttering woeful statistics about their work: "I have eleven papers due tomorrow and five exams in the same hour." No matter how overworked you feel, someone else will feel more so. The more you talk about this grim subject, the less energy you'll have for getting it behind you. Ease up on the word "time." Saying it only makes it weigh more, and turns you from a person into a beast of burden. Beasts of burden don't write.*

☞ Fourth, a good writer revises.

Revising a paper is like saying to it, "You were going out there a chorus-kid, but now I'm gonna make you a STAR." But it is not a magical process, any more than is struggling from chorus line to center stage. Revision means **looking again**: testing to see if your earlier draft has met the requirements; marking weak places; tightening your argument; polishing your words; checking spelling, mechanics, and typing. More critically, revision asks you to rethink your idea for logic, persuasiveness, and clarity, and to groom your words so that they help you look good.

Learning to revise can help improve every stage of writing. Knowing that you're going to revise will free you of the pressure to make the first draft perfect, something a first draft should never have to be.

Becoming your own editor will heighten your sensitivity to words and how they work. And it will give you a sense of competence which will increase with every paper.

Chapter 35

Brainstorming

Cheryl McKnight, California State University Dominguez Hills
Center for Learning and Academic Support Services (CLASS)
Carson, California

Brainstorming is the term commonly used to refer to any type of pre-writing that authors use to help themselves generate ideas and work out the connections between larger and smaller concepts.

Brainstorming is an invaluable process used by writers at all skill levels, regardless of their experience. Good writing is understood to be not the product of a "genius strike of lightening" but the product of a series of trials and errors, beginning with the early stages of prewriting that are generated through brainstorming.

It is also important to note that writers are not permanently linked to their original outlines. During the research and/or writing processes, authors usually find that their initial "Plan of Action" needs to be revised and, in some cases, completely rethought. Don't be afraid to see your writing as a work in progress that can and, in some cases, must be modified to match the evolution of your work. All writers go through this very normal process. This is good writing in action!!

Common Prewriting Techniques

Word Map: Use circles or arrows to show relation between ideas.

List: List any and all ideas/items about your topic.

Scratch Outline: Highlight the main points of your paper.

Question and Answer: Ask yourself questions about the topic.

Freewrite: Be the creator, not the editor of your work.

Samples of Brainstorming Strategies

☞ **Writing Prompt:** Read the topic or idea presented as the prompt for the writing assignment. The social and political movements of the past thirty years have contributed to a more "open" society with increased rights for the citizens of our country. This openness has, in turn, led to an expanded desire – if not demand – for increased personal freedoms. This evolution in thought is generally regarded as an overall positive development. Many, however, debate the nature and degree of the rights that should be afforded to our society's children and adolescents.

As the pace of the culture speeds up, many are concerned that our young people are engaging in increasingly "adult" behavior; this is especially true with respect to dress standards and norms. To remedy the perceived threat as embodied by current dress fashions, many parents and educators have begun to advocate for dress codes in the public school systems.

☞ **Writing Task:** Develop a position paragraph in which you either support or reject the school uniform policy and in which you state clear reasons and examples for your claims.

Brainstorming Strategy 1: Word Map

Make a word map with key terms related to the topic. Use circles to show the relation between ideas. Allow the spatial relationships on the page to provide you with a visual representation of the ways in which your topics and subtopics can be connected with one another.

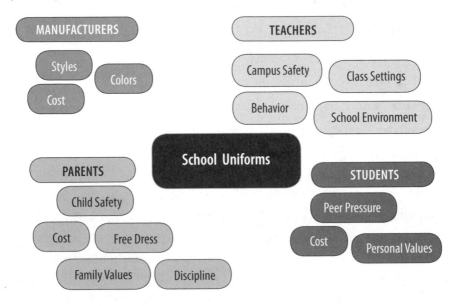

Brainstorming Strategy 2: List

List any and all ideas/items about your topic. Using a list allows the writer a great deal of freedom. You do not have to conform to any preset standards or ideas. Just allow any and all of your ideas to come forward, writing them down as you think of them. After you have completed your first draft of the list, review it and eliminate those ideas that you are certain will not benefit the draft you are working on. You can use the remaining items to begin to determine which are the main ideas, which are the supporting ideas, and in which order you would like to arrange them in your document.

Initial List	Revised List (shows unnecessary items)
Cost of uniforms	Cost of uniforms
Uniform manufacturers	*
Cost of clothes	Cost of clothes
Colors of uniforms	*
Behavior control	Behavior control

Fewer fights?	Fewer fights?
Styles of dress for girls	Styles of dress for girls
Styles of dress for boys	Styles of dress for boys
Competition	Competition
Parental attitudes	Parental attitudes

Brainstorming Strategy 3: Scratch Outline

Briefly highlight the main points of your paper. Using the list you have generated, make an informal outline that will serve as a starting point in your efforts to organize your work. Remember, though, that this is just a starting point and you are not obliged to keep the order you establish during this prewriting activity. Allow this to be a springboard exercise that helps you to think about order and structure.

> **Sample Outline:**
> I. Current Styles of Dress
>   A. Girls
>   B. Boys
>   C. Cost
> II. Behavior Control
>   A. Fewer fights
>   B. Better Attitudes
> III. Parental Concerns

Brainstorming Strategy 4: Question and Answer

Ask as many questions about the topic as you can think of. During this process, allow your mind to flow freely and ask as many questions as pop into your head. These may be questions that you would like to know more about and/or they may be the questions that you think your audience will be asking and looking for answers to. Use the list to determine which questions you know the answers to and which questions you will need to research further. Begin your list free form, allowing the questions to emerge as they come to you. Eventually, you can use this to determine what type of order/structure you wish the paper to take.

Questions	Answers
Who benefits the most from uniforms?	Parents, Administrators
What is the cost of the average uniform?	???
What is the cost of kids' clothes?	???
Have uniforms actually been shown to improve school conditions?	???
Whose rights matter more? The school? The individual?	I think it depends
What about freedom of expression?	Not sure what I think yet

Brainstorming Strategy 5: Freewrite

Be the creator, not the editor of your work. Let your thoughts flow freely without interruption for five minutes. This process will allow you to "get the juices flowing" and may help you to uncover your thoughts and feelings surrounding the topic. It may also help you to remember long-forgotten experiences and ideas, all of which can help to guide you towards the position you will take in your writing.

Just remember that your freewriting is not your first draft. Instead, it is a warm-up exercise to help you formulate your ideas. Read through your freewriting and then work with the information that relates to your prompt. You can do this by highlighting the sentences or ideas that can be used in your first draft and adding notes to help you find ideas that address your prompt. Your notes can then be used to create a scratch outline, Q & A list and/or word map.

The following is an example of freewriting:

Well, I'm not sure how I feel about school uniforms…I don't know if I would force my kids to wear one to school but then again **I had to wear one and it turned out OK…***I didn't really like the colors that were chosen, but then again everybody had to wear the same thing so after awhile* **we didn't really notice** *the difference. Also, it was* **so much easier to not have to spend time picking out an outfit in the morning,** *especially since I had to get up early to catch the early bus. I did* **hate** *that the girls had to wear* **skirts**…*it used to get so cold in the winter and the tights didn't really help…I would certainly make sure my kids could wear pants!…Also, I guess we* **looked better**—*with* **everybody wearing the same thing,** *it gave us a nice* *uniform (pardon the pun!) look. Since we all kind of looked the same, I noticed that* **people fought less** *and teased each other less about clothes (although that didn't stop them from finding other things to pick on each other about)....* **The uniforms, once bought, probably end up saving parents money** *too b/c they don't have to constantly spend money trying to keep their kids in the latest styles (at least not at school)*.

Q & A to Expand Ideas

Ask questions to help formulate or support your view:
1. How can uniforms be acceptable?
2. How are they time efficient?
3. How can they promote safety/ standardization?
4. How does the cost of uniforms affect students' acceptance?

Scratch Outline:

Personal experience examples reveal
1.   *Uniforms are acceptable*
2. *Are time efficient*
3. *Can promote safety/ standardization*
4.   *Are cost efficient*

☞ **Final Draft/Completed Paragraph:** After reviewing your preliminary drafts, create a final draft. For example: *School uniforms provide many benefits to students, parents, and educators. First, students will always know what they are wearing, and they will not need to rush or feel pressured to find a "cool" outfit each morning. Additionally, they can spend their allowance on fun clothes for their free/play time. Second, parents will have the benefit of knowing there is structure in their children's educational environment, and they can rest assured knowing that, at least while they are in school, their children are not wearing "objectionable" styles. Furthermore, parents can save money. Third, educators can also enjoy the benefits of the uniforms in so much as the student body will usually have a presentable appearance. Moreover, educators will be less likely to encounter the types of arguments and fights that are generated by teasing and/or competition related to style choice. For all concerned, school uniforms are an invaluable addition to the academic learning environment.*

Chapter 36

Steps to Organization

Reprinted with permission from Susan Snively, former Director of the Amherst College Writing Center, Amherst, Massachusetts

Getting papers started often seems to be the hardest part of the process. Anxious to get the paper from inside the head onto the page, writers may become so obsessed with the product that they flounder about in the process. An outline may seem slightly constraining or restrictive, but making a plan for a paper need not inhibit the flow of ideas. A plan help you decide what is most important to say.

What follows is a list of methods for shaping the raw material of a paper. Not all of them will work for all kinds of papers, or for all people. Experimenting with various methods will help you see what works best when. Often writers who have "always done it that way" find that trying a new way releases energy and improves the prose.

Using the Paper Topic

When you receive a paper assignment, **read it aloud** once or twice; you'll be surprised how much more sense it makes. Then make a list of the questions you need to answer. Writing them down on a separate sheet of paper, in a computer file, or on notecards will help you see the assignment as yours, not simply as a regurgitation of others' ideas.

You may find that these questions form an outline which you can follow to set down information and draft ideas. Or the topic's questions may lead to one big question, problem, or definition which you may use as a focal point. If you become entangled in questions and possible lines of approach, pick the one that makes the most sense and start there. It may be the real beginning or it may lead you to the right start.

However you arrange the questions, **try to make the paper topic your own.** Take some time to figure out what preparation you need before you start writing: a trip through class notes, some re-reading of the class materials, some research in the library. Don't be afraid to **draft a series of preliminary questions** whose answers might give you a place to start. A snappy quotation from a primary source can often get a first paragraph going, whereas a large generalization might stop you in your tracks.

Rough Magic

In this method, the writer does not use an outline, but simply begins to write, steadily and quickly, until all the ideas have taken rough shape on the page. It often works when papers are short, when the subject is narrow in scope (a speech from a play, a painting, a controversial political document, a treaty, etc.) and the writer feels confident and familiar with the material. This method works best if the writer plans in advance to put in some time revising.

After completing the rough writing, the writer then goes back and **marks** (with numbers, underlining, or brackets) **the important points, and arranges them in a logical order.** Putting these points in a sequence and then reviewing them to see what the whole thing looks like will help control the wayward drifts of the rough writing, and lead to a careful rewrite.

It is often wise to take breaks between the rough writing and the reorganizing, in order to be re-charged for the final draft.

Grocery Lists

Most people start a paper with a list: it's comforting, it tells the writer he or she is going somewhere, it gives a sense of control by suggesting limits, and it doesn't take too much time.

However, list-making needs the same balanced treatment of freedom and discipline as rough magic. Proceed steadily and quickly, putting down everything that might be important, and then examine the list. Are all the ingredients here? Anything left out?

After you've made your list and checked it twice, write your first draft with one item to a paragraph. It's okay if the paragraphs look long and unwieldy; before the rewrite you'll examine them for proper balance and consistency. For now, the list is telling you simply to put things down.

Up Against the Wall

Many students have difficulties in the early stages of writing because they think that everything that turns into the paper must look like the paper. The result of this approach is a tight-looking series of pages, with paragraphs all bunched up (if there are paragraphs), no margins, and microscopic inserts tucked wherever possible.

This disorganized writing often happens when a student has a lot of material to cover or a series of questions to ask, each with a subordinate topic. As he writes he finds he must look up quotes again and again, sometimes losing track or changing direction in mid-draft. In fact, the student knows the material and has good ideas, but he seems to have too many ideas at once.

In this situation, the blank wall which faces him might help. He might make a list of points for each major category in the paper. Plato, Machiavelli and Hobbes might serve him better if he hung them on the wall, each with a list of nifty quotes and page references. Using different-colored paper for each category may help him see the way to clear, coherent drafting, and placing the lists beside each other may encourage comparative thinking.

For papers which require some knowledge of chronological events or reactions happening in a sequence, the blank wall might help again. Tacking up a blank piece of paper and drawing a horizontal line, the writer marks points of development along the line to consider before starting to write.

The Paragraph Outline: The Inside Authority

Some writers feel more comfortable with methods that prescribe what they should do when writing a paper. For such writers, a modified form of the traditional outline (Roman numeral, A.B.C., 1.2.3.) might work. This technique concentrates on shaping the structure of a paper by weighing each of its paragraphs.

The writer begins her outline by roughing out a paragraph which presents a thesis or problem. The paragraph may contain a list of questions the writer is promising to answer.

After drafting this paragraph, the writer then goes on to block out the rest of the paper. She roughs out a main idea for each succeeding paragraph in outline form, and lists the evidence she'll need to support the idea.

The process has begun to shape a coherent paper, covering important points and arranging them in a reasonable order. Presenting more details, sharpening focus, and working on transitions can come later, along with polishing up that first paragraph.

Building on Evidence

The paragraph outline works best when the writer feels sure of a line of argument and thoroughly understands the topic. Sometimes, however, a writer needs to write a draft or two in order to decide what her thesis is. This is known as the "how-can-I-know-what-I-think-till-I-see-what-I-say?" problem, and it often crops up when you confront material which offers no easy answer.

The paper topic asks you to look at the evidence from more than one point of view: to keep questions alive in your mind while writing, before emerging with conclusions, judgments, or definitions. You may write much better using such questions to focus on a selection of specifics (e.g., incidents, political changes, significant statistics, signs of the times) and build the whole paper out of "mini-papers," separate sections that take bits of evidence and evaluate them. With each of these sections you may want to assemble materials, asking simply "What do I need to refer to when I talk about this?" Building on facts, you can then raise questions and answer them. Or if the answers are ambiguous, the ambiguity may lead you to a more interesting conclusion than a dead-certain approach might have done.

Good Old Traditional Outlines

For some papers, particularly long ones, the good old traditional outline still works. It allows the writer to focus in both large and small units; it suggests a coherent procedure and gives the writer a sense of mastery. Advice about traditional outlines is likely to be so commonsensical that it's just plain boring. Nevertheless, for writers who want to improve their skills at outlining, here are four suggestions.

☞ **Keep thoughts and details of equal weight parallel in structure.**
It is also important to use a logical order.

☞ **Use complete sentences** in outlining the major points of your argument, preferably sentences that illustrate cause and effect or show the relation of the part to the whole. Putting subjects with verbs helps writers feel more in charge of their arguments. In addition complete sentences will fit better into the first draft. Using a reasonable number of quotations will help unite the paper with its sources, and save time and trouble.

Though the writer may change some of these sentences, they can lead to a reasonable paragraph; this is the advantage of a sentence-outline over a phrase-outline. It often works best when the writer is feeling confident and prepared, has a strong interest in the subject and has allowed several days or weeks to get the paper done.

☞ **Try writing outlines and putting them aside; or, trash your way to glory.**
An outline can get you thinking, organizing, matching evidence to
ideas, noticing what quotes you need, helping you figure out a line of
argument. **And then you can go ahead without it.** To stick too
closely to it in some cases might not work, especially if it is elaborate.

Writing an **outline summary,** a list of major points derived from
the outline, might serve you just as well and make you less tense
when you start to write. This technique of turning the big outline
into a kind of trial outline helps writers who characteristically begin
their papers with a page covered in doodles, and bits of ideas scrib-
bled all over in a kind of three-ring circus effect. Whatever structure
the writer comes to use, preliminary outlining can help clear the
head.

☞ **Last but not least, try starting your paper with the last paragraph of a
rough draft.** Scrap the rest of it and begin at the end, making it the
introductory paragraph of your next draft. Believe it or not, this
method often works. Writing a rough draft often clears your head,
so that by the time your last paragraph rolls out, you're writing and
thinking more clearly. To put it another way, **rough writing is
often a way of giving yourself permission to say what you
mean.** A last paragraph summons up will and energy, allowing your
thoughts to crystallize, your ideas to become decisive. If, on re-
reading the rough draft, you find the ideas are weak or non-existent,
check the last paragraph to see if it has started to work better. If so,
then summon up your courage, take out your scissors, and carve out
a new start.

Chapter 37

How to Write Better Introductions and Conclusions

Cheryl McKnight, California State University Dominguez Hills
Center for Learning and Academic Support Services (CLASS)
Carson, California

Guidelines for Creating Strong Introductions

☞ Purpose of the Introduction

The introduction presents the main idea of the paper and captures the reader's attention. It should be clear and not cluttered with details.

☞ Steps of an Introduction

Generally, the introduction contains the following three parts:

1. Broad opening, attention-getting statement

» *Strong introductions will usually start with a broad opening statement that is relatively neutral and engages the reader's interest.*

» *This opening statement should usually make a claim that most people can understand.*

» *The purpose of this statement is twofold: to catch the reader's attention and to avoid alienating the reader*

» *A good example of a broad opening statement would be "Everybody has the right to be happy."*

» *After the opening statement, the writing moves towards the topic of the paper.*

2. Background information

» *After the writer has captured the reader's attention and slowly brought her/ him towards the context surrounding the topic of the essay, the writer should begin to reveal what position s/he will take in the paper.*

» *A good way to set the stage and prepare the reader for the claim that will be made in the thesis statement is to provide some factual background information about the topic.*

» *If the paper is arguing a certain position, after providing the background information, it is often helpful to provide a general overview of the opposition's position on the topic.*

» *The background information in the introduction should be limited to the "big picture"; specifics will occur in the body paragraphs and are not necessary in the introduction.*

3. Thesis statement

The thesis statement usually occurs near or at the end of the introduction and serves:

» *To announce the topic to the reader*

» *To state a position and/or make a claim about the topic*

» *To provide the reader with a blueprint for what is to come in the paper*

☞ Diagram of an Introduction

1. Broad opening, attention-getting statement

2. Background information

3. Thesis statement

☞ Sample Introduction

Opening: Welfare was created during the Great Depression to address a rampant epidemic of poverty in the United States.

Background: Thousands upon thousands of people could not find work and were starving. The government stepped in to provide assistance. But an unfortunate by-product of this initially philanthropic institution is generational dependency on the "dole," which strips the nation's poor of respect and empowerment and in turn engenders resentment in tax paying citizens.

Thesis statement: In order to keep the welfare system alive and healthy, it must incorporate time limits, more job training programs, and incentives to encourage recipients to move beyond the system.

Guidelines for Creating Strong Conclusions

☞ Purpose of the Conclusion

The conclusion is the writer's way of summing up the main purpose of the essay and reviewing the relevant issues that were discussed in the body of the essay for the reader. The conclusion allows the writer to remind the reader of the most important concepts relating to the issue under discussion and to demonstrate their interconnectedness. This, in turn, allows the reader to see the "big picture" as it relates to the topic being addressed.

☞ Steps of a Conclusion

By and large, the conclusion contains the following three parts:

1. A return to the big picture

Strong conclusions will usually start by restating the general/big picture idea of the essay, thereby reminding the reader of the ideas that have been argued and demonstrated in the previous body paragraphs.

2. Summary of relevant points

» *After restating the main claim of the composition, the author should sum-marize the main points of the essay, so the reader can see the relationship between the initial claim and the evidence provided in the essay.*

» *A good way to summarize the relevant points is to provide one or two strong sentences that assert the facts / details of each of the preceding body paragraphs.*

3. Learning statement

» *The "learning statement" is the broadest part of the conclusion.*

» *In the "learning statement," the author offers the reader some of the insights that s / he has learned and / or insights that s / he hopes the reader has become aware of as a result of the composition.*

» *There is no exact formula for the "learning statement," but it usually reflects one of the following categories:*

  » ***Statement of a new view***

  » ***Hope for the future***

  » ***Suggestion for change***

  » ***Suggestion for future research***

☞ Diagram of a Conclusion

1. Return to the big picture
2. Summary of relevant points
3. Learning statement

☞ Sample Conclusion

Return to the big picture: To eliminate welfare would be to deny an essential part of our nation's ideology, that of offering assistance to all citizens who may need it. The elimination of welfare would actually create even more problems in society.

Summary of relevant points: Homelessness and crime would rise as the desperate poor try to survive. Welfare should offer incentives to encourage people toward self-sufficiency and to discourage people from taking advantage of the system. A program with time limits should be adopted in order to obliterate the possibility of generational welfare as children watch their parents work towards these goals and have a model to follow.

Learning statement: Welfare must stay in place and reforms must be made to the system before the stress between the recipients and contributors causes the system to break altogether, creating a situation reminiscent of the Great Depression.

Chapter 38

Learning to Write a Research Paper

Starting Out!® Research Group

Writing a research paper is a much bigger job than writing a short essay, story, or report, but it is a very satisfying process because of the knowledge we gain. It involves a series of organized steps beginning with the selection of a topic, followed by research and writing, and ending with a carefully prepared piece of work that serves a real purpose.

Research papers are not designed to be a tedious exercise for an English or history class. Rather, they represent an orderly process of collecting, organizing, and presenting information that increases our knowledge, documents an argument or line of reasoning, or serves as the basis for making a decision.

In an academic setting, research papers serve as a way to learn a great deal about a small, specialized topic. After writing a paper, we often feel we are almost an expert on a single topic. In the working world, companies make decisions based upon research and reporting in a very similar way. Information on a given topic is collected, analyzed, assembled, and presented, and then decisions are made about whether to create a new product, re-design a product, offer a new service, open a new market, or change other ways in which business is being conducted. To write a research paper you must first do some research to learn all about your topic. Examine books, journals, newspapers, or the Internet to gather the facts that will be used in the paper. Sometimes the research requires interviewing others or performing a series of experiments. The information that is gathered in this way can then form the basis of your paper and the position that you will ultimately take.

Writing a research paper also involves documenting your sources of information with footnotes or endnotes. This way the reader knows where you obtained your information and can judge whether it is reliable.

Steps to Follow when Writing a Research Paper

☞ **1. Selecting a topic**

» Choose a topic that interests or challenges you. You will definitely work harder on your paper if you enjoy the process and feel you are learning something worthwhile.

» Give yourself time to select a topic by doing some preliminary reading or research in some of the possible areas that you are considering. For example, do you want to understand why alternative sources of energy is important? If so, you might formulate a research paper about the differences between solar, wind, and tidal energy. Do you want to learn more about a figure in history, a life-changing event, such as the collapse of the World Trade Center on September 11, 2001, or a current political controversy, such as whether we should have a simpler income tax code. Good research ideas often come from looking at the headlines in a newspaper and wondering what is behind the news.

» Be sure the topic you select is not too broad or complex. It is always easier to write a research paper about a very specific subject or idea, so that the paper does not get too long or cover too much ground. For example, it is preferable to write a paper about the contributions of Martin Luther King, Jr. than about the entire history of the civil rights movement. Similarly, rather than writing about Egyptian history, it would be better to select a single topic, such as theories as to how the pyramids were constructed.

☞ **2. Researching information sources**

» Visit your college library and use the catalog to locate possible books or articles on your topic. Get some guidance from the librarian. When you go to the library shelves, don't just look at one book. Look at those books nearby that may offer additional information on the same subject.

» Try to use as many different types of sources as you can, including books, magazines or journals, and Internet articles. Don't rely on just one source for all your information.

» Keep a list of all the sources that you use. Include the title of the source, the author, publisher, and place and date of publication. Make note of the URL if the article is from the Internet. This information will be needed when you put together a final bibliography of all the sources you used. You may want to put the information on file cards or separate sheets of paper within a binder, so they don't get lost.

☞ **3. Read your sources and take careful notes:** After you've gathered a group of sources, begin reading about your topic or question and taking notes.

» Use 3 x 5 index cards or a separate sheet of paper for each fact, theory, or idea that you feel is important, and that helps advance your overall paper's objectives. Be sure to make a note of the source of each piece of information.

» Group similar ideas or related information from different sources together.

» If you copy something directly from a book, such as a quotation or specialized concept or opinion, without putting it in your own words, put quotation marks around it, and write down the source where you found the quotation, including book name, publisher, date, and page number. If you use other people's ideas or quotations without giving them credit, you will be guilty of plagiarism, which is a serious literary offense, because it is equivalent to stealing someone else's ideas and presenting them as your own.

» Always keep your note cards or materials carefully organized so that they can be found and placed into an outline and then a rough draft for the final paper.

☞ **4. Organize your ideas into an outline:** Once you feel you have collected sufficient information about your topic on the note cards, you can begin to create a rough outline of your paper, which will help you organize how you present the information you have collected. Normally an outline includes the points you intend to make, in a logical order, each followed by the evidence, facts, or information you have found to support your points.

For example, if you have determined that there are four major points or arguments you wish to make in support of your position, list them in outline form, and have subheads below them which include the key supporting facts from your note cards that you intend to include.

You should organize your outline into major sections, such as the following:

» **An introduction**, which states the subject or argument you intend to investigate in the paper.

» **The body of your paper**, consisting of the key ideas or arguments you wish to make, including the supporting information you have found.

» **A conclusion**, which brings together the results of your research and writing into a series of organized results, arguments, or positions.

☞ **5. Prepare a first draft:** Since your outline should have organized your research into three main sections, your paper will also follow this order of presentation and give you a clear goal for each section.

☞ **6. Writing an introduction:** The introduction is the first paragraph of the paper. It often begins with a general statement about the topic and ends with a more specific statement of the main idea of your paper. The purpose of the introduction is to:

» Present the topic so the reader knows the intent of the research paper.

» Provide a general overview of your position, point of view, or goal in writing the paper.

» Draw the reader into your subject so he or she wants to read the rest of the paper to find out what you have to say or what you have discovered.

☞ **7. Drafting the body of the paper**: The body of the paper follows the introduction. It consists of a number of paragraphs in which you develop your ideas in detail.

» Limit each paragraph to one main idea, argument, or theme. It is never good to mix different ideas in one paragraph, since the reader may become confused.

» Support your ideas, position, and points with specific facts, examples, quotations, or references to the sources you researched.

» Think about the order of presentation of your ideas, so the paper builds from a foundation of distinct facts or arguments toward a conclusion.

☞ **8. Writing a conclusion:** The conclusion is the last paragraph of the paper. Its purpose is to:

» Summarize your prior points, arguments, or facts (without the examples) that set the stage for your concluding statement. Think of your concluding paragraph as a lawyer's final statement to the jury about the most convincing reasons for finding the defendant guilty or innocence.

» End your paper with a concluding statement that indicates that you have arrived at your position as a result of the facts and arguments presented in the paper.

☞ **9. Include footnotes or endnotes to document sources:** As you write your first draft, including the introduction, body, and conclusion, add the information or quotations on your note cards to support your ideas.

» Use footnotes or endnotes to identify the sources of this information. If you are using footnotes, the note will appear on the same page as the information you are documenting, at the bottom (or "foot") of the page. If you are using endnotes, the note will appear together with all other notes on a separate page at the end of your report, just before the bibliography.

» There are different formats for footnotes (and endnotes), so be sure to use the one your teacher prefers.

» Note that footnotes can be shortened if the source has already been given in full in a previous footnote.

☞ **10. Prepare a bibliography:** A bibliography is a list of the sources you used to get information for your research paper. It is included at the end of your paper, after your conclusion and endnotes.

» It is very easy to prepare a complete bibliography if you keep track of each book, encyclopedia, or article you use as you are reading and taking notes. Therefore, you should build your bibliography as you build your paper, always writing down each source you use, including full title, author, publisher, place of publication, and date.

» When assembling a final bibliography, list your sources (texts, articles, interviews, and so on) in alphabetical order by authors' last names. Sources that don't have authors (encyclopedias, movies) should be alphabetized by title. There are different formats for bibliographies, so be sure to use the one your teacher prefers.

☞ 11. Revising and polishing the first draft

» It is helpful to think about your first draft for several days before revising and improving it. Try to be very objective in reading your own work, and decide whether you have made clear points, or whether some of your ideas need further explanation or supporting evidence.

» If necessary, add to your research to fill in holes that you find in your paper or the evidence that you are assembling.

» Have somebody else read your paper and tell you if it follows a logical order and clearly makes your points. A fresh opinion of a first draft will help make the final draft much better.

☞ 12. Proofread the Final Draft

» Check your final draft carefully, avoiding spelling, punctuation, capitalization, or other formatting or stylistic errors. Be sure all sentences stand on their own.

» Ask a friend to proofread your paper as well, since two sets of eyes are better than one. If you are unsure about a word, look it up in the dictionary to be sure it is the best word to use and that you have spelled it correctly.

» Put your paper together in a neat document, since presentation is always an important part of a research paper. Be proud of the final product.

Chapter 39

Editing and Proofreading Strategies

University of Minnesota Center for Writing
Minneapolis, Minnesota

Problem

Editing and proofreading are essential aspects of effective writing. However, they are the later steps in the ongoing process of brainstorming, planning, drafting, and revising. Writers who rush or ignore any of these earlier steps can end up with a paper that is unclear, underdeveloped, and very difficult to correct in the later stages of the writing process. When you are ready to edit and proofread your draft, you should do so carefully and thoroughly. In reviewing your work and seeking feedback, the following strategies may prove useful.

Solutions

☞ **Leave yourself plenty of time for all steps of the writing process, including editing.** By making and following a timeline for the paper, you are more likely to have time to finish everything with the proper amount of care and attention. Also, keep in mind that it may be best to lay your paper aside for a day or so before proofreading and editing, as you may be more likely to catch errors or notice structural problems if your writing isn't so "fresh" in your mind.

☞ **Get acquainted with your resources.** You don't need to memorize every grammatical citation rule that may apply to the genre or discipline in which you're writing—you can look them up. Take advantage of the resources available to you: dictionaries, thesauruses, handbooks, citation guides, handouts from class, librarians, and writing center consultants.

☞ **Know your weaknesses.** Keep a list of errors you tend to make; it will help you know what to look for when you edit. You can also read the paper once for each error type—if you're only looking for one thing, you'll be more likely to notice it.

☞ **Print a copy of your paper to use when editing and proofreading.** It is much harder to catch errors on a screen than on paper.

☞ **Read your paper out loud.** Often, when we read silently, our eyes skip over small errors, awkward or run-on sentences, and typos. By reading out loud, you force yourself to notice everything from spelling and word choice to the structure of sentences. You can also have someone read your paper aloud and tell you where they are confused.

☞ **Read your paper backwards.** Another way to force yourself to notice small details is to take things out of context. Try reading your paper backwards, sentence-by-sentence or paragraph-by-paragraph, so that you are focusing on the text, not the ideas. This technique is especially helpful for catching sentence fragments.

☞ **Check the punctuation.** Look over the paper on a sentence-by-sentence level to see if your punctuation is correct. Are commas in the right places? Are there any run-on sentences? If you aren't sure about how to use certain kinds of punctuation, look in a manual, explore other quick tips, and/or ask a writing consultant for help.

☞ **Check each in-text citation for correct format,** and verify that the source is in the Works Cited or References list. This is also a good time to double-check the spelling of authors' names, book or article titles, and so on.

☞ **Reread quotations;** it is all too easy to mistype when copying words.

☞ **Get feedback from other people.** Because we are such a part of what we write, it can be difficult to step outside our work and view it critically. When you seek outside opinions, you can break free of the isolation and absorption of writing and receive perspectives and insights that you may have otherwise not considered. You are no longer left wondering whether you followed the guidelines of the assignment, whether your structure and language are clear, etc. By asking for feedback from other people, you are taking essential measures to improve your writing and to develop as a writer.

☞ **Don't rely solely on computer help.** Spell-check and grammar-check tools are useful, but they do not constitute or substitute for proofreading. Develop and follow your own editing strategies, and don't be fooled into thinking that computer tools alone are adequate for the job.

☞ **Rest. Relax. Reread.** Leave your paper alone for a day or two. Having some distance from what you've written can make your proofreader's eye more clinical and perceptive. In addition, you may find changes you would like to make after you read your text later.

Chapter 40

Completing Your Paper: The Final Draft

Patrick Rael, *Reading, Writing, and Researching for History: A Guide for College Students*, Bowdoin College, Brunswick, Maine

Before submitting your paper, complete the following checklist.

CHECKLIST

Introduction

✓ My introductory paragraph tells the reader the subject of my research, and defines key terms I will use in my thesis.

✓ My introduction contains a clearly-stated thesis which explains how and why something happened.

Paragraphs

✓ I have thought about how my paragraphs are arranged, and they are structured in a way that best supports my argument or findings.

✓ I have checked to make sure that I completely tackle one part of my argument before moving on to the next, and I have checked to make sure that I do not unnecessarily revisit arguments I began earlier in the paper.

✓ Each paragraph is focused around a main idea ("mini-thesis"), which is stated in the paragraph's first sentence ("topic sentence").

✓   Each paragraph employs evidence supporting that idea. That evidence is analyzed; that is, I have used my own words to tell the reader why and how my evidence supports the topic sentence.

✓   Each paragraph has a workable transition from its predecessor.

Argumentation

✓   I have thought about the arguments that could be marshaled against mine, and I have addressed those through refutation or concession.

Quoting and Citation

✓   All material I have quoted appears between quotation marks.

✓   I have minimized or eliminated block quotes. When I have used them, I have indented them on the left, single-spaced them, and not placed quotations at the start and end.

✓   Each time I bring in evidence that is not clearly common knowledge, I have cited the source of that information with a footnote or endnote.

✓   Each time I quote I have checked to make sure the quotation is properly integrated into the sentence.

✓   Each of my quotes clearly relates to a footnote or endnote which offers the source and page number of the quotation.

✓   For each of my quotes, it is clear who the speaker of the quote is, and the circumstances in which the speaker authored the quote (relevant time, place, and context).

✓   My footnote or endnote style conforms to the style in my style manual.

✓   I have included a bibliography of my sources, which conforms to my style manual.

Style

✓ Each page is numbered consecutively.

✓ I have used a common typeface, like Arial or Times Roman.

✓ I have double-spaced the paper, and have left one-inch margins at top, bottom, and sides.

✓ The title of my paper clearly relates to its contents, or to the question I have been asked to answer.

Editing

✓ I have proofread the paper for spelling and grammar errors.

✓ I have re-written the paper at least once, identifying and eliminating instances of:

> » *passive voice*
> » *inconsistent tenses*
> » *subject / verb disagreement*
> » *dangling clauses*
> » *improper pronoun references*
> » *comma splices, run-on sentences, and sentence fragments*
> » *colloquial phrases*

✓ I have read the paper aloud to myself or to someone else, listening for sentences that do not work.

Part X

Study Skills

Chapter 41

Where and When You Study: Choosing Your Best Place

Massachusetts Institute of Technology
Office of Undergraduate Advising and Academic Programming
Cambridge, Massachusetts

Where to Study

Your surroundings have a big effect on your efficiency. Answer each question in this section, and then read the advice that follows it. What changes do you need to make?

☞ **Is my study place available to me whenever I need it?**

» Your study place does you little good if you cannot use it when you need it.

» If you are using a shared study place, work out a schedule so that you know when you can use it without distractions and as long as you need it.

☞ **Is my study place free from interruptions and distractions?**

» It is important to have uninterrupted study time. Even one hour of study without distraction is more effective than four hours of study with interruptions.

» Turn off your cell phone or set it to silent. No ring tones + no vibrations = no distractions.

» Turn off the IM feature on your computer, unless you are using it as a means to communicate with members of a study group.

» Don't check your e-mail while studying. Set aside time to read it before you start studying or once you have finished.

☞ Does my study place have all the materials I need?

» Be certain that your study place includes reference sources and all of the supplies you generally need (e.g., graph paper, pens/pencils, rulers, calculator, a computer with Internet access).

» If you study best outside your room, check your backpack or bag before heading for the library or another study area to make sure you have everything you'll need.

☞ Does my study place have a large enough desk/table?

» Use a desk or table large enough to spread out everything you need, so that you don't waste time moving things around.

» Allow enough room for writing.

» Try to avoid clutter.

☞ Does my study place have a comfortable chair?

» A chair that makes you stiff or fidget will interfere with your studying.

» A chair that is too comfortable might make you sleepy.

» Find a chair in which you can sit for at least an hour and still maintain your attention. Then take a stretch break.

☞ Does my study place have enough light?

» Straining to see the page or screen burns through your energy more quickly.

» If you use a dark room as a study place, add a lamp or use a reading light.

☞ **Does my study place have a comfortable temperature?**

» If it's too warm, you might become sleepy.

» If it's too cold, you may become distracted.

» Select a temperature at which your mind and body function best.

When to Study

☞ **Make studying a regular part of your schedule.** Let it become routine like brushing your teeth or tying your shoes. For example, once your class times are set, find times when you have a two-hour block, say 2–4 p.m. on Tuesday/Thursday and 8:30-10:30 p.m. Monday/Wednesday. Do not ever schedule something else at those times: make them sacred!

☞ **Choose study times and days when you're likely to feel energetic** and have enough time to complete assignments before class.

☞ **Use daylight hours** (as much as possible). Research shows that 60 minutes of study during the day is the equivalent of 90 minutes of study at night (Pauk, 1989).

☞ **Plan to study for blocks of time.** Generally, studying in one-hour blocks is most effective (50 minutes of study with a ten-minute break). Shorter periods can be fine for studying notes and memorizing materials, but longer periods are needed for problem-solving tasks, projects, and writing papers.

☞ **Determine how long you need to study** to fully engage with the material you are learning. One recommendation is to study one hour for every hour you spend in class. You may find, over time, that you need more or less than this.

☞ **Study soon after lecture.** You'll remember and understand more if you review your lecture notes immediately after class. If questions arise then or something is unclear, you'll have plenty of time to check with a classmate or the instructor to clarify what you missed; it may be something important that you need for your homework and might even appear on an exam.

☞ **List and do tasks according to priorities.** Remember Parkinson's Law: "Work expands to fill the time available for its completion." If you allot two hours to read ten pages, it will probably take you the full two hours to complete this 30-minute task.

☞ **Start long or involved assignments ahead of time.** In your heart you know it's true: cramming and rushing = poor quality work.

☞ **Set an agenda for each study period.** Be specific, and plan ahead so that you know exactly what task you will accomplish during each study period.

☞ **Once you find a schedule that works for you, stick to it.** Some days you may not feel like studying at the appointed time, but habit will help you settle down.

Chapter 42

Technology Tips: Studying in the 21st Century

 Reprinted with permission of the Harold W. McGraw, Jr. Center for Teaching and Learning, Princeton University, Princeton, NJ

Y ou can find scholarly resources from your dorm room, communicate instantly with friends in another state, and get an instant answer to a factual question using a search engine. Yet the technology that facilitates so many activities for you can also be a source of distraction and even inefficiency. How can you make technology work for you?

Limit Distractions from Technology

☞ **Set out a certain time of day** that you will devote to fun with technology—browsing the Internet, playing games, chatting with friends, or checking e-mail. If you allocate time for this, you will not be tempted to let these activities interrupt your schedule.

☞ **When you need to concentrate on your studies, find quiet spaces,** and leave your cell phone, laptop, and other electronic devices at home.

☞ **Check e-mail only a few times per day,** and only handle it once: respond, archive, and/or delete.

☞ **Limit the number of listservs you are on** so that you can control the amount of junk mail you receive and must sort through.

☞ **To limit your time Instant Messaging,** use occasional e-mails to keep in touch with friends from other schools.

☞ **If all else fails, unplug** the Ethernet cord, remove the wireless cord, or work in an area without wireless. You might also make a habit of turning off the computer when not in use.

☞ **Assess what technology is truly needed when you study,** and proceed from there. Often all you need are the relevant books and papers to outline your paper, start a problem set, or practice conjugations. Don't discount the value of a clear, well-written textbook with loads of examples or diagrams to follow.

Use Technology to Your Advantage

☞ **When looking for scholarly articles and resources, go to the library home page** rather than using a general search engine. From there you can narrow your search, find legitimate peer-reviewed articles and accomplish quite a bit of research in a short amount of time.

☞ **Search the web with clear goals in mind.** What information do you need? What information do you already have? It is very easy to get thrown off course on the information superhighway, so the more specific the question you ask, the better off you will be.

☞ **Put a cap** on how much time you spend looking up things online. If you have searched three to five sites and are getting nowhere, you are probably better off talking to a TA or professor about your question.

☞ **Use your computer to monitor your computer.** Several different and free programs (e.g., Slife and Personal Task Manager) can track your computer usage and generate reports revealing how much time you spend on your computer and what you're doing. It can be quite revealing.

☞ **Consider the source of online information.** A web page created by a professor is likely to be more valuable than one created by a high school class. The better pages often contain more information, are more detailed, and make more sense.

☞ **If you are studying a foreign language, you can use the Internet to read foreign language newspapers.** This is an excellent way to practice the language, and learn more about the culture.

☞ **If your professors place slides, articles, and other needed resources on the class Blackboard site,** save time by printing out several weeks of class materials at a time rather than printing several times a week.

Chapter 43

Concept Mapping

Dennis H. Congos, M.S.Ed.,
University of Central Florida, Orlando, Florida

Concept mapping is a tool that can make even the most boring task fun and interesting, thereby improving concentration and recall. It encourages thoughts to flow and connect more easily. The ability to remember is increased and creativity is enhanced. Concept mapping focuses on using visuals along with the traditional verbiage from lectures and tests. This has a powerful effect on increasing learning speed and later recall.

Concept maps can eliminate gaps and omissions in important information. They can be used to take notes, design a project, solve a problem, summarize history, improve recall, and organize notes to speed learning. The only limitation for making concept maps is your own imagination and that is a part of learning that makes it fun. The fun and love of learning is in the process.

Simply put, one part of the human mind learns in words and another part learns best with visual designs such as diagrams, charts, sketches, pictures, graphics, drawings, or numbers and symbols. Concept mapping brings together both the verbal and visual parts in learning which can speed up the process enormously.

How to Make a Concept Map

Concept mapping, sometimes called mind mapping, involves diagramming a main idea and attaching related ideas which radiate out from the center. By focusing on key ideas written down in your own words, and then making branches and connections with important details, you are mapping knowledge in a manner that will help you understand and remember new information.

☞ **1. Look for relationships:** Use lines, colors, arrows, or some other way of showing connections between the main idea and its related details on your concept maps. These relationships are important in helping you understand new information which speeds learning and later recall. By including your own symbols and designs you are building meaningful relationships between main ideas and details which are essential for understanding and later recall.

☞ **2. Use capitals for major ideas:** Using capital letters for main ideas is one way to identify the most important ideas on the map. Details are added later with lines, arrows, etc.

☞ **3. Put main ideas in the middle:** This leaves space around the main idea for important and related details to radiate out from the main idea.

☞ **4. Use space:** The separation visually of material to be learned is easier to recall when main ideas and details have space between them.

☞ **5. Reserve some space:** As you go along, you may think of new ideas to add, or information to add to existing ideas. Make sure you have enough space to add things later.

☞ **6. Draw quickly:** By jotting the information down quickly, you'll find out how much you really know.

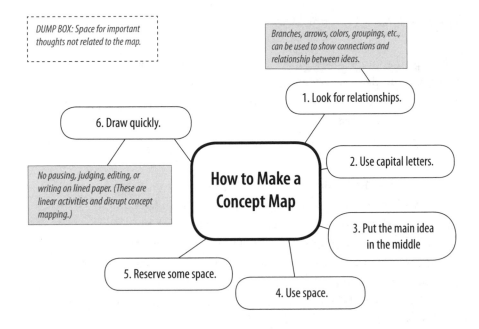

DUMP BOX: Space for important thoughts not related to the map.

Branches, arrows, colors, groupings, etc., can be used to show connections and relationship between ideas.

6. Draw quickly.

1. Look for relationships.

No pausing, judging, editing, or writing on lined paper. (These are linear activities and disrupt concept mapping.)

How to Make a Concept Map

2. Use capital letters.

3. Put the main idea in the middle

5. Reserve some space.

4. Use space.

Organization Patterns in Concepts Maps

Branches. May be used for details and sub-details to clarify relationships.

Arrows. Are used to join ideas or show a progression from one idea to another.

Groupings. Are important to aid in recall of details related to the same idea.

Lists. Numbered lists aid recall.

Making Concept Maps of Readings

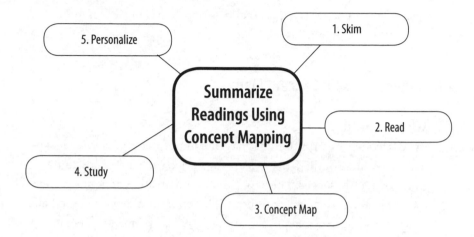

☞ **1. Skim:** Skim over outlines, introduction, chapter headings, bold print, summaries, questions at the end of a chapter, and marginal notes. Pay attention to diagrams, pictures, graphs, etc. and bring them to the part of the brain that learns best with visuals. These provide a kind of mental preparation for what you are about to read, providing advance organizers—categories into which to place information which facilitates learning. Do this quickly. Skimming shouldn't take more than 2 to 3 minutes overall.

☞ **2. Read:** Some students can read a whole chapter in one sitting while others find it more comfortable to break the reading into more bite-size pieces, making it easier for the brain to absorb.

☞ **3. Concept Map:** Create your concept map using the techniques shown in this chapter.

☞ **4. Study:** When you are finished with your concept map, see how completely and accurately you can reproduce the map from memory as a test to see how much you can recall. Draw as much of the map as you can on a separate piece of paper without looking and then compare it with the concept map you just made.

☞ **5. Personalize:** After reviewing your concept map, see if there are any details that are missing and add them. Study and personalize your concept map as much as necessary, until you feel that all the important information is there.

Advantages to Using Concept Maps

✓ **Adds structure**
Structure and organization that has meaning to you promotes learning. It also incorporates many learning styles such as visual, auditory, and tactile senses. This is an important strategy for increasing understanding, learning, and recall. The content may be detailed and complicated but a concept map allows you to organize information into a format that works for you, promoting better memory.

✓ **Speeds review and facilitates the benefits of self-testing**
When students self-test, it is easier to identify material not yet learned and determine where time and effort need to be focused. Learned information is also recognized and students should review regularly so they don't forget. It is normal for forgetting to begin immediately after something is heard, read, or studied; thus, regular review is essential.

Fair Game

What is fair game to be included on a college level test after weeks of lecture notes, textbook chapters, and outside articles and readings? As many students say with dismayed expressions. "All of it." So, any material that could appear on an exam can be enhanced by using concept maps.

Chapter 44

Working in Groups

Russell Conwell Center, Office of the Senior Vice Provost for Undergraduate Studies, Temple University, Philadelphia, Pennsylvania

Working effectively in groups is an important skill to master. Whether taking a class that requires group work or working in a student, civic, or other type of organization, working collaboratively is a skill that you will use throughout your life. Successful teamwork requires various components as listed in this chapter:

Having a leader

Most groups, formal (club, organization or group class project) and informal (ad-hoc study group), work best when the roles of the participants are defined. Leaders are either chosen (elected and voted upon) or emerge organically. In either case, a group leader is necessary to help the group members identify and stay focused on the task. Some characteristics of an effective leader include:

» *Good listening skills.*

» *The ability to be fair and impartial.*

» *Not having his or her own agenda—treating all members equally.*

» *Having a clear understanding of the task and goal.*

» *Maximizing everyone's talents and contributions by matching their roles to their skills.*

Scheduling times

In order for groups to work well for all the members, scheduling time that is convenient for all is **paramount**. It is not fair to the members of the group if decisions are made by only a few because meeting times are not suitable to all. This is especially true for groups in school in which each group member's participation is required and schedules vary greatly.

Socialization

Social time is valuable in developing a productive group. It is important for group member to get to know fellow members, whom they will interact with closely on a task or project. Arrive early or stay later, but build in time to share, talk, and get to know one another.

Agenda

Set an agenda for each meeting and be prepared. If all group members are prepared, the sessions will be more productive.

Courtesy

It is critical for the members to be courteous and considerate towards one another. This means the following:

» *Attend all scheduled meetings.*

» *Arrive on time to all meetings.*

» *Be prepared with any work that was assigned.*

» *Be ready to contribute and/or assist other members.*

» *Be open, honest, and respectful of each member.*

Doing your part

It is often the case that in groups there are those people who are "workers" and those who are "watchers." Groups work best however, when all the members work together toward the common goal. The "watchers" should be encouraged to work with a "worker." By assisting someone who is motivated and involved, the "watcher" will be able to learn how to do the things required, as well as be held more accountable. Also, the energy of the "worker" often rubs off on the "watcher" and gets him or her more involved.

Part XI

Memory Skills

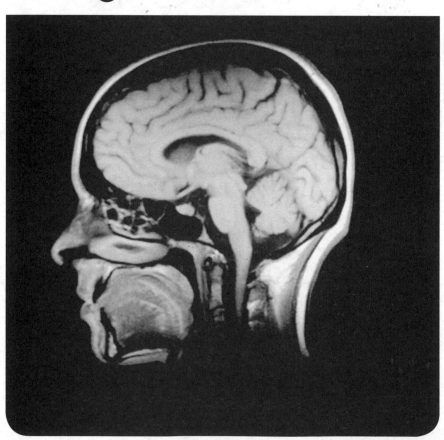

Chapter 45

The Basics of Memory

Dennis H. Congos, M.S.Ed.,
University of Central Florida, Orlando, Florida

Part 1: Reasons Why We Forget

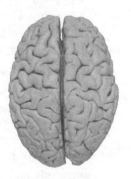

Forgetting is normal under certain circumstances, but in college, forgetting leads to low grades and sometimes academic dismissal. Below are seven reasons why students forget and some suggestions on what you can do to overcome each one.

☞ **1. Under-Learning** The most common reason why students forget is because the material is under-learned. To remember something, it must first be thoroughly learned, that is, stored in long-term memory. If you don't do what is necessary to get information into your long-term memory, you have under-learned the material and poor recall is normal.

To combat under-learning, repeatedly recite or quiz yourself on your reading and lecture notes. Discover what you have learned and have not learned before you take a test. Learning is a process that takes time and repetition for humans to move information from short-term memory toward long-term memory. That is why when material is reviewed only once or twice, it is difficult to remember for quizzes and exams.

Neurochemical and biochemical studies of the brain during the past fifteen years have revealed another factor in the remembering-forgetting cycle. Long-term memory does not occur unless protein synthesis takes place in the brain. Protein synthesis can now be measured using brain-imaging technology. In 1992, Steven Rose in his book *The Making of Memory*, shows that when something new is introduced to and understood by the learner that sufficient review of this material must take place during the following 24 hours for protein synthesis to happen and to achieve long-term memory retention. With the tight schedules of today's college students and those who have not yet mastered college-level time-management, students either do not or cannot prevent other activities from interfering with this crucial 24-hour window for learning. Timely and sufficient review is critical to learning.

☞ **2. Changed Clues** You may have information stored away in your mind but are unable to recall it if the right cue or "handle" is missing. In other words, if you study material one way and a test question asks for the material another way, it is normal to have difficulty recalling it.

To prevent this problem, it is important that you *learn* material using as many of your own words as possible. When you can put something completely and accurately in your own words, it significantly increases your ability to remember.

☞ **3. Interference** Psychologists have discovered that recently learned material interferes with recall of previously learned materials.

To deal with this situation, all material to be remembered must be refreshed in the mind by regular review and repetition.

☞ **4. Mental Overcrowding** This condition cannot only inhibit memory, but can also prevent learning. Too much input at one time into the senses impedes learning and remembering. That is why it is normal to experience poor learning and recall when studying with the stereo playing, TV blaring, talking in the background, and worrying about personal problems. All sound slows learning because all sound interferes with proper storage of information in the mind. Study where it is quiet and where it is going to stay quiet until you are finished studying.

☞ **5. Negative Thinking** Students who believe that they cannot remember are more likely to forget. You must believe you can remember before you can actually do it.

If believing in your ability to remember is difficult for you, see a counselor, or a learning skills specialist, or start reprogramming your mind with positive self-talk such as "I will remember this" and "I have a good memory."

☞ **6. Disuse** Forgetting something because you don't use it is another normal and unavoidable human characteristic. Most forgetting takes place immediately after hearing or seeing new material. To address disuse, you must regularly recite and review material to be remembered until it is stored in long-term memory. Then, it is less likely that you will forget it.

☞ **7. Effort and Intention Are Lacking** It is necessary to find out what you need to do (the "effort") in order to remember, and then do it. "Intention" means to make a deliberate choice to remember.

The art of remembering is a direct result of the amount of effort exerted coupled with the intention to remember. Recall is the outcome of the effort you choose to allot to the task of remembering. Furthermore, your mind does what you tell it to do, for the most part. If you don't intend to remember something, you are telling your mind, indirectly, not to remember, so you don't.

Part 2: Ebbinghaus's Curve of Forgetting

In 1885, Hermann Ebbinghaus discovered the exponential nature of forgetting newly acquired information, illustrated by the rapidly declining curve shown in the graph on the following page.

The Ebbinghaus Curve vs. Regular Review and Reinforcement

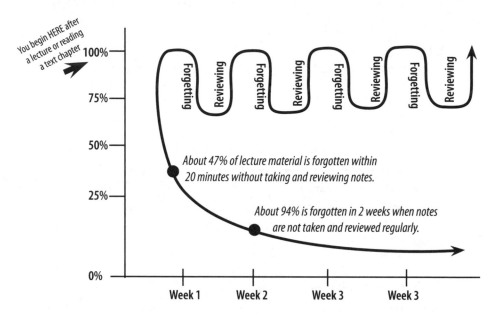

Overall, forgetting takes place immediately after information is acquired, unless we reinforce our memory through regular review. The top part of the graphic is the author's depiction of the need for constant review and reinforcement of new knowledge in order to retain that knowledge in long-term memory.

Part 3: Memorizing vs. Understanding

With all the previous discussion of memory and memorizing, it's good to include a brief discussion of the concept of understanding, a critical step in the learning process. The following is a chart juxtaposing the differences between memorizing and understanding.

Memorizing	Understanding
Tries to learn ideas and concepts word for word only.	Converts ideas and concepts into own words.
Difficult to explain ideas to someone else other than word for word.	Able to use own words to explain something clearly to someone else.
Difficult to see how ideas apply in real-life situations or case studies.	Can apply ideas to real-life situations or case studies.
Relevance of ideas outside the classroom is difficult to see and explanations are typically not sought.	Seeks connections between knowledge from the classroom and the outside world.
Does not see differences, similarities, and implications of ideas.	Can identify differences and similarities between ideas, and implications of these ideas.
Interprets ideas literally.	Realizes that there can be figurative as well as literal interpretations of ideas.
Strives for rote learning and has trouble solving problems when numbers or components are changed.	Strives to see how parts are related to each other and why things are done certain ways and can solve problems even when numbers or components are changed.
Believes there is one "right" answer for every question.	Accepts that there may be more than one "right" answer to a question depending on circumstances.
Has trouble seeing beyond the basic concept or idea.	Can see meaning, effects, results, and consequences beyond the basic idea or concept.

Chapter 46

Mnemonics for Better Memory

Dennis H. Congos, M.S.Ed.,
University of Central Florida, Orlando, Florida

Mnemonics are memory devices that help learners recall larger pieces of information, especially in the form of lists like characteristics, steps, stages, parts, etc. We knew back in 1967 from a study by Gerald R. Miller that mnemonics increased recall. He found that students who regularly used mnemonic devices increased test scores up to 77 percent!

Why Mnemonics Work

Take this quiz:

» Name ten Oscar winners for best actor.

» Who were the coaches of the last five NFL Champions?

» Who were the five richest people in the United States during the 1990s?

» Name any five Heisman trophy winners.

» Who are five winners of the Miss America pageant?

» List three people who have won the Nobel Prize.

How did you do? Few of us can remember many individuals from the past that were famous at one point. The people who are the answers to the questions are not unknowns. They were the tops in their fields and received much publicity, but what meaning did they have for you at the time?

See how you do with this quiz:

» List three teachers who were helpful to you in high school.

» Name three friends who have helped you through a difficult emotional time.

» Name five people you believe are very wise.

» List three people who have made you feel important and appreciated.

» Think of five people you enjoy being with the most.

Was this a bit easier?

What makes the difference in recall for these two lists is the meaningfulness to you. Meaningfulness is a powerful memory technique. That is the principle behind mnemonics and why they work so powerfully, because they have meaning to YOU. The term "meaning" refers to associating something to be remembered with something already known. For example, it is easier to remember how many books there are in the old and new testaments with this mnemonic:

Old testament = 39 books
New testament = 27 books

$3 \times 9 = 27$.

Most people already know the multiplication table and once the association is made between the numbers of 39 and 27, recall is much easier.

Nine Types of Mnemonics

Many types of mnemonics exist and which type works best is limited only by the imagination of each individual learner. The nine basic types of mnemonics presented in this chapter include Music, Name, Expression/Word, Model, Ode/Rhyme, Note Organization, Image, Connection, and Spelling Mnemonics.

☞ **1. Music Mnemonics** How many lyrics to songs do you remember? How did you come to remember them? Music is a powerful memory technique and it can work just as well in school. Many learners have made songs out of information when a list of items must be learned. Advertising on radio and TV uses this technique to help potential customers remember their products when shopping.

You can make a song or jingle using any type of music you choose for a list of items. Music Mnemonics work best with long lists. For example, some children learn the ABC's by singing the "ABC" song. Other children learn the states in alphabetical order using the "50 Nifty United States" song.

☞ **2. Name Mnemonics** Name Mnemonics uses the first letter of each word in a list of items to make a name of a person or thing. An example is:

ROY G. BIV = colors of the spectrum (**R**ed, **O**range, **Y**ellow, **G**reen, **B**lue, **I**ndigo, **V**iolet.)

☞ **3. Expression or Word Mnemonics** This is by far the most popularly used mnemonic. To make an Expression or Word mnemonic, the first letter of each item in a list is arranged to form a phrase or word. Examples include:

» In English, the seven coordinating conjunctions are **F**or, **A**nd, **N**or, **B**ut, **O**r, **Y**et, **S**o = **FANBOYS**.

In math, The order of operations is **P**arentheses, **E**xponents, **M**ultiply, **D**ivide, **A**dd, and **S**ubtract = **PLEASE EXCUSE MY DEAR AUNT SALLY**.

» Almost every anatomy class has to remember the eight small bones in the wrist: **NAVICULAR, LUNATE, TRIQUETRUM, PISIFORM, MULTONGULAR (GREATER), MULTONGULAR (LESSER), CAPITATE (and) HAMATE**.

Never **L**ower **T**illy's **P**ants, **M**other **M**ight **C**ome **H**ome.

» Now try to create an Expression Mnemonic for remembering the order of the planets from the sun outward: Mercury, Venus, Earth, Mars, Jupiter, Saturn, Uranus, Neptune, and Pluto (maybe).

☞ **4. Model Mnemonics** In a Model Mnemonic, some type of representation is constructed to help with understanding and recalling important information.

Examples Include the following:

1. A family tree

2. A pyramid model, such as the food pyramid for understanding nutrition

3. A pie chart to show the components of a budget

4. A circular sequence model showing the stages of combustion, below:

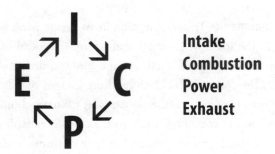

Intake
Combustion
Power
Exhaust

☞ **5. Ode or Rhyme Mnemonics** An Ode or Rhyme Mnemonic puts information to be recalled in the form of a poem.

Examples include:

1. A commonly used Rhyme Mnemonic for the number of days in each month is:

30 days hath September,
April, June, and November.
All the rest have 31, Fine!
February 28 except when 29.

2. You'd probably like your doctor to know the difference between cyanate and cyanide: **Cyanate "I ate"** and **Cyanide "I died."** Cyanide is a deadly poison.

☞ **6. Note Organization Mnemonics** The way textbook and lecture notes are organized can promote memory, especially when we can visualize our notes on notecards in our memory, or visualize a study outline we have created.

Three examples:

a) notecards
b) outlines
c) Cornell System (see chapter 19)

☞ **7. Image Mnemonics** The information in an Image Mnemonic is constructed in the form of a picture that promotes recall of information when you need it. The sillier the Image Mnemonic is, the easier it is to recall the related information. These images may be mental or sketched into text and lecture notes. Don't worry about your artistic ability. As long as you know what your sketch means, Image Mnemonics will help you learn and remember. For example, you may better remember a new acquaintance's name, such as Tom **Car**ter if you imagine him driving an automobile.

☞ **8. Connection Mnemonics** In this type of mnemonic, the information to be remembered is connected to something already known.

Examples include:

Remembering the direction of longitude and latitude is easier to do when you realize that lines on a globe that run North and South are long and that coincides with **LONG**itude. Another Connection Mnemonic points out that there is an **N** in **LONG**itude and an **N** in <u>N</u>orth. Latitude lines must run east to west, then. There is no **N** in Latitude.

Another Connection Mnemonic is related to sound. The first part of the word latitude sounds like "flat" and flat runs horizontal or East and West.

☞ **9. Spelling Mnemonics** An example of a spelling mnemonic: A princi**pal** at a school is your **pal**, and a princip**le** is something that you believe or follow as in "ru**le**," which ends in "**le**."

Chapter 47

Mental Manipulation:
The Key to Remembering

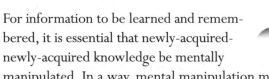

Dennis H. Congos, M.S.Ed.,
University of Central Florida, Orlando, Florida

If you haven't been mentally manipu-
lating what it is you have to learn and
remember, and then you don't remember
what you think you learned when it comes
to test and quiz time, don't worry: **You
are normal!**

For information to be learned and remembered, it is essential that newly-acquired-
newly-acquired knowledge be mentally
manipulated. In a way, mental manipulation means repeatedly getting the
hands and fingers of your mind on material to be learned and then doing
something with that material.

☞ **Practice by Self-Testing** If you want to learn and remember material in
the shortest time possible, use the techniques for mental manipulation
shown on the chart on the next page.

Keep the Following Guidelines in Mind:

1. Set up your notes so that you can easily test yourself on the material
    you wish to remember.

2. Create your own questions in your notes, and highlight the answers
    you want to remember.

3. To reinforce memory, you can create a set of notecards, with questions on one side, and answers on the other.

4. Answer questions concisely in the form that is suggested.

How to Formulate Questions:

Types of Details	Possible Questions/Statements You Can Make From Details
Definitions	A *definition* question requires details in an answer that simply define and do not necessitate elaboration. Some example of formulating such questions are: *"What is the definition of....?"* *"What is.....?"*
Lists: Characteristics, Parts, Sections, Causes, Effects, Steps, Stages, Phases, Processes, Elements, Summaries	For details consisting of lists, make a question that requires a listing of details in an answer. An example of a listing question begins with "What are...." Some examples are: *"What are the characteristics of....?"* *"What are the sections in....?"* *"Outline the causes and effects of.....?"* *"What are the [steps, stages, phases, etc.] in....?"*
Application: Analyzing, Summarizing, Describing, Predicting, Translating, Criticizing, Justifying	When details consist of the application of knowledge, answer the question of "What is happening...." Make questions or statements that require a presentation of what is happening such as: *"Analyze what happens when...."* *"Summarize the actions you see in...."* *"Describe what happens when..."* *"Translate this statement according to...."* *"Criticize the performance of...."* *"An example of this is....."*

How Something Works	When details consist of how something works, construct a question that requires you to present a description or explanation of how that thing works. Some examples are: *"Describe how _____works when…."* *"What are the [steps, stages, phases, etc.] in….?"* *"What are the essential roles of each character as….?"*
Two or More Sets of Information	When there are details that consist of two or more sets of information, formulate your question to include such verbs as compare or contrast or connect. Make questions or statements that require presenting similarities, differences, and relationships such as: *"Compare the….."* *"Contrast the…."* *"Compare and contrast….."* *"Make connections between….."* *"What is the relationship of ____ to ____?"*
Solutions to Problems	When details consist of solutions to problems, organize your questions to require a presentation of steps. Some examples are: *"What are the steps in solving a __ type problem?"* *"What are the steps to solve [list problem here]?"* *"What are the steps for solving __ problems?"*

Take a main idea and make a question out of it based on the type of details you are given in textbooks and lectures.

Sample Notecards with questions and answers:

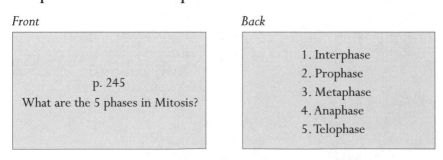

Front

p. 245
What are the 5 phases in Mitosis?

Back

1. Interphase
2. Prophase
3. Metaphase
4. Anaphase
5. Telophase

p. 256 What happens in Interphase?	Chromatin spreads out in an indistinct mass.

It is important for learning and recall to: **Make questions match the details.**

Once notes are rewritten and better organized, here is what you do to speed your learning. Notecards are used in the description below:

1. Look at a question and then recite aloud and without looking, as much of the detail as you can. If you are looking at a problem, work the solution out on scrap paper.

2. Next, turn the card over to check for completeness and accuracy of your recitation or solution on scrap paper.

3. If your recitation or solution was correct, put that card in the "I know this" pile.

4. If your recitation or solution was incorrect or incomplete, read the answer out loud or correct your solution until you think you can recall it from memory, then turn the card over and read the question or problem again. Recite the answer aloud or write it out again without looking, and then check again. Do this as many times as you need to in order to get the answer correct from memory and then place that card in the "I don't know this yet" pile. Don't move on to the next notecard until the present one is recited or written correctly from memory.

5. Review your "I don't know this yet" pile every day or at least every other day to speed your learning and remembering. Go over your "I know this" pile every two or three days to prevent forgetting.

☞ **Ways to Mentally Manipulate Material** You must learn something before you can remember it or forget it and learning requires *mental manipulation.* Here are some suggestions of ways to mentally manipulate material.

» *Pay attention in class and while reading textbooks.*

» *Take notes in lectures and from textbooks.*

» *Make questions based on the details.*

» *Use a neat and organized format for notes that speeds, not impedes, learning.*

» *Visually separate main ideas from other main ideas and each main idea and its details from other main ideas and their details.*

» *Paraphrase main ideas and details in your own words as much as possible.*

» *Condense lecture and textbook material into short phrases and abbreviations.*

» *Relate something to learn to something similar you already know.*

» *Discuss what you have learned with a colleague or in a study group.*

» *Practice remembering by looking only at main ideas or questions you made and recite answers aloud, without looking, as if you are lecturing a class.*

» *Have someone quiz you or quiz someone else.*

» *Include diagrams, charts, sketches, and pictures in notes on material to be learned.*

» *Tutor someone on the subject matter that you have to learn and remember.*

» *Practice recalling, when you are not in class, what it is you need to remember.*

» *Make mnemonics out of details.*

» *Explain what you need to remember to someone else using as many of your own words as possible.*

» *Go into an empty classroom, conduct a lecture from memory, and use your notes to check your recall.*

☞ **The Difference Between Recognition and Recall** Remembering is divided into two basic types: recognition and recall. Each requires a different type of practice to optimize learning from memory.

You are RECOGNIZING *something when…*

You can spot information and pick it out of a set of similar pieces of information such as among options in multiple-choice questions. You need to see all or most of the actual information in order to remember it.

You are RECALLING *something when…*

You can produce larger amounts of information from memory from key words, mental cues, test questions, or when needed in responses to conversational cues. This kind of recall demonstrates knowledge and intelligence.

Chapter 48

Strategies for Better Memory

Dennis H. Congos, M.S.Ed.,
University of Central Florida, Orlando, Florida

A good memory is a key ingredient for academic success, and it is an ability that you can enhance over time by following several proven techniques. Here are seven strategies for enhancing your memory:

☞ **Intend to Remember** If you do not *intend* to consciously remember, it is normal to have difficulty remembering what you read, hear, or study. On the other hand, if you choose to remember what you read or study, you will enlist the use of a powerful memory strategy. When you intend to remember, your mind begins the tasks needed to build a better memory.

☞ **Organize What You Need to Remember** Make QUESTIONS out of main ideas using details as a guide. Number steps, stages, characteristics, arguments, procedures, etc. Visuals such as **sketches, diagrams, charts,** etc. increase understanding, learning, and recall.

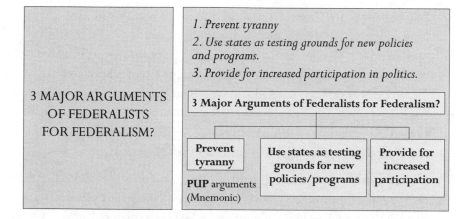

☞ **Use Mnemonics** As you will recall from Chapter 47, a mnemonic is simply a memory device which helps increase recall. It may consist of a name, word, or phrase. Be sure to include a key word with the mnemonic from the main idea to reduce chances of confusion with other mnemonics.

☞ **Use Spaced Reviews** Cramming overloads the short term memory and for most people results in statements such as, "I thought I knew the material." There is a difference between recognition and recall. Recognizing something is not the same a recall as many college students have discovered when taking a test. **Recognition** means one remembers going over the material and may even remember portions of details. **Recall** means that all or most of the details can be remembered by seeing clues in a question on a test. One's ability to recall is increased after repeated reviews of material are spaced over time. Eight reviews spaced over two weeks are more effective than eight reviews a day or two before a test.

☞ **Proper Sleep and Diet** While some students appear to survive on too little sleep and a poor diet, the vast majority of students suffer academic performance far below potential when there is not enough sleep or is an unbalanced diet. The average college students needs between seven and nine hours of nighttime sleep to maximize learning. A poor diet can lower one's ability to think, reason, learn, remember, and feel motivation and have an interest in academics.

☞ **Self-Test Regularly** The worst time to discover whether you have learned the material for a test or not is after a test is graded. Little to nothing can be done about the grade at that point, so students are out of control in this situation. Set up a study system where you can identify what you have learned and what you have not learned before you take a test, so you can still do something about it. Making questions from main ideas and answers out of details provides a self-testing potential that puts you more in control of what you learn.

If you are using notecards, self-testing consists of looking at a question on one side of the notecard, saying an answer aloud as best you can, then turning the card over to see if you remembered the material.

☞ **Get Actively Involved With the Material** It is normal for passive reading or rereading text or lecture material to result in little improved recall at test time. Smaller amounts of fairly simple material may be absorbed by rereading for some students. But a larger amount of knowledge with lots of detail is difficult to impossible to absorb and recall later by simply rereading over and over.

Quizzing oneself, rewriting notes, including visuals in notes, organizing notes more clearly, and helping others learn the material all entail active involvement with material to be learned and remembered. The result is better learning and recall.

Part XII

Test Preparation

Chapter 49

Preparing for Tests

Dennis H. Congos, M.S.Ed.,
University of Central Florida, Orlando, Florida

Ten Test Preparation Techniques

Test preparation is the practical short-term goal of studying. Learning is the longer-term goal. Whether given frequently, on small amounts of information, or only once or twice a semester, exams serve to motivate students to do their assignments and master the necessary material. Here are ten test preparation steps worth following to improve your success rate.

☞ **1. Prepare for exams from the first day assignments are made.**

☞ **2. Recite notes aloud from memory.** As the number of recitations increases, information is moved from short-term memory toward long-term memory where it must go to be stored and recalled when needed. One way to recite is to look at a main idea and recite the details aloud without looking. Then check the details to see how much was recalled correctly. Read aloud any material that was recalled incorrectly and go through this process repeatedly until it is recited correctly from memory, then move on to the next idea.

☞ **3. Review notes on a regular basis**, for example, every other day. This improves memory, reduces test anxiety, and allows time between reviews for the information to consolidate in the mind. Spacing out reviews also results in better recall at test time. It is normal to forget on tests when notes are reviewed only once or twice.

☞ **4. Rewrite notes after each lecture.** Condense main ideas and clarifying details into a more organized format that promotes and speeds learning. For example, turn main ideas into questions and details into answers. Put one question on the front of the notecard and its answer on the back. Do the same as you take notes from textbooks.

☞ **5. Self-test** using a study system that includes a step to reveal how much has been learned and not yet learned before a test is taken, when something can still be done about it.

☞ **6. Use the instructor's clues** to ideas that are likely to appear on exams. Did the instructor narrow down potential testable material? What clues were given about what may appear on the test? Were sample test questions or review sheets provided? How much time was devoted to each topic? What questions did the instructor ask in class? What did the instructor repeat?

☞ **7. Check to see if old tests from previous semesters are available for review.** This will provide a clue on how test questions may be constructed and the types of information instructors believe are important for you to learn.

☞ **8. Utilize study groups.** If there are no study groups, start one. Study groups provide opportunities to check the completeness and accuracy of notes with others and to quiz each other. Research shows that study group members typically earn higher grades than non-study group students.

☞ **9. Use the five types of studying to increase chances of academic success.**

» **1. Studying to gather information.** *Its purpose is to formulate complete and accurate sets of lecture and textbook notes.*

» **2. Studying to learn.** *Its purpose is to move information from short-term memory toward long-term memory.*

» **3. Studying to check for learning.** *Its purpose is to reveal what has and has not yet been learned before a test is taken.*

» **4. Studying to refresh.** *Its purpose is to prevent forgetting. This type of studying requires regular review of material already learned.*

One way to do this is to have a calendar book and make time in your schedule to review the material you have learned on a regular basis.

» **5. Study to improve learning skills.** *It has two purposes: (1) identify which skills for learning worked, so they may be repeated, and (2) identity which skills did not work well, so they may be modified and not repeated.*

☞ **10. Cramming doesn't work** for most students because it limits learning which in turn limits grades. Start studying to gather information early. Spend most of your time studying to learn and studying to check for learning. Study to refresh every two or three days. Don't forget to use studying to improve learning skills to earn those higher grades.

Chapter 50

Self-Testing

Dennis H. Congos, M.S.Ed.,
University of Central Florida, Orlando, Florida

The Self-Testing Concept

O ne of the most dangerous things college students can do academically is to go into a test thinking, feeling, assuming, hoping, or believing they have learned the material. This is dangerous academically because in all five of these cases students don't find out if they have learned the material until after a test is returned when little to nothing can be done about the test grade. This approach is like waiting to discover if you can swim only after someone throws you into the deep end of the lake miles from shore. It would be better to develop swimming skills before going in the deep water.

What is self-testing?

One way to identify what has and has not been learned before a test is taken is to become a self-tester along the way. The Self-Testing Concept uses the mighty weapon of recitation to avoid forgetting key ideas, and **doubles its effectiveness** for use in learning.

Using Notecards for Self-Testing

Using notecards to organize notes is the easiest way to self-test. Note-cards are recommended because they are:

☞ **Easy to carry.**

☞ **Easy to review** in the short time periods which are normally wasted such as between classes, at meals, on the bus, walking to and from class, etc. This reduces study time to the minimum without a sacrifice in grades.

☞ **A very simple way to organize notes.**

☞ **A very fast way to recite material to be learned.** Regular recitation of material to be learned speeds the movement of information toward long-term memory which is where it needs to be for accurate recall on exams and after graduation.

Steps for Self-Testing

☞ **Step 1:** Take each set of ideas or facts from lectures or assigned readings or chapters that could be on a test and use them as a guide to formulate a typical exam question.

☞ **Step 2:** Visibly separate answers from questions by placing questions on one side of a notecard and answers on the other. For notecards, use one question (main idea) and its answer (related details) per notecard.

☞ **Step 3: Recite.** In this step, students read the question aloud, recite answers containing related details aloud from memory, as if lecturing a class. Some students may prefer writing answers from memory, as if taking an exam. Verbalizing or writing in complete sentences requires the kinds of thinking skills that move information into long term memory more quickly.

☞ **Step 4:** Look at answers to check for completeness and accuracy.

☞ **Step 5:** If ANSWERS are recited correctly from memory on the first try, that notecard should be placed in the "learned" pile.

☞ **Step 6:** When ANSWERS are inaccurately recited, redo the five previous steps.

☞ **Step 7:** As long as answers are recited incorrectly on the first try each time students review, they must be considered "not yet learned."

☞ **Step 8:** Review by reciting/writing answers as often as it takes until you can recall all answers correctly, by memory, on the first try.

Watch out for Fading!

It is normal for fading (forgetting) to begin immediately after a human being hears or reads something. Therefore, it seems wise to attack the normal process of forgetting. Regular reviews of notecards that have been learned is the best way to combat the normal process of forgetting.

Students should re-self-test learned material two to three times per week to avoid fading and reinforce learning and memory.

Learning Speed

Learning speed is individual and has no correlation with intelligence. Learning speed does affect how many reviews each person must do to earn an "A".

How many reviews each student needs in order to earn an "A" is revealed when: 1) the number of reviews is identified that the student performed to effectively prepare for the test or quiz and 2) the completeness and accuracy of the material on the notecards is determined in a post-test review. If grades are less than desired, students should verify if notes were complete and accurate and increase the number of reviews for the next exam.

Develop an Individual Style

Students should feel free to develop an individual self-testing style using the previously described basic fundamentals as a guide. Grades earned on tests and quizzes will provide feedback if further refinement is needed in self-testing methods. The advice and guidance of a campus learning skills specialist can be very helpful here.

Don't give up if desired results are not obtained on the first try. How well did you do the first time you rode a bike without training wheels? Persistence to refine self-testing methods will eventually earn the grades that students are capable of achieving when this powerful technique for learning is mastered.

Chapter 51

To Cram or Not to Cram

Russell Conwell Center, Office of the Senior Vice Provost for Undergraduate Studies, Temple University, Philadelphia, Pennsylvania

Why is cramming frowned upon, yet so popular amongst college students? Is it wrong? If the goal is to get a good grade on an exam and cramming can help you "learn" large amounts of information, what is the harm? Read on, then you can decide whether to: Cram or not to cram!

What is cramming?

Cramming is defined as hurried, last-minute studying. When students cram, the most common technique used is memorization. Memorizing is a good technique for learning terms and dates, but for complex concepts it doesn't work as well. In order to learn a concept, you have to spend quality time studying and reviewing the material and gaining an understanding of the relationship among the concepts so that you can manipulate the information.

Even with exams that are true/false or multiple choice, information is presented in such a way to test your understanding, not memory. In a multiple-choice test, two answers usually seem right—that's to test what you know, not what you remember.

Perhaps the biggest difference between learning and memorizing is seen over time. Information that is memorized tends to fade from short-term memory, as opposed to information learned, which will stay with you.

Tips for Extended Study Periods or "All Nighters"

☞ **Do not use over the counter (OTC) stimulants.**
OTC stimulants may seem harmless. They are sold legally and you do not need a prescription to buy them. The truth is, they are not healthy. They raise your heart rate and blood pressure.

☞ **Do not abuse caffeine.**
Drinking gallons of soda or coffee is not recommended. Sure, you get a jolt of energy, but the come-down crash is more severe and leaves you more drained than if you stayed up the natural way. You will wind up more tired, which will negatively affect your memory and cognition.

☞ **Stay off the sweets.**
So you want a sugar rush. Again, not a wise idea. It's bad for your teeth, not to mention the stomach and hips! As with coffee, the crash may prove worse than the natural tired feeling of staying awake.

Healthier Alternatives are:

☞ **Natural sugars**
Try fruit instead of chocolate. It is healthier for your body and has less of a crash afterwards.

☞ **Exercise**
Need to get the blood pumping? Try exercise. Run around the block, up the stairs, or do some jumping jacks. That will wake you up and help your refocus.

☞ **The power nap**
This is not recommended for those inclined to hit the snooze button. Set your alarm for a 15–30 minute nap. Wake up and get back to studying.

Your body needs sleep—do not deprive it. You may think that you need to pull an all-nighter, but not if you practice proper planning! The use of appropriate study skills and time management will help you get the most out of your academic experience.

Last-Minute Study Suggestions

» Go through your flash cards one last time.

» Focus on critical concepts (don't go over the text page by page).

» Create a last-minute study sheet with the key facts, definitions, formulas, and so forth.

» Arrive early and study in your seat until you are asked to stop.

» Use Mnemonic Devices: connect information you are trying to learn with simpler information you know. Instead of learning by rote, associate the work with something familiar—this will give you familiar cues to retrieve the information while under the stress of the test.

» Create visual images: turn the information into mental pictures to help improve memory.

» Create acronyms: create a word from the first letters of a series of words to help you remember the series.

Chapter 52

Test Anxiety

Dennis H. Congos, M.S.Ed.,
University of Central Florida, Orlando, Florida

Anxiety often stems from a fear of losing control or of being out of control. With test anxiety, there is a direct correlation between knowing and understanding the material that could appear on an exam and resulting anxiety. As knowledge and understanding increase, test anxiety commonly decreases.

Test anxiety in college students is fairly common and never fatal. In fact, a small amount of anxiety may be beneficial because it sharpens the senses and the mind. In excess though, test anxiety may become overwhelming and cause discomforting physical symptoms and recall impediments.

The good news is that there are many strategies that students may use to combat test anxiety. Like tools, they don't work unless they are used in proper time and manner.

Techniques to Reduce Anxiety

Test anxiety, to a large degree, is related to test preparation. The more certain you are that you *know* the material, the less you experience test anxiety. Beware. There is a huge difference between *thinking* you know material and *knowing* that you know the material that could appear on a test. You can use the list of techniques below to combat test anxiety.

☞ **1. Set up and follow a study schedule and begin studying from the day of the first assignment.** A large part of the anxiety experienced by students is due to the fact that they don't make enough time to prepare for a test. Once a realistic schedule is set up for study time, some of this anxiety is relieved. You can bring back the anxiety with a thud if you don't stick to your schedule.

☞ **2. Self-test to discover what has and has not yet been learned before taking a test, when something can still be done about it.** One way to self-test is to make questions from main ideas and answers from the details and put them on notecards. Do this for lecture and text notes. Include one main idea and its details per notecard.

☞ **3. Ask the instructor what types of questions will be on an exam (multiple choice, true-false, essay, etc.) and how many questions there might be.** If a review sheet or sample test is provided by the instructor, rely on that more than anything else in preparing for an exam. Exams from previous semesters are also excellent tools for determining the format of future exams. They can tell you how questions may be formatted and the score of expected answers.

☞ **4. Rework all of the problems assigned for homework and any others that apply to the material.** The more problems you tackle and the more often you do them, the more skill and confidence you acquire.

Write out all the steps for solving each type of problem in math, chemistry, and physics; do not do this work in your head and assume you know the solution. Set up a system to review the steps for solving each type of problem that could appear on an exam.

☞ **5. Do not cram.** In most cases, cramming leads only to confusion of concepts and raises anxiety. Eight to 10 hours of study is much more beneficial when it is spread out over a week or even several days rather than doing it in one sitting. It is a known fact that the brain needs time to absorb new material. So, take frequent breaks and schedule your study time evenly over many days or weeks.

☞ **6. Eat well and sensibly.** Your body is an engine that must have proper vitamins and minerals to think, concentrate, learn, and recall properly. To emphasize the effect of nutrition on learning, we can use an analogy. Ask a mechanic what would happen if you filled your car's gas tank with Kool-Aid instead of gas and then you tried to drive away. A balanced diet is the proper fuel to promote learning.

☞ **6. Get a reasonable amount of nighttime sleep.** Too little sleep negatively affects learning and recall. College students typically need 7 to 9 hours of nighttime sleep.

☞ **7. Choose a positive attitude.** Anytime fears come rushing in, regularly visualize yourself taking the exam, doing well, and seeing an A on the paper. Make a list of affirmations i.e., "I'm doing well in math," "I can learn this material," "I enjoy math," etc. Even if you do not initially believe what you are saying to yourself, it sends a message to your subconscious that, in turn, affects your belief system. It is your belief system that controls your behavior.

On Test Day: Before the Test

☞ **Arrive at the exam room at least 10 minutes early.** Get settled, relaxed and focus on deep breathing. Don't think about the material.

☞ **Read the whole exam over before beginning** and figure out how much time you need to allot for each question or problem. If you spend more than your allotted time on one problem, leave it and go on. If there is time at the end, you can always go back.

☞ **Visualize yourself at home or at the library doing your homework.** This will help you create a more relaxed atmosphere, thus allowing that part of your brain needed for complex thinking to function.

On Test Day: During the Test

☞ **Do all the problems and questions that you are totally sure of first.** This will increase your confidence level and start the information flowing. A result is often encouragement to try those problems you are not so sure of.

☞ **Always go with your first instincts in solving a problem or writing an answer.** Don't second-guess yourself unless you are *absolutely certain* you have the wrong answer. If in doubt, leave it. Have confidence in your preparation and ability to do well.

☞ **Answer the questions and problems with the most points first.** Do problems and questions with fewer points per item later.

☞ **Work at a reasonable pace and work carefully.** Divide the time allotted for the test by the number of problems. This will give you a rough estimate of how much time you should spend on each answer.

☞ **Think positively.** Tell yourself over and over that "you can do it, that you have studied, that you are smart." Remember positive comments from teachers and friends. At the very least think, *"I am doing the best I can do and that is all I can do."*

☞ **Focus** on breathing deeply and regularly.

☞ **If your mind begins racing or you start to panic,** say to yourself, *"Stop!"* This can reduce or stop the racing. Breathe deeply. Visualize yourself in a calm peaceful place like a summer meadow or a forest or by a stream, and keep on breathing deeply. Take a *few minutes* to do this with your eyes closed. Then tell yourself you can only do your best and that is all you can do. Then go back to the test.

If test anxiety persists in spite of your efforts to control it, see a counselor in your college counseling center. They help students with test anxiety all the time.

Use Your Brain to Cut Stress

Here is what the experts say about relieving stress in general. To begin, you need to understand which brain hemisphere is stressed.

If you feel depressed or emotionally overwrought, your stress is in the right hemisphere—the creative, emotional, holistic side.

What to do: Switch to your matter-of-fact left hemisphere by doing math, writing facts, or organizing something. The emotional right brain will calm down.

If you feel stressed and overloaded, the left hemisphere is involved.

What to do: Switch to your right brain by singing, playing a sport, or doing something creative.

Part XIII

Test Taking

Chapter 53

All About Essay Tests

Dennis H. Congos, M.S.Ed.,
University of Central Florida, Orlando, Florida

The four most important points to remember in answering essay questions are to:

» *Read all questions carefully, noting the direction words.*

» *Mark all key words in questions before answering.*

» *Do what the questions ask or what the instructions say.*

» *If uncertain about a question, check with the instructor before answering.*

Instructors frequently remark that a major reason that students don't receive higher grades on essay exams is because they do not follow directions even when these directions are included in the question. These instructors add that many students don't seem to know how to recognize words in questions that give directions on how to construct an essay answer and what to include.

Here are some ideas you can use to better understand what the instructor is asking and to write a better answer.

Understanding the Question: Direction Words

Aside from the major key words, there are other clues given in test questions or statements that direct how to select and compose a correct answer. These clues are called <u>direction</u> <u>words</u>.

There are four types of direction words in essay questions:

» *Subject Words*

» *Aspect Words*

» *Qualifying Words*

» *Presentation Words*

☞ **Type 1. Subject Words**

The purpose of **Subject Words** is to tell the test taker what to write about. **Subject Words** used on exams will vary with each class that you take. For example, a biology class will use words like "cell," "osmosis," and "mitosis." On the other hand, examples of **Subject Words** for a history class are "age," "period," and "event."

<u>Sample Essay Test Question</u>: Describe the four techniques that use positive reinforcement to modify most **[Subject Word]** behavior?

☞ **Type 2: Aspect Words:**

These are words that identify which aspects of the subject you are asked to write about. Examples of **Aspect Words** are "stages," "characteristics," and "proof."

<u>Sample Essay test question</u>: Describe the four **[Aspect Word]** that use positive reinforcement to modify most [Subject Word] behavior?

☞ **Type 3: Qualifying Words**

Qualifying Words are words that define or limit the scope of answers. Examples of **Qualifying Words** are "never," "always," "all," and "few" or they may be numbers such as "5" and "three".

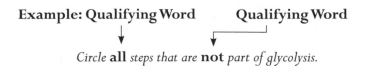

Circle **all** *steps that are* **not** *part of glycolysis.*

Sample Essay test question: Describe the four [Aspect Word] that use positive reinforcement to modify **[Qualifying Word]** [Subject Word] behavior?

☞ **Type 4. Presentation Words**

These are words in exam questions that indicate how an instructor wants to see information presented in answers. Examples of **Presentation Words** are "compare," "explain," "trace," and "list". **Presentation Words** often begin with the 5 W's, H, and I. They are:

Who? What? Where? When? Why? How? If?

Examples: Describe when... Explain where... Define what...
Justify why... Analyze how... List those who...

Sample Essay test question: **[Presentation Word]** the four [Aspect Word] that use positive reinforcement to modify [Qualifying Word] [Subject Word] behavior?

Understanding the Question: Keywords

A list of important words in essay questions is given below to help students answer essay questions with the kinds of responses that instructors seek. These words are called keywords.

One suggestion students have found helpful is to mark all the keywords in all test directions and questions before beginning to answer. This step makes it easier to organize an answer, know what to say, and know when enough has been written. If there is ever doubt about the clarity of a test question, ask the professor for clarification before beginning your answer.

Some keywords include:

☞ **Analyze:** Explain, step-by-step, point-by-point, while writing. Pay attention to who, what, where, when, why, and how in the answer. Include strengths, weaknesses, pros and cons, research for and against.

☞ **Compare:** Stress similarities and differences between objects, concepts, or ideas. (For example: "Compare Operant and Classical Conditioning")

☞ **Contrast:** Emphasize the dissimilarities, differences, or unique and distinguishing characteristics in the response.

☞ **Define:** Clearly state the meaning, list qualities, traits, or characteristics.

☞ **Describe:** Include traits, characteristics, or retell a story including those facts that summarize the essential features.

☞ **Discuss:** Present significant characteristics, pros and cons, pertinent research, and the significance of each. Develop the arguments for and against or analyze the advantages, disadvantages, or problems.

☞ **Evaluate:** Emphasize positive and negative aspects. Include opinions and support these with proof, information, or examples. Normally, instructors don't value unsupported opinions.

☞ **Examples:** Use brief stories, analogies, relevant events, or similar instances to support general statements and main ideas.

☞ **Explain:** Give reasons or justifications for something, or present causes, rationalizations, or how or why something occurred.

☞ **Interpret:** Cover existing understandings of a topic. Paraphrase, translate, condense, simplify, and/or diagnose as you write.

☞ **Justify:** Present rationale, reasons for conclusions, recommendations, or results. Use proof, research, examples, or quotes to support justifications.

☞ **List:** Record topics in numerical, developmental, or chronological order. Many times a brief description or explanation is expected but the questions will usually request it if desired. If in doubt, ask your instructor.

☞ **Outline:** Present your answer in terms of major points followed by clarifying details or facts. No elaboration is usually necessary. It is wise to find out if your instructors wishes for you to outline by listing only main and subordinate points in short numbered phrases or if they want you to use the narrative format with complete sentences and paragraphs.

☞ **Prove:** Include factual evidence, research, logic, and/or scientific proof that substantiates a case, a specific position, or a set of hypotheses.

☞ **Relate:** Clearly point out connections or relationships between two or more ideas.

☞ **Review:** Mention important ideas, major points, and/or list topics from lectures or the textbook. Sometimes review means critically evaluate and/or give your opinion.

☞ **Summarize:** List major ideas, concepts, and consequences in a short paragraph or a sentence. This could also mean present a brief abstract of main ideas, compose a concise resume covering only the highlights and relevant details. Little elaboration is necessary.

☞ **Trace:** Discuss according to a pattern such as chronological order, according to a definite sequence, or by presenting phases or stages in order.

Chapter 54

Strategies for Multiple-Choice Tests

Dennis H. Congos, M.S.Ed.,
University of Central Florida, Orlando, Florida

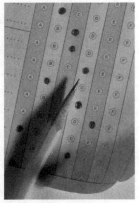

One way to improve scores on multiple-choice exams is to do what "A" students do. Below are eight tips for earning better scores from students who earn high grades. **Keep in mind that the number one test-taking tip is to know your subject well.**

☞ **1. Evaluate each possible answer in relation to the question or statement** and NOT in relation to other answers unless choosing the best answer among several correct ones.

☞ **2.** If the correct answer isn't obvious, **read the question along with each answer**. It's easier to spot a match this way.

☞ **3. Analyze questions and code answers.** For example, mark obviously incorrect answers with a "–" and possible correct answers with a "+" and then choose among the "+" options.

☞ **4.** If the correct answer to a question is not known, code the question to be considered later (possibly with a large ? in the margin) and **skip the question for now**. Look for clues to this answer in later questions and answers. Jot these clues in the margin to use when reconsidering skipped questions.

☞ **5.** Before turning in an exam, **reread each question and an-**

swer. Unless you are *absolutely certain* an answer is wrong, DO NOT CHANGE IT. First impressions are more often right than wrong

☞ **6. Circle "keywords."** "Keywords" reveal the subject of a question and what to look for in an answer.

Example: *Which is a false statement about the nucleolus?*

The keyword "false" tells you to look for a wrong answer while the word nucleolus tells you the subject to which the false statement relates.

☞ **7.** Budget time for each question. **Divide the number of minutes available for taking an exam by the number of questions plus one.** This way you'll know approximately how much time to spend on each question and leave time to recheck answers. Allow more time for essay answers.

☞ **8.** The number one test taking technique is to **know your facts cold.** There is no substitute for knowing your subject well when taking a test. All the test-taking techniques in the world won't help much if you don't know your material.

Chapter 55

Tips for Other Types of Tests

Reprinted with permission from Texas A&M
University Student Counseling Service
College Station, Texas

Multiple-choice and essay tests are not the only types of tests out there. Continue reading to find suggestions for other types of exams.

Matching

Matching is an exercise in recalling memorized information. The tests are divided into two columns. Items on the left side are usually matched with responses on the right side.

» *Ask if you can use alternatives more than once.*

» *Do not match if you are not sure.*

» *Cover one column and try to think of the answer before reading the choices.*

» *Choose the best answer and mark the answer sheet according to the directions.*

» *Narrow down the field, by completing those answers you know are correct.*

» *Avoid changing answers.*

Fill-in-the-Blank

This test item also requires recalling specific types of information. Unlike multiple-choice and matching questions, you must supply the appropriate word or number to complete the entry.

» *Look for clues (e.g., grammar, tenses).*

» *Use common sense.*

» *Choose the best word.*

» *Pay attention to the length of line given or to the number of lines.*

» *Read through after you answer to make sure it sounds right.*

Short Answer

» *Pay attention to grammar.*

» *Answer within the context of the course.*

» *Use terms the instructor used.*

» *If you are having a problem, answer by giving an example.*

» *Beef up your answers if you have time.*

True/False

» *Pay attention to qualifying words (e.g., always, never).*

» *The answer is false if any part is false.*

» *Do not look for patterns.*

» *Guess if you don't know.*

» *Stick with your first answer unless you are sure you are wrong.*

Problem Solving

» *Read the question.*

» *Re-read to get more important information.*

» *If there are multiple options, estimate your answer.*

» *Work backwards (e.g., 2 + 3 = 5, 5 - 2 = 3)*

» *Watch for careless errors.*

A Few More Final Tips…

☞ **Plan your arrival so that you have plenty of time.** Be sure to check your test taking material prior to leaving for the exam. (Showing up for an exam late is a sure way to focus unfavorable attention on yourself.)

☞ **Read all directions.** Underline key words in the directions that give indication as to how your answers are to be recorded and how they should be worded.

☞ **Budget your time.** Survey the test to determine the type and number of questions to be answered. Determine where you will start on the test. Check yourself at 15 or 20 minute intervals to determine if you are progressing at an acceptable rate.

☞ **Be aware that you may have problems remembering from time to time.** If you find yourself blocking, move on to the next question.

☞ **Ask for help in interpreting test questions which you do not understand.**

☞ **Be aware of any negative statements you are telling yourself about the test.** Such statements as "I'm failing, I didn't study for this, and the test is too hard for me" are sure ways of increasing anxiety.

☞ **Do not be concerned with what the other students are doing.** (Another sure way of increasing anxiety is to tell yourself that you are the only one having trouble.)

☞ **As a general rule answer the easy questions first.**

Chapter 56

Post-Test Survey

Dennis H. Congos, M.S.Ed.,
University of Central Florida, Orlando, Florida

**The Post-Test Survey is the single most ne-
glected and underutilized skill for learning in college.**

The Post-Test Survey (PTS) has the potential to
provide the most useful feedback a learner
can get to increase knowledge and improve
grades. Without knowledge about how well skills
for learning work, learners are more likely to
repeat unproductive study skills and ignore productive ones.

The time *immediately after an exam* is a very important time for learners.
When a test is graded and returned, going over exam answers is the best opportunity for learners to discover which study skills worked well and which
didn't. Information from the PTS can be the basis for refinements in skills for
learning that lead to better grades.

Two Keys to Raising Grades

1. *Study skills that worked must be identified so they may be repeated.*

2. *Study skills that didn't work must be identified, modified, or replaced so they
    won't be repeated.*

Without knowing these *two key pieces of information*, learners are likely to *repeat nonproductive study skills that produce lower grades* and remain ignorant of the study skills they use that are effective.

Implementing a Post-Test Survey

Below is one model for properly implementing a Post-Test Survey. The focus is on faster, more productive ways to gain the knowledge needed for better grades. When you get a quiz or test back, follow these **five easy steps** to analyze the effectiveness of learning skills you used.

☞ **Step 1: Identify the Sources of Questions and Answers on Tests**

Determine the lecture date or textbook page numbers where test questions or problems came from. Jot this information down next to the question or problem on the returned test. *This will help you spot clues to main ideas in textbooks and lectures that instructors use when selecting information for future exam questions.* For example:

» *Main ideas in bold print, italics, a summary, an outline at the beginning of a chapter, information in list form or numbered, pictures / charts / drawings, margin notes, etc.*

» *How much time did the instructor spend on this topic in lecture or what was done to emphasize the importance of this material in lecture?*

» *How much text was devoted to this topic in the textbook?*

More importantly, this will be of great help to organize notes for future quizzes and exams.

☞ **Step 2: Use the solutions below to solve study skills problems**

PROBLEM	SOLUTION
My notes were incomplete and/or inaccurate.	• Compare notes with an A student. • Tape lectures and use the tape later as an aid to build a complete set of notes. • Join/form a study group and compare notes. • Sit in the first row in class to make listening easier.
Piece(s) of an answer or solution are missing in my notes and my test answer.	• For any test, be certain you include ALL the main ideas and their details from lectures and texts in your notes. • Recognize and use the clues to important ideas in the texts or lectures as a signal for what to include in notes. • If notes were complete and accurate, determine how many times you reviewed the material, and increase the number of reviews.
I have trouble spotting the clues in the text or lecture that identify information that could be used in a likely test question.	• *In textbooks*, look for bold print, italics, headings, sub-headings, outlines, summaries, end-of-chapter questions, pictures, graphs, charts, diagrams, examples, lists, numbered items, etc. • *In lectures*, listen for repeated ideas, delivered in a louder or softer tone of voice. Notice introductions of topics to be covered in each day's lecture. Be sure to include all of what is put on the board in your notes, included in hand-outs, and answers to questions the instructor raises.

I have the information in my notes but forget it when I take a test.	• Determine how many times you recited and reviewed the material to get it into memory. • Organize notes so that you can self-test to discover how much you have learned or have not yet learned before you take a test. • Use more mnemonics, pictures, diagrams, and charts in your notes to aid recall.
I have too many or too few details in my notes.	• Ask instructors to review notes and offer suggestions on adding or deleting details. • Look at past tests to see how much detail was required for a perfect answer. • Look at an A student's answer to see how much detail s/he included. • See a learning skills counselor for advice.

☞ **Step 3: Determine How Many Times You Reviewed the Material That Could Have Been on the Test**

*Too few reviews are **a major** cause of low grades!*

In general, people become better at that which they practice. That applies to sports as well as learning. Unfortunately, learners are not usually taught that they must practice what they need to learn. The results are the same if an athlete does not practice: poor performance. To practice in learning, a learner must recite and review material a number of times.

Reciting means practice by saying answers to questions or details to main ideas aloud, without looking at notes and then check for completeness and accuracy. With math, chemistry, or physics problems, practice involves doing solutions over and over after looking only at the problem. Practice allows learners to know immediately how well material is or is not learned and remembered.

Reviewing means reciting material a number of times on a regular basis. Going over material only once or twice before a test for most people results in poor learning and recall on exams. Some learners can review material 2–3 times to get an A, while others must review 5–8 times or more to get an A. It is normal to forget, misorder ideas, make careless mistakes, or have difficulty in recall at test time when not enough reciting and reviewing is done.

☞ **Step 4: Evaluate**

Identify which study skills you used for answers you got correct and which study skills you used for answers on which you lost points. Find the source of information for answers where you lost points. If the information was complete and accurate in your notes, this suggests more reviews and recitations are necessary. If the information was not in your notes, what were the clues that this information was important? (Bold print, italics, numbered items, recorded on the chalkboard, etc.) Evaluation reveals where changes need to be made in your learning skills in preparation for the next test.

☞ **Step 5: Modify**

In learning, unless you have the proper tools (learning skills) for doing the job of learning and the knowledge of how to use these tools properly, grades are not likely to improve. *Specific changes* are needed in those learning skills that were used for the last test if higher grades are to be achieved in the future.

Part XIV

Utilizing College Resources

Chapter 57

Tapping into College Resources

Starting Out!® Research Group

Every college and university offers extensive resources to help
students with problems or decisions.
Get to know what your school has to
offer in these important areas:

☞ **College counseling center:** Whether
you are suffering from homesickness or depression, or are having difficulty with your courses, visit your college's counseling center and seek
out assistance immediately. Caring counselors will listen to your concerns
and give you valuable support and guidance. If they cannot assist you, or
feel you need other help, they will give you referrals to other appropriate
resources or health facilities.

☞ **Study skills center:** Many students enter college with weak study skills.
Every college offers remedial and tutoring assistance to students to
improve basic reading and study skills. Strong study skills are vital for
college success. Identify the areas where you need help, and spend
the time to build the missing skills that you need. If you need tutoring
there are always students and faculty members who will help you.

☞ **International student help:** Many international students attend colleges
and universities in every state, often needing assistance with documents, transcripts, health issues, visas, and other matters. If you need
help from your college, see if there is either an international student

office or advisor, or speak with the college counseling center.

☞ **Health center:** Health issues often become major concerns to students, including both physical and mental health problems. Visit your student health center immediately with any questions, concerns, or medical problems. There will be caring individuals to help with all types of problems including mental health concerns and women's health issues.

☞ **Library resources and reference tools:** A key part of your college experience involves writing and research. Aside from resources available on the Internet, get to know your library and especially the reference librarian and take advantage of the valuable services offered by your college library. Learning about the numerous types of reference sources and tools will help throughout your college career.

☞ **Computer facilities:** Learn about the public computer facilities available on your campus, especially at the library. Your college bookstore will direct you to computer repair facilities, or sell you new software or equipment.

☞ **Mental health services:** Every college offers immediate assistance to students experiencing mental health issues, especially depression and suicidal thoughts. Such services can often help you deal with family problems, including grief and loss over the death of a family member, relative, or friend, or concern over the loss of a parent's job.

☞ **Drug and alcohol counseling:** Alcohol consumption is a major college problem in the U.S. today as is the use of street and party drugs, and the misuse of prescription medications. Do not permit such problems to overwhelm you. Visit your campus health center or alcohol and drug abuse counseling center.

☞ **Financial aid:** Your college financial aid office is an important resource to get to know and utilize during your college career. Learn about different types of financial aid, including low-cost student loans, scholarships, and grants.

☞ **Campus jobs:** To provide spending money during college, campus jobs can be invaluable. Hours and schedules for different types of jobs can be very flexible to mesh with your academic schedule. Learn about jobs in research labs, food service, the library, tutoring, grounds maintenance, and other areas.

☞ **Career placement center:** Information about part-time, summer, and full-time jobs can be obtained from your college placement office. Get to know the resources available on campus, and plan well ahead of your graduation date for help locating a full-time job.

☞ **Housing problems:** On and off-campus housing can present many problems for students, including both availability and cost. Check with your campus housing office to solve your housing needs. Consider house-sharing with a group of students to keep your costs as low as possible.

☞ **Religious services:** Students of most faiths will find religious centers or groups on campus catering to their needs and interests. If you prefer, visit a local place of worship, or consider forming your own group with like-minded students.

☞ **Registrar services:** Aside from keeping track of your courses and grades, the registrar's office will provide you with an official transcript of your academic record at any time. This document is very important when you apply for a full-time job.

☞ **Testing services:** Do you want to be tested to identify you aptitudes or interests? Do you want to get credit for courses that you have previously taken? Find out from your campus counseling office how to get the tests you need. Special competence in a foreign language, mathematics, and other areas can sometimes get you immediate course credits, which will save you time and money.

☞ **Emergency services:** Have you experienced date rape, violence, theft, or other serious crimes? Are you aware of another student who is having a personal crisis? Visit your campus police office or call 911 for immediate help.

☞ **Alumni affairs:** As a freshman, you may not be thinking about the college alumni office. However, as you progress through college you may want to meet or network with other graduates, especially in your future career field. Many colleges have websites or can provide networking opportunities that can be extremely valuable to help you find a job, or to get advice from someone with real experience.

☞ **ROTC:** Larger colleges and universities often have very active ROTC programs on campus (reserve officers' training corps). Visit with officers from the ROTC to learn about careers in military service.

☞ **Volunteer office:** Do you want to volunteer helping people in your college community? Do you have time to volunteer at the local hospital, schools, or prison? Colleges usually have an office or staff member who coordinates community volunteer activities for students. Volunteering is a wonderful way to help others and gain valuable experience outside the classroom.

Chapter 58

Building an Advising Relationship

Hiram College, Student Services
Hiram, Ohio

The Advisor's Role

Having an advisor who can serve you during your college experience, can result in a very valuable relationship. **Here are some ways an advisor can assist you:**

» Your advisor will come to know you, your interests, and abilities throughout your first years. He/she will listen to you describe your goals and your options and suggest alternatives for you to consider.

» Your advisor can interpret placement test results and help you choose courses suitable for your educational background.

» You and your faculty advisor will meet regularly prior to registration each semester to discuss your academic plans and progress and your options for the next registration.

» Your advisor may maintain and regularly update an academic file for you. This file will include copies of all official correspondence including registration records and grade reports. You will also want to keep your own copies of these documents.

» Your advisor will be knowledgeable about college requirements for general education, for majors and minors, and will encourage you to fulfill them in a timely and appropriate way.

» Your advisor will encourage you to seek the opinions and advice of other faculty members. Although you are primarily responsible for your own academic planning, it will be helpful to have input from faculty with different perspectives and from different disciplines.

» Your advisor will help you develop oral and written communication skills by suggesting appropriate courses and experiences to strengthen those abilities.

» If you need additional help to be successful academically, your advisor will be aware of campus resources and refer you to academic services, tutors, writing assistants, or other resources.

» Since your advisor will come to know your abilities well, your advisor may provide letters of reference for summer jobs, programs, internships, or graduate school.

Your Role

These are ways you can help your advisor be most effective:

» Make an appointment to see your advisor as soon as possible. Be on time and be prepared for the meeting. If you miss an advising appointment, it is your responsibility to schedule another.

» Share information about yourself with your advisor. Your educational goals, tentative career plans, your understanding of your own abilities, and milestones in your life will help your advisor know you better and help you make better curricular choices.

» Familiarize yourself with academic procedures and graduation requirements by reading your school's course catalog and student manual.

» Be knowledgeable about requirements for any majors you are considering; requirements are listed in your school's course catalog.

» Discuss your choice of a major with a department faculty member;

they may also have handouts for you.

» It is your responsibility to keep records and to record your progress towards graduation.

» Print a transcript and bring it with you to your advising appointments.

» Ask your advisor questions. He or she may assume you know more about the curriculum than you do. Your advisor may also assume you understand the reason for any advice he or she gives you. If you are not sure why a particular course of action is appropriate for you, ASK.

» When you have questions about majors or special programs, ask your advisor to refer you to another faculty member for more information.

» Contact your advisor immediately if:

• you are having problems with a class,
• an emergency prevents you from keeping up with your course work,
• you need help solving a problem.

» Everyone changes and grows during college. Tell your advisor when you want to try a different approach, and discuss the advantages of the change. Sometimes there is more than one way to reach a goal. If other faculty or students suggest alternatives to you, discuss them with your advisor.

Chapter 59

Taking Advantage of Office Hours

Cornell University, Learning Strategies Center
Ithaca, New York

What Are Office Hours?

Professors and teaching assistants schedule time outside of class to meet with
students. These are called office hours. Office
hours are times when you can meet with your
professors and teaching assistants to discuss
the material being presented in class or other
related interests you have. Course-related discussions include asking for
extra help, seeking clarification of material presented in class and following up on aspects of the class you find compelling. In addition, students
also discuss majors and programs of study, and graduation requirements,
as well as summer internships, graduate schools, campus events, and much
more.

Most professors do not require that students attend office hours. They expect students to decide for themselves when they need or want to participate. Professors usually announce their office hours on the first day of class
or on their print or web-based course material.

Most professors and teaching assistants do not have lessons planned for
office hours. They expect students to "drive" these meetings with their
questions and their thoughts. A good way to prepare for office hours is to
attempt your homework and review your notes from class and from readings and identify as clearly as you can what you do not understand.

Do not be surprised when the professors and teaching assistants reply to your questions with questions of their own. They are working with you to uncover the source of your questions. Often they will ask students to show them their work and where they got stuck. They may ask you to explain what you were thinking as you moved from step to step. They may ask you to generate alternative ways to solve a problem. Hopefully they will help you change how you think about the material so that you can answer many different kinds of questions about it — not just the question on the homework that is stumping you. Don't be surprised if they ask you to solve another problem before you leave the office.

Current students state that:

"Office hours are a great asset to learning."
"(Office hours are) very helpful!"

What Office Hours Are Not

Office hours are not related to activities in high school that *require* students to stay after school. They are not detention sessions. They are not a place where the instructor will do your homework for you.

What Are My Responsibilities as a Student Going to Office Hours?

To make the very most of your time with your instructor during office hours, you should:

☞ **Study your textbook and lecture notes thoroughly** and attempt the assigned problems before you go to office hours.

☞ **Try to identify specific questions or concepts** you need to address during the office hours.

☞ **Expect instructors to ask you questions about the material.** They do this to find out what you understand, and to provide you with information and strategies tailored to your individual needs.

☞ **Be patient!** Several students often come for office hours at the same time. If the instructor is especially busy, you may have to wait a little longer for individual assistance. Use this time to study the material.

☞ **Expect the instructor to suggest general study strategies to help you improve your overall academic performance.** These strategies will help in all of your courses.

☞ **Avoid waiting until the day before the test or the day before an assignment is due to seek assistance.** Study a few hours each day, and keep up with your assignments. It is EASIER to keep up than to catch up!

☞ **Keep a positive attitude about the subject and about your potential to excel.** Your attitude will go a long way in determining how well you do in the course!

Chapter 60

Communicating with College Professors

Reprinted with permission from Texas A&M
University Student Counseling Service
College Station, Texas

Getting Along with Your College Professor

☞ **Go to class!** Regular attendance is
important not only for good rela-
tions with the professor, but also for
ensuring that you don't miss anything. Professors may say they don't
care about class attendance. Don't
believe it! They notice who's there
and who's not.

☞ **If emergencies arise that cause you to miss class, be sure to get notes from
someone in the class whose work you respect.** At the next class meeting
after your absence, tell the professor you've gotten the notes, but that
you want to double-check to make sure you didn't miss announce-
ments of upcoming tests, etc. Don't dwell on the reason for your
absence. The professor has probably heard it before!

☞ **Don't be late!** The first few minutes of class are often used for vital an-
nouncements of upcoming tests, due dates for assignments, etc.

☞ **"Better late than never" is usually a good rule of thumb, but not always**
Note the professor's reaction when other students are late, then guide
your own actions accordingly. If he/she ignores students walking in late,
that doesn't mean it's okay, but it's better than missing class entirely. If
the reaction to student tardiness is somewhat stormy, it may be better to

miss class than to call attention to yourself in an unfavorable light.

☞ **Professors usually announce office hours at the first class meeting each semester.** It is to your advantage to know your professors and for them to know you. Make an appointment to see each of your professors no later than the fifth class meeting. Appointments may be made before or after class or over the telephone. If for some reason you must cancel, be sure to call! Remember, teaching is not your professor's only responsibility. Don't expect that he/she will always be available at your convenience.

☞ **The purpose of meeting with a professor, regardless of your level of interest in the course, is to enhance your understanding of what is going on in class.** Before your appointment, be sure you have done the following:

» *Previewed your text to familiarize yourself with topics for the remainder of the course.*

» *Reviewed your notes up to that point and identified topics or issues that you don't understand.*

» *Written down at least three or four good questions about the course, such as potential topics for papers or projects, questions about the most effective ways to study the material, etc.*

» *Located the professor's office so that you won't be late for the appointment due to wandering around the halls at the last minute.*

» *Make sure you know the professor's title (Dr., Mr., Ms.) and how to pronounce his/her name.*

☞ **Getting to know professors can have other benefits as well.** Most of them are interesting people, knowledgeable about many topics beyond their own discipline. You may discover that you have common interests that can be the basis for a good relationship long after you have finished the course. You may also find that a particular field is much more interesting to you than you previously thought. It is not unusual for decisions about college majors to originate with a good student-professor relationship. Professors may have information about special opportunities that you may find useful. Summer internships, competitive awards, graduate programs, etc., are usually posted on cluttered bulletin boards and are sometimes hard to spot. A professor who knows you may be the key to your becoming aware of these special opportunities. A single office visit won't change your life, but it could lead eventually to many "fringe" benefits that wouldn't have come your way if you hadn't gotten to know your professors.

☞ **Get assignments in on time!** Earthquake, fire, flood, and catastrophic illness are the only excuses for turning assignments in late. You've got 24 hours in your day just like everyone else. You want the professor to know who you are for the right reasons! There is a definite relationship between students who do poorly on tests, receive low final grades, or fail courses, and those who turn assignments in late.

☞ **Being courteous in class doesn't mean you have to agree with everything that's being said.** When asking questions, don't be hostile or demanding and don't back the professor into a corner. When you disagree or don't understand a point, be positive. Preface your question with leads like "Could you clarify the relationship between . . . ?" or "Could you elaborate on . . . ?" Avoid negative leads like "I don't see how . . ." or "Don't you think . . . ?"

☞ **Grades are another area in which professors and students sometimes disagree.** Never discuss a grade when you are angry. A test may have seemed unfair to you, but don't label it as such when you're discussing it with the professor. Be specific but courteous when making your points. Remember, regardless of how skillful your arguments are, the odds are that your grade won't be changed on that particular test. But, if you make your points well, the next test may be much better constructed and may seem to you to be a fairer measure of your knowledge of the material.

☞ **Most professors are experts in their fields.** Many of them are not experts in psychometrics or applied learning. Realizing that very few of them have had formal training in test construction or in how to teach may help you to understand their occasional shortcomings in these areas.

Most good professors have gotten that way by trial and error. Improved teaching often depends on the kind of feedback they receive from students. Avoid being negative in your comments. Specific, positive, constructive feedback can really improve the learning situation.

☞ **Sit toward the front of the class and act like you're paying attention.** There is a strange but definite relationship between your distance from the professor and your distance from an "A". Regardless of how dry a lecture might be, there is always something communicated that you will be responsible for.

☞ **Always bring a notebook and textbook to class.** This communicates preparedness and interest, even if neither of these qualities applies to you.

Talking With a Professor About a Grade

 Reprinted with permission from Tom Sebok, Director, Ombuds Office, University of Colorado at Boulder

Assigning grades is one of the most protected of faculty rights and responsibilities. Talking with your professor about a grade—particularly if you differ in your perceptions about what the grade should be—can be very difficult. The following guidelines are  suggested to assist you in having a productive discussion with your professor about your grade.

☞ **Ask specific questions that focus the discussion on how your grade was derived. There are at least four possibilities:**

» *The professor made an honest mistake. This is easy to fix!*

» *You made mistakes you did not realize. (In this case, the conversation is a learning opportunity for you. Also, by taking the time to have this discussion with your professor, you can convey to him/her that you are serious about learning).*

» *You and the professor have an honest disagreement about the weight your professor gave to one or more aspects of your performance.*

» *Your professor used non-academic criteria in determining your grade.*

☞ **You might suspect your grade is based on non-academic criteria for any number of reasons:**

» *You have seen the work of other students and it seems obvious to you that your work is stronger, yet your grade is the same or lower. Hint: Look carefully at "objective criteria," as much as possible, in making this comparison. For example, in looking at papers or essays:*

- *Were more specific details cited in one student's work than in another's?*

- *Did one student present his / her ideas more clearly?*

- *Does one student present a clearer context, demonstrating a better grasp of the "big picture?"*

» *You strongly disagreed with your professor in class or in one or more previous discussions and now you suspect you are being "punished" for doing so.*

» *You have heard or observed that your professor has demonstrated prejudice against people with whom you have significant things in common (i.e., race, gender, sexual orientation, national origin, etc.).*

» *Your professor disagrees with your political or social views.*

☞ **When having the discussion, here are some "do's" and "don'ts"**
DO:

» *Ask appropriate questions about how your grade was calculated.*

» *Ask for examples of what would have made your work stronger.*

» *Try to understand what your professor thinks is missing or incorrect about your work.*

» *Focus on objective criteria (i.e. things that can be measured or valid and recognized standards for evaluating the merits of work).*

» *Use a flat, neutral, inquisitive tone of voice.*

DON'T:

»   *Accuse her/him of cheating you - even if you believe s/he has done that. Making such an accusation is much more likely to cause the professor to resist hearing your point of view!).*

»   *Give up trying to gain a clear understanding of the professor's stated reasons for assigning you the grade.*

»   *Use a tone of voice which conveys anger or disrespect.*

If, after discussing the issue with the professor, you are convinced that your grade does not reflect the merits of your work, politely indicate that you and the professor appear to be in disagreement about how the grade should have been calculated (e.g., "It looks like we disagree about the calculation of my grade" rather than "I think you are wrong" or, worse, "You are trying to rip me off!") Ask if s/he can suggest any alternatives for resolving the disagreement.

At this point, informal options to resolve the issue are limited to choices with which both you and the professor can agree. Any professor who is convinced s/he is assigning a fair grade is unlikely to change the grade. However, if s/he believes there may be room for different interpretations, s/he may be willing to consider feedback from another professor. From the professor's perspective, one disadvantage of this alternative is that another professor is unlikely to have read the work of other students in the class. But if the professor is willing to consider the comments of a colleague, an informal resolution might still be possible.

If the professor suggests no other alternatives and you still wish to pursue the matter, you will need to speak with the department chair (in the professor's department). If s/he is unable to help you resolve the matter informally, you may initiate a formal grade appeal procedure with the chair.

Chapter 62

Working with a Tutor

California State University Dominguez Hills,
Center for Learning and Academic Support Services
Carson, California

Tips for Working With a Tutor

☞ **Never wait until the last minute.**

☞ **Come prepared!** Bring your assignment, books, notes and any other
necessary materials to your session.

☞ **Read your assignments and review your
notes** before meeting with a tutor.

☞ **Attempt to do your assignment before you
meet with a tutor,** or bring questions about your assignment.

☞ **Don't expect your tutor to do or check your work.**

☞ **Don't expect your tutor to take the place of your instructor or a missed
lecture.**

☞ **Expect your tutor to help you develop your study skills.**

☞ **Expect your tutor to help you develop your writing skills.**

☞ **Expect your tutor to help you develop your critical thinking skills.**

☞ **Expect your tutor to help you learn how to review material.**

☞ **Expect your tutor to help you learn about our other services.**

When working with a writing tutor . . . .

☞ **Bring your writing prompt.**

☞ **Bring a typed or legible draft** or questions about your assignment.

☞ **Make sure you have read your textbooks** and all your assigned course materials thoroughly.

☞ **Expect your tutor to help you with strategies to revise your paper.**

☞ **Expect your tutor to suggest strategies** to help your develop better writing skills.

☞ **Expect your tutor to work with you on the patterns of errors that he/she sees in your paper.**

☞ **Expect to write another draft of your paper after your session.**

☞ **Don't expect your tutor to proofread for errors or write your paper.**

☞ **If you have a paper longer than eight pages:**

  » *Seek assistance early*

  » *Identify specific sections that you want discussed*

  » *Remember sessions are often limited to 30 minutes, so don't expect tutors to review the entire paper.*

☞ **Find out if you need proof that you've worked with a tutor** and get it, if necessary.

Part XV

Communication Skills

Chapter 63

What's Your Communication Style?

Reprinted by permission of the publisher, from *How to Become a Better Negotiator*, Second Edition, by Richard A. Luecke and James G. Patterson

©2008 American Management Association, New York, New York. *www.amacombooks.org*

O ur accomplishments often depend on how well we can communicate our needs and objectives to others. Truly effective communication requires an understanding of other people's styles as well as our own. Take this quiz from *How to Become a Better Negotiator* by James G. Patterson to determine your personal dominant communication style—Listener, Creator, Doer or Thinker—then read on for some insight into each style.

Communication Style Quiz:

Read each of the following phrases and check the word that best describes you. Then count up the check marks in each of the four columns and consult the Scoring Key to determine your dominant style.

1	**Manner is basically:**		Accepting		Friendly		Controlling		Evaluative
2	**Decision making:**		Slow		Emotional		Impulsive		Fact-based
3	**I talk about:**		Personal things		People		Achievements		Organization
4	**Using time:**		Not rushed		Socializer		Rushed		Runs late

5	Relates to others:		Accepting		Empathizer		Commands		Assessing
6	Gestures:		Sparse		Open		Impatient		Closed
7	Clothing:		Conforms		Very stylish		Formal		Conservative
8	Work pace:		Steady		Enthusiastic		Fast		Controlled
9	Listening:		Interested		Distracted		Impatient		Selective
10	Study area has:		Keepsakes		Pictures		Awards		Charts
11	Oriented toward:		Support		People		Results		Facts
12	Basic personality:		Easygoing		Outgoing		Dominating		No-nonsense
13	Communication:		Low-key		Animated		Direct		Reserved
14	Responsive to others:		Steady		Friendly		Restless		Distant
	TOTAL:	1	Listener	2	Creator	3	Doer	4	Thinker

SCORING KEY:

7 or more = Strong Preference

5–6 = Moderate Preference

0–2 = Low Preference Characteristics of Each Communication Style

☞ **1. Listeners**

> » *People oriented*

> » *Believe there is more than one method to achieve the same results*

> » *Demand a voice in decisions that affect them*

> » *Place a high premium on relationships*

> » *Can be slow decision makers*

> » *Don't delegate well*

> » *Seek security; don't take risks*

Conflict: Mainly with Doers

Advice: Try to be more assertive. Focus less on relationships and more on tasks. Learn to make observations based on facts, not subjective judgments.

☞ **2. Creators**

» *Enthusiastic, excitement driven*

» *Like public speaking and attention*

» *May be too talkative*

» *Persuasive and optimistic*

» *Creative*

» *Good sense of humor*

» *Can be impulsive, make snap decisions*

» *Have problems following through with an idea*

Conflict: Mainly with Thinkers

Advice: Slow down. Try to be less intense

☞ **3. Doers**

» *Pragmatic*

» *Assertive*

» *Results oriented*

» *Competitive*

» *Competent*

» *Very verbal*

» *Excellent problem solver*

» *Risk taker*

» *Can be arrogant and domineering*

» *Can be poor listener and impatient*

Conflict: Mainly with Listeners

Advice: Slow down. Count to ten before responding. Learn to listen more. Work at showing your feelings, being more interested in relationships and being more open.

☞ 4. Thinkers

» *Detail oriented*

» *Can be slow decision makers*

» *Like rules and predictability*

» *Lowest risk taker*

» *Analytical*

» *Conservative*

» *Can be rigid, overly serious and indecisive*

Conflict: Mainly with Creators

Advice: Try to move faster, show less need for endless detail, be less rigid about following policies. Take more risks. Show more personal concern for others.

Chapter 64

Nonverbal Communication Skills

It is not only what you say that is important, but it's how you say it that can make the difference. Nonverbal messages are an essential component of communication.

Part 1: Nonverbal Communication Techniques Department of Veterans Affairs, Office of the Dispute Resolution Specialist

Nonverbal communication skills can be applied in your personal life, to improve understanding between you and your friends, family, and professors. These skills are most important when you are on the listening end of the conversation.

Listening is an art, a skill, a discipline, and like other skills, it needs self-control. You must understand what is involved in listening and develop the necessary techniques to be silent and listen. You must ignore your own needs and concentrate attention on the person speaking. Hearing becomes listening only when you pay attention to what is said and follow it very closely.

☞ **You demonstrate that you are listening by:**

» *using your body language*

» *echoing words*

» *making eye contact*

» *nodding your head*

» *keeping your body open*

» *leaning toward the speaker*

☞ **You listen to:**

» *show your support and help the other person(s) relax*

» *show you are accepting them, and open to them*

» *enable each person to speak and be heard*

» *be able to ask questions to clarify*

» *check assumptions*

» *clear up misperceptions*

» *re-state or paraphrase*

» *find the key points or issues*

» *provide the silence necessary to encourage speech*

» *know when to bring to closure and when to test for agreements*

☞ **You need to show you are listening carefully; this is called "attending." Attending skills build rapport and help people feel at ease.**

» *Listen without interrupting.*

» *Pay attention.*

» *Use supportive body language.*

» *Paraphrase facts and feelings.*

☞ **You also need to practice reacting and responding in positive ways. Using good responding skills help people understand the things you care about and help you collect information about the situation.**

» *Ask clarifying questions.*

» *Ask probing questions.*

» *Restate what the other person is saying catching the essence, but trying to take out any volatile phrases or language. This is called "laundering" language and it can reduce friction.*

» *Summarize facts and feelings.*

» *Reframe issues; focus on the interests, not positions.*

» *Try to always use "I" language instead of "You" Not: "When you do that, you make me feel . . ." instead say, "When you do that I feel . . ."*

» *Try to communicate directly with the other person.*

» *Be forward thinking; try to focus on the future.*

When dealing with a conflict, paying attention and listening without interruption allows the other person to "let off some steam." Before any serious resolutions can occur, you need to let the other person know that you understand where they are coming from and you understand that they feel strongly about the issues you are discussing with them. Their intense emotions must be acknowledged and affirmed before serious solutions can be discussed.

☞ **You should encourage the other person to explain his or her views by using verbal cues such as:**

» *"I see."*

» *"I understand."*

> » *"That's a good point."*

> » *"I can see that you feel strongly about that."*

> » *"I can understand how you could see it like that."*

☞ **These nonverbal actions also show the other person that you hear what they are saying:**

> » *Squarely face the other person.*

> » *Adopt an open posture.*

> » *Lean discreetly toward the other person, not threateningly.*

> » *Maintain eye contact; take cues from the other person as to how much eye contact s/he is comfortable with.*

> » *Try to relax as you interact with the other person.*

Of course, for the other person to know that you are listening, you must make a response. The effectiveness of your listening will be determined by the style and quality of your response.

Part 2: Six Ways to Improve Your Nonverbal Communications While Giving a Presentation

Vicki Ritts, Ph.D., Professor of Psychology, St. Louis Community College-Meramac, St. Louis, Missouri

Nonverbal communication can also help improve a presentation. People should be aware of nonverbal behavior for three major reasons:

1. *An awareness of nonverbal behavior will allow you to become better receivers of messages.*

2. *You will become a better sender of signals that reinforce communication.*

3. *This mode of communication increases the degree of the perceived psychological closeness between speaker and listener.*

Some major areas of nonverbal behaviors to explore are:

✓ *Eye contact*

✓ *Facial expressions*

✓ *Gestures*

✓ *Posture and body orientation*

✓ *Proximity*

✓ *Paralinguistics*

✓ *Humor*

☞ Eye contact:

Eye contact, an important channel of interpersonal communication, helps regulate the flow of communication. And it signals interest in others. Furthermore, eye contact with audiences increases the speaker's credibility. Speakers who make eye contact open the flow of communication and convey interest, concern, warmth, and credibility.

☞ Facial expressions: Smiling is a powerful cue that transmits:

- » Happiness
- » Friendliness
- » Warmth
- » Liking
- » Affiliation

Thus, if you smile frequently you will be perceived as more likable, friendly, warm, and approachable. Smiling is often contagious and listeners will react favorably and retain more.

☞ Gestures:

If you fail to gesture while speaking, you may be perceived as boring, stiff, and unanimated. A lively and animated speaking style captures listeners' attention, makes the material more interesting, facilitates learning, and provides a bit of entertainment. Head nods, a form of gestures, communicate positive reinforcement and indicate that you are listening.

☞ **Posture and body orientation:**

You communicate numerous messages by the way you walk, talk, stand, and sit. Standing erect, but not rigid, and leaning slightly forward communicates to people that you are approachable, receptive, and friendly. Furthermore, interpersonal closeness results when you and the person you're speaking to face each other. Speaking with your back turned or looking at the floor or ceiling should be avoided; it communicates disinterest.

☞ **Proximity:**

Cultural norms dictate a comfortable distance for interaction. You should look for signals of discomfort caused by invading another's space. Some of these are:

» *Rocking*

» *Leg swinging*

» *Tapping*

» *Gaze aversion*

Typically, in large classrooms, space invasion is not a problem. In fact, there is usually too much distance. Increasing proximity enables you to make better eye contact and increases the opportunities for listeners to speak.

☞ **Paralinguistics:**

This facet of nonverbal communication includes such vocal elements as:

» *Tone*

» *Pitch*

» *Rhythm*

» *Timbre*

» *Loudness*

» *Inflection*

For maximum effectiveness, learn to vary these six elements of your voice. One of the major criticisms is of speakers who talk in a monotone. Listeners perceive these speakers as boring and dull. Listeners report that they retain less and lose interest more quickly when listening to speakers who have not learned to modulate their voices.

☞ **Humor:**

Humor is often overlooked as a speaking tool, and it is too often not encouraged in college classrooms. Laughter releases stress and tension for both speaker and audience. You should develop the ability to laugh at yourself and encourage others to do the same. It fosters a friendly environment.

Obviously, adequate knowledge of the subject matter is crucial to your success; however, it's not the only crucial element. Creating an interesting speech demands good nonverbal and verbal skills. To improve your nonverbal skills, record your speaking on video tape. Then ask a friend or a study skills counselor to suggest refinements.

Assertiveness

Reprinted with permission from the University of Texas at Dallas Student Counseling Center, Dallas, Texas

Does This Sound Like You?

» *You find yourself saying "yes" to requests when you really want to say "no."*

» *It is hard for you to make a decision.*

» *You are unable to express your discontent with a friend or partner, even if you think it's justified.*

» *It is difficult for you to ask for help or assistance.*

» *It is hard for you to express an opinion that is different from other people's opinions.*

» *It is hard for you to share something positive about yourself.*

» *You do not speak up in class, even when you know the answer to a question.*

» *You find it difficult to accept a compliment.*

If any of these sound like you, you may have difficulty using assertive communication.

Defining Assertiveness

Communication styles can be seen as on a continuum from passive to aggressive, with assertive communication in the middle.

Passiveness is more indirect communication. It lets other people choose for you and puts other people's rights ahead of your rights.

Assertiveness is standing up for yourself in a way that does not violate the rights of another person. It is a direct and honest expression of your feelings and opinions. Your rights and the rights of others are equally valued, expressed, and respected.

You may have been uncomfortable being assertive in the past because you confused it with aggressiveness. Aggressiveness is a way of standing up for yourself that violates the rights of other people. It results in humiliating and putting down the other person. Aggressiveness assumes your rights are more important than other people's rights.

Common Challenges to Being Assertive

You may have also found assertive communication uncomfortable to use due to cultural norms, gender norms, or social norms. Cultures vary in how acceptable it is to communicate directly. You may not choose to use the same communication style in every situation. For example, while you might decide to express yourself more assertively in a salary negotiation at work, you might choose to be less assertive in communicating with your elderly relatives.

Sometimes people would like to be more assertive, but find this difficult. They may be afraid of what will happen if their views or feelings differ from other people. They may fear that other people will not like them if they share themselves honestly. Fear of conflict is another reason people avoid assertive communication. A belief that they should be perfect and handle all challenges alone can also lead people to communicate in a nonassertive way.

When you find yourself wishing you were communicating more assertively, ask yourself what is challenging to you personally or in the specific situation about being assertive. If you think it would be helpful to be more assertive in your communication, use the following tips on increasing assertive communication:

☞ **Specific Techniques for Assertiveness**

» **Start by identifying your thoughts, feelings, and wants**. Think of what you want to communicate and how you want to phrase your message.

» **Make your communication clear and specific.** Talk about another person's behavior, not the person. "I-statements" are one way to communicate assertively. With I-statements, you start by briefly describing the other person's behavior. Then you state how their actions affect you, starting with the words "I think" or "I feel." You may choose to make a request. For example, "When you are late picking me up and do not call, I feel afraid that something has happened to you and I feel angry that I am waiting. I would prefer it if you call to let me know if you are going to be more than 10 minutes late picking me up."

» **Think about your non-verbal communication.** Try to remain calm. Use a level tone and volume. Don't hesitate with your words. Face the person you are talking to and maintain some direct eye contact.

» **It is o.k. to say no.** You do not have to explain or justify your reasons for saying no to a request.

» **Ask others for feedback on your message** and how the other person sees the situation. Communicate that other people's thoughts and feelings are as important as your thoughts and feelings.

» **Practice!** Communicating assertively is a skill that can improve with practice.

Chapter 66

Dealing With Difficult People and Difficult Situations

University of Kansas Counseling and Psychological Services (CAPS), Lawrence, Kansas

Setting the Stage for Success

College life involves frequent interaction with people in a multitude of situations, ranging from getting along with roommates to negotiating group projects. Part of your success and happiness in college depends on your ability to effectively negotiate problems. Here are some tips for dealing with difficult people and difficult situations:

Meet privately—having an audience causes more defensiveness. **Expect that difficult situations will take time to resolve**—if you feel rushed, ask to meet at a later, specific time. Don't take things personally. Recognize that your role is to be calm and objective. (Vent later with a friend or colleague if you need to.)

☞ **Use Active Listening Skills**

Clarification: Ask questions to clarify if you are unsure.

Paraphrasing: Rephrase content.

Reflection: Rephrase feelings.

Summarization: Listen for themes or main points.

Physical cues: Use head nods, eye contact, open body posture; this lets the listener know that you are listening.

☞ **Identify the Problem**

Clarify the expectations of the interaction.

Encourage the person to talk—this provides you more understanding of the "real" issues involved and often provides clues for possible solutions.

Reframe the problem so that it is not personal. For example, the problem is usage of room time, not that one roommate is a jerk who plays music too loudly, and the other is a jerk who sleeps too much.

Make the problem something that you are both working on collaboratively to solve.

☞ **Problem Solve**

As much as possible, solve problems **collaboratively.**

Ask what he or she has done to try to resolve the problem.

Provide the opportunity for **everyone to "save face."**

☞ **Know Your Limits**

You are not responsible for **solving all problems**.

Once you have done what you reasonably can do, **don't beat yourself up** if the outcome is not totally satisfactory to each of you.

Don't let the other person's problem become your problem. Your job is to problem solve, not to simply take on other people's problems.

☞ **Refine Your Problem Solving**

Make requests, not ultimatums.

Focus on the present not the past. Focus on what you want, not on what you don't want.

☞ **Note progress**

Acknowledge progress to the other person.

Reward yourself for achievements.

☞ **Improving Communication in Your Relationships**

Communication problems are the most common reason for seeking counseling, accounting for 40 percent of all counseling issues.

Problem-solving training changes communication skills and aids in creating interpersonal relationship satisfaction.

Tips

☞ **Be Realistic.** Change takes time; appreciate the small steps of improvement.

☞ **Stay friendly.** Work up to the more difficult topics; don't make negative comments. Focus on the positive.

☞ **Be optimistic.** Remember the good things about this person; try not to generalize criticisms (do not use "always" or "never").

☞ **Say things in ways that will be easy to hear.** Make sure you understand what is being said. "What I heard you say was. . . "Is that what you meant?"

Chapter 67

How to Be a Good Listener

Starting Out!® Research Group

A significant part of what we learn comes from listening and observing. But being a good listener is not simply being present in class when a teacher is giving a lesson or being in the same room when a parent is giving instructions. Rather, listening is an active *process*, and we can get better at it over time and with practice.

Hearing vs. Listening

The first thing you need to know is the difference between *hearing* and *listening*.

Hearing is simply the act of perceiving sound through the ear. If you are not hearing-impaired, hearing simply happens as one of our primary sensory experiences. In most settings we are subjected to a combination of voices, sounds, and other environmental distractions, and we filter out what we want to hear, disregarding other noises and interference.

Listening, however, is something you consciously <u>choose to do</u>. Listening requires concentration so that your brain processes meaning from words and sentences. Paying attention through attentive listening leads to learning.

Learning Follows Listening

Listening is a cognitive act, and the first step in <u>absorbing new information</u> that then must be processed by our brain. From listening comes comprehension, or understanding, and from understanding comes action or response. We become educated through listening to others and by observing and reading. How we use the knowledge we gain through listening, observing, and reading directly impacts our everyday lives and our careers.

Ten Steps to Becoming a Better Listener and Learner

Because so much of our learning comes through listening, it is worth finding ways to become a better listener, and to derive more information from speakers, instructors, and other communicators. Here are a few recommendations:

1. Be alert and awake. Be ready to listen in a class or lecture. Come to the class well-rested so you can focus on what is being presented. Don't be late, and avoid missing classes.

2. Have a constructive attitude about listening. Commit yourself to listen to what is being presented, even if it is on a subject that does not interest you. There is always something valuable we can learn from others. We are often surprised at the new and interesting knowledge that comes to us through careful listening.

3. Listen with a purpose. When possible, be aware of the intended subject of discussion, and prepare for the class ahead of time by doing any advance reading or preparation, so you will get the most out of the class. Lectures on specialized topics will have greater meaning if you understand something about the topic ahead of time.

4. Be open-minded when you listen. Absorb what is being presented, even if you do not agree with the speaker or share the same point of view. You always have the right to challenge or disagree, but that should come later.

5. Be respectful of the speaker. Do not talk during a lecture or presentation. Instead, give the teacher your undivided attention.

6. Put aside distractions. Do not engage in other tasks while you are trying to listen. Turn off your hand-held devices and do not look at them during a class or lecture.

7. Take careful notes. Learn to take notes during a class or lecture so you can read them over later and think about what you have learned.

8. Be an active listener. You can think faster than your teacher can speak. Use this ability to your advantage by evaluating what is being said and trying to anticipate what will be said next. Don't arrive at conclusions until you have heard everything.

9. Meet the challenge. Don't give up and stop listening when you find information to be difficult to understand. Listen even more carefully at these times and work hard to understand what is being said.

10. Ask questions. Don't be reluctant to ask questions if you don't understand ideas or concepts, or if you wish to engage the teacher in further discussion. Some classes allow Q&A sessions or have separate group discussions.

Part XVI

Oral Presentations: Preparation for Excellence Can Eliminate Anxiety

Chapter 68

The Fear of Public Speaking

Reprinted with permission from Ron St. John, Assistant Professor of Speech, University of Hawai'i, Maui College

As a public speaking professor for the past 18 years, I have come in contact with thousands of students who were terrified of speaking in front of others. Some speakers tremble and get sweaty palms. Some speakers talk extremely fast and some go blank. For some speakers it's their heart that races, and some experience red blotches on their neck and face.

Do you suffer from anxieties when faced with speaking in front of a group? Many people do. In fact, the fear of public speaking has been listed as greater than the fear of death (but not as much as the fear of snakes).

Most of my students have bought into the myth that public speaking is something to be feared and avoided at all costs. They have convinced themselves that there is no way to address this fear and deliver a superior speech. Many people have bought into this myth about public speaking. Most people believe that they will never enjoy public speaking. Many people have decided that they will be nervous every time they present and are incapable of presenting a superior speech.

However, there are ways to reduce the anxiety associated with speaking in public, and therefore anyone is capable of presenting a superior speech.

Why are we afraid of speaking in public?

The reason most people get anxious when required to speak to a group is that they are afraid of looking "foolish" or "stupid" in front of their peers and other important people. Many speakers think that their audience is waiting for them to mess up or judging them the minute they walk up to the lectern. Speakers are often afraid that their lack of speaking skills will lower the opinion others have of them. The thought of being humiliated in front of an audience can lower a person's self esteem and confidence, even if it is a myth. It can really ruin their day, too. There are many fears that we have about speaking in public; however, most of them are unfounded fears. One rational fear of public speaking is the fear of the unknown, so if you have never presented a speech in front of an audience, the first time can be a fearful situation. Fortunately, there are steps that you can take to reduce the fear.

In most cases the fear, anxiety, and nervousness a speaker experiences can be considered as just extra energy. This extra energy can be incorporated in the presentation if it is controlled, however, we first must attempt to reduce the fear and try to control everything that we can control prior to the presentation. The easiest way to reduce the fear and learn to control the energy is through preparation and practice.

There are several steps that can be taken to reduce the fear of "making a mistake," "boring an audience to tears" or "looking foolish" when you speak to an audience, and these will be discussed in the following chapters.

The steps include:

☛ Be well prepared in what you do before an audience.

☛ Prepare a superior outline or manuscript.

☛ Realize that the audience is on your team and wants you to succeed.

☛ Practice, practice, practice for excellence, engagement, and inspiration.

Chapter 69

Mental Preparations
for Excellence

Reprinted with permission from Ron St. John, Assistant
Professor of Speech, University of Hawai'i, Maui College

One of the best ways to make sure you don't make embarrassing mistakes during a presentation is to be well-prepared before you speak to a group. Being well-prepared doesn't mean you need to memorize exactly what you plan to say. Many people think that if they write

down word-for-word everything that they will say in their speech and then memorize the information, that they will be prepared to present a speech. Memorization is not an effective preparation method to present a speech.

Writing down everything that will be said during the speech in essay format and then trying to memorize the word-for-word information is the type of preparation that most people are familiar with and fear. This type of preparation often makes for a robotic speech where information is thrown at the audience and there is very little engagement.

In essence, the speech is read word-for-word to the audience. This is called public reading and not public speaking. It produces anxiety in the speaker and can be a traumatic experience for the speaker and a waste of time for the audience.

If you have been asked to share information with an audience in the form of a meeting, seminar, workshop, or formal presentation, it is because you can give an audience much more than just the information. If a presentation was meant to be a simple transfer of information to the audience, you could just send out e-mails or provide the audience with an article or handouts with all the information that you wanted to share. This would be easy, and it would get the information to the audience in an efficient way.

A well-prepared speaker can bring information to life. A well-prepared speaker can engage an audience and create understanding. A well-prepared speaker can motivate and inspire an audience.

Preparation for excellence, engagement, and inspiration begins with the end. Before you start to prepare for your speech take some time to think about the day of the presentation. First ask yourself what the specific purpose is of your presentation. You want your preparation to center around the audience. This is audience-centered preparation.

You will want to decide what you want your audience to know, do, or feel at the end of your speech. What do you want your audience to take away from your presentation? If you start your preparation focusing on the outcome you seek, you will be more likely to arrive at your desired objective.

Always be audience-centered and think about the audience every step of the way. Be audience-centered in the preparation process as you are gathering, composing, and organizing your speech. Be audience-centered as you are practicing your speech. Be audience-centered as you are delivering your speech.

A professional in any field does not leave anything to chance before a big event, important performance, critical presentation to corporate executives, or even a speech in a classroom setting. Any speaker can be successful when strategies are laid out, all material is ready, contingency plans are made, and every detail is taken care of in advance allowing plenty of time to practice for engagement.

Preparation for excellence and engagement takes time (excellence usually does), and knowing the way to do this will save time. Once you have determined the outcome you seek and what you want your audience to take away with them after your presentation, you will want to begin organizing your information thoroughly and logically.

It is often a waste of time trying to start at the beginning of the speech. Start with the body of the speech and save the introduction and conclusion for last. The introduction and the conclusion of the speech can only be created effectively after the body of the speech is complete. The organization process begins with the body of the speech and the main points.

Main points are composed for engagement. They are statements that create a dialogue with the audience and engage the audience. Main points are supported using logical details. The supporting points are supported by further logical support and so on until the support is crystal clear to the audience. Each point is only one point in a complete, clear, short, concise sentence.

Everything is broken down in the preparation outline. Each and every element is composed to engage the audience. Your audience is informed, persuaded, or inspired by how well you compose and organize your information.

When we fail to prepare; we prepare to fail. When we are well-prepared, success is not left to chance; it is prepared for. When we prepare for excellence, we feel more relaxed and sure of ourselves because we have all the bases covered and have taken all the steps to prepare for a superior speech. So simply prepare and practice for excellence and engagement. This is the key to success in public speaking.

Preparing for excellence in an oral presentation begins with preparing a superior outline, which is the best way to deliver a speech for maximum engagement with your audience.

Chapter 70

Prepare a Superior Outline or Manuscript

 Reprinted with permission from Ron St. John, Assistant
Professor of Speech, University of Hawai'i, Maui College

Referring to your notes during a presentation is certainly acceptable to refresh your knowledge of your speech and keep you on track. Don't use your notes or outline as a crutch, however, but as a guide to keep you on track so that you can include all the points that  you prepared and to demonstrate to your audience that you are knowledgeable about your topic.

An **outline** is used to prepare for most speeches that you will present in class, at work, or in the community when you are informing or persuading an audience. There are two types of outlines that can be developed:

The Preparation Outline

1. This outline is prepared first.
2. It includes complete sentences that are short, clear, concise and made up of one point.
3. Logical reasoning is used to organize the information into your introduction, body, and conclusion.

The Speaking Outline

1. Use 20pt font for easy readability
2. The speaking outline should follow the same structure as the preparation outline, but use keywords and abbreviations rather than complete sentences.

3. Place visual cues written in the margins. For example:

   a. Visually alert yourself to "slow down," "pause," or "walk out into the audience."

   b. Note when to show visual aids and when to take them away.

   These cues are essential in a speaking outline when slides are being used; they allow you to synchronize your slide presentation with your verbal presentation so that you don't forget to show a slide or change a slide when you are done talking about it.

4. If you will be moving around during your speech, write your outline on 5x7 cards. Be sure to practice with the cards so they don't suppress your gestures or cause a distraction.

A **manuscript** is used for special occasion speaking. A manuscript is a word-for-word script of your presentation. A manuscript can be used well when a speaker practices for engagement. Do not use it during a presentation because it lessens the engagement of the audience. The manuscript is used when you are commemorating someone, introducing someone, accepting an award, making a toast, or any other special occasion when it is imperative that you say exactly what you have prepared to say in the exact words and order.

☛ **Well-prepared manuscripts use 20pt font and are single-spaced.**

☛ **Each sentence starts on the left hand margin** and there is a line space between sentences.

☛ **There are no "widows" or "orphans,"** which are sentences that are broken up between pages and set the speaker up for

[hypothetical page break]

awkward pauses.

☛ **You don't want to use paragraph format for the manuscript.** If you use paragraph format, then you have to fish around in the paragraph to find the start of each sentence when speaking.

☞ **Some people like to bold the first word or couple of words** of each sentence so that the start of each sentence can be easily picked out of the manuscript. It may also help to bold or italicize the words that you want to emphasize.

☞ **If you start every sentence on the left hand margin** then you know exactly where each sentence starts.

Chapter 71

Your Audience Wants You to Succeed

Reprinted with permission from Ron St. John, Assistant
Professor of Speech, University of Hawai'i, Maui College

Once you have thoroughly prepared your
content and have a superior speaking
outline or superior manuscript, you are ready
to get your mindset right. It is imperative that
you realize your audience is there to help you
present a successful speech. After all, they are
the reason for the speech in the first place.
Don't be afraid of your audience.

**Embrace your audience. Befriend your audience.
Engage your audience.** Your reason for presenting a speech is for the benefit of the audience. You want to include your audience and be audience-
centered every step of the way: From topic selection, through preparation,
and while practicing.

It is important to know who your audience members are and something
about their demographics (age range, gender mix, ethnicities, back-
grounds) and their knowledge (or lack of knowledge) of your topic. The
more you know about your audience, the better you can tailor your message to the needs of your audience.

**As a public speaker, your main objectives are to deliver a clear message that your
audience can understand and to engage the audience so that they will want to
listen to you.** However, presenting information, whether to peers,
classmates, colleagues, employers, instructors, or dignitaries, can create
fear and/or anxiety in any speaker. This can potentially interfere with your

ability to engage your audiences or present information clearly.

Visualizing these types of audience members as equals can begin to reduce the fear. First you need to realize that the audience is there to hear what you have to say. The audience is not waiting for you to "mess up" or "make a mistake." This is an unfounded fear and a myth associated with public speaking. Think about your audience as an integral part of your speech and a part of "your team."

Become one with your audience. Don't build an artificial wall between you and your audience. Some speakers use the lectern as something to hide behind. They won't venture out from behind the lectern and they often have a grip of death on the lectern or their outline. Some speakers try to avoid eye contact with the audience and look over their heads (any audience member recognizes this immediately). Some believe that if they don't look at the audience the audience can't see them.

Direct eye contact can create a oneness between you and your audience and allow you to gather positive energy from your audience. Use the abundance of energy that your audience is capable of projecting to your benefit. Use "the Force" (of natural eye contact) and tap into the energy that your audience wants to give you.

Energy comes from audience members who are listening to you. You can see that they are listening by their positive feedback. You want to focus on the audience members who are giving you positive feedback in the form of direct eye contact, smiles, and nods of their heads in agreement. As your audience showers you with positive energy, let the force be with you and reap their abundance of energy.

Unfortunately, people in any audience can also take energy away from a speaker just as fast as they can give it. These people, referred to as "energy-suckers," can be found in every audience. Avoid eye contact with the energy-suckers in your audience. Energy-suckers' phones go off during a speech, they are often reading (the paper, a book, their notes, or anything so they don't have to look at the speaker), they are looking out the window or into space, texting, whispering to a neighbor, clicking their pen incessantly, cracking their knuckles, sleeping, or just not paying attention to the speaker.

They should be shunned and banned from the audience, but you can excommunicate them by just not looking at them, unless you are going to reprimand them for a phone going off or other energy-sucking disturbances.

Chapter 72

Practice for Engagement... and Excellence

 Reprinted with permission from Ron St. John, Assistant Professor of Speech, University of Hawai'i, Maui College

Many people use the mantra "Practice Makes Perfect," even though perfection is unrealistic. Everyone, however, is capable of excellence.

Even if you know your material very well, practicing it is extremely important. The more you practice, the more automatic it becomes, the more energy it can have, and the more confidence you have in your abilities to give the speech.

Many people think that if they practice their speech enough, they will memorize it and that will make for a perfect speech. This is contrary to what I teach. When people try to memorize a speech, they often end up further away from engaging their audience then when they just read the speech. Because when a speech is just partially memorized, the speaker often robotically regurgitates the information and if one word is forgotten they end up like a deer in the headlights and freeze or want to start all over. Memorization is not the key to success. I have seen this look of terror on the faces of hundreds of students who try to memorize a speech. I have equated attempts at presenting a partially memorized speech to running after the words in their own mind and trying to grasp at each word. Sometimes the speaker stumbles and sometimes they don't, but they always seem to be going faster and faster as the speech continues in an effort to finish the speech. The race is an internal one in order to "get it over with" and engagement falls by the wayside. The audience just watches as the speaker throws the information at them.

Guided practice for engagement is the key to success. Practicing with a few people who will give you feedback is one of the best ways to practice. The "Interruption Method of Practice" is one of the best ways to get feedback during practice. This method uses interruption at any point during the speech to give the speaker feedback. If a practice audience member identifies anything the speaker is doing that could be improved or should be eliminated, the audience member immediately interrupts the speaker and gives the appropriate feedback. Using the same method, if a practice audience member sees the speaker doing something natural and engaging, the speaker could be interrupted and told something like: "That is what we want to see on speech day. That is the natural and engaging speaker we want to see. You were using natural gestures."

Other Practice Do's

☞ **Practice out loud to small groups; to friends; to relatives; to strangers; to pets; to roommates; alone.**

☞ **Go to the room where you will give your presentation** to get a feel for the environment/set-up. Practice in front of a friend or friends without stopping, just as you will do on speech day.

☞ **Practice in front of a mirror** (full length if possible).

☞ **Practice using visual aids** so you know how much time they will take up and how to incorporate them into your speech. Make sure that you have all of your visual cues on your speaking outline.

☞ **Practice with background noise** (e.g., turn on the TV, radio, etc.) in order to practice with distractions.

☞ **Practice with the actual speaking outline** you will use in your presentation.

☞ **Practice your speech dressed as you plan to dress for your actual presentation** so that you can feel comfortable.

☛ **Time yourself.** Make sure that you are consistently within your time frame.

☛ **If possible, videotape yourself practicing your speech.** This is the best way for you to be able to see any mistakes, so that you can fix them before you give your presentation.

☛ **Become aware of your posture and mannerisms** as you speak. If you are going to use movement or gestures on speech day, you need to practice moving to keep them controlled and natural. Avoid distracting mannerisms, such as shuffling your notes or cracking your knuckles.

Practice and Speech Day Don'ts

☛ **Never have change or keys in your pockets.** You do not want to have the sound of objects competing with your voice.

☛ **Never wear a hat, unless it is part of your presentation.** Dress appropriately any time you give a presentation. Make a credible first impression by looking as if you are interested in giving a good speech.

☛ **Do not stand with your arms crossed or your hands in your pockets.** This type of posture prevents you from gesturing and may even make your audience uncomfortable.

☛ **Never apologize if you make a mistake while giving a speech.** Simply correct the mistake and move on. You never want to draw attention to an error; chances are most people will miss it anyway.

☛ **Don't put your visual aids up in front of the audience before you explain them.** Rather introduce them as you are speaking. Also, don't keep visual aids up after you are no longer referring to them. Use visual cues on your speaking outline to easily avoid these blunders.

☛ **Don't practice your speech holding on to your speaking outline.** When you are practicing, put your outline on something—a music stand, a box, a high counter, anything to simulate the lectern that you will be presenting with.

Other Practice Tips

☞ **Practice with natural energy and enthusiasm.** If you don't care about your information, why should your audience? Your enthusiasm builds your audience's enthusiasm.

☞ **Practice with precise articulation** so the members of your audience will understand you. If you tend to speak fast while you are presenting, then over articulate when you are practicing; this may produce a more conversational speaking rate during your speech.

☞ **A pause can be used to provide emphasis**. Pauses can also replace many filler words like "um" or "like" or other similar filler words.

☞ **Practice with natural posture and confidence.** Correct posture conveys confidence.

☞ *Practice. Practice. Practice.*

Conclusion

The way to reduce the fear, nervousness, and anxiety of speaking is to make sure you are well-prepared, have a superior outline (note cards or a speaking outline) ready, visualize your audience as part of your team, and practice the way you want to give the speech on speech day.

So the next time you are asked to speak, you will be confident that you can successfully present a speech and engage your audience. Everyone is capable of presenting a superior speech. The key is to prepare and practice for excellence and engagement.

Part XVII

Social Adjustment in College

Chapter 73

College Friendships

Part 1: Friendship Building

Reprinted with permission from the University of Texas at Dallas Student Counseling Center

People who successfully build intimate relationships with friends and/or a significant other often utilize the five following skills that can foster closeness with others:

☞ 1. Be Yourself

Don't try to relate to others by acting like you think they would want/expect you to act. Being real from the start gives each person a chance to see if he or she can be comfortable with each other's beliefs, interests, values, and lifestyle.

☞ 2. Communicate Better

This is an essential skill in a good relationship of any type.

» *Use "I" statements when talking to others about your thoughts or feelings. This promotes ownership of what you are saying, which establishes a strong, direct position.*

» *Self disclose at a slow, but steady rate. This is the art of sharing your private thoughts and feelings with people you trust. Revealing too much too soon can cause the speaker to feel overly vulnerable and the listener to feel uncomfortable and obligated to reciprocate. Take your time. You can increase your rate of sharing as you get to know the person better.*

» *Ask for what you need/want. Limit your expectations of the other person's ability to guess what you prefer. The best chance of receiving what you want is to speak up and ask for it!*

» *Check your assumptions. You are no mind reader either. Misunderstandings can arise from acting on what you guess your friend/partner wants.*

» *Give each other permission to peacefully refuse each other's requests at times.*

☞ 3. Resolve Conflicts

Take the relationship from my way or your way to our way through negotiation and compromise. Start the problem solving by listening to and respecting each other's point of view. Conflicts are more easily addressed when both people participate in the solution, instead of one person dominating the decision-making process. Aim for a balance of power.

☞ 4. Reciprocate

Give equal importance to the feelings, interests, and needs of each person in the relationship. Develop the skill of both giving and receiving emotional support.

☞ 5. Enjoy Each Other!

Let good humor and fun together be a part of your regular schedule.

Part 2: Roommate Relationships

Web article reprinted with permission by The Office of Admissions and the Office of Communications and Marketing at Spring Hill College, Mobile, AL c. 2009-1010

Living with a Roommate

"They were the best of times, they were the worst of times." These words of Charles Dickens from *A Tale of Two Cities* might accurately summarize the experience of living together as roommates for many people. Sharing space with other people can sometimes be very rewarding, yet other times may be quite challenging.

A key point for students to remember is that in order to have a good roommate, you have to be a good roommate. Here are some tips on being a good roommate:

» *Be willing to share common ground and recognize the needs of your roommate. Being on common ground, though, should not imply that everything is common property.*

» *Keep in mind that living together successfully is a give-and-take proposition.*

» *Spend time with your roommate outside of your room. Try to do things you both enjoy. These types of activities create cohesion and make living together more enjoyable.*

» *Get to know your roommate. The more you know about each other, the easier it will be to build and maintain your new relationship.*

» *Don't expect too much—no one ever said roommates have to be best friends.*

» *Be open—ask, listen, discuss. Don't wait until things get out of hand.*

» *Don't forget to say what's going right too.*

» *Be sensitive to each other's moods. Everybody has bad days, so try to be understanding when that happens.*

» *Remember that being willing to compromise is the key to happiness!*

Getting Acquainted with Your Roommate

Living with a roommate is a new experience for many students. At the same time, it can provide some of the best memories. In order to help with this transition, the following are a few suggestions for questions that you and your roommate may want to discuss from the beginning. Try to talk about how each of you will handle the various topics. Share what you are comfortable sharing. It is helpful to find out at least a little bit about the person you will be living with before you move in together.

» *Where are you from? Can you tell me a little bit about your family?*

» *Have you ever shared a room before? Why did you choose this school?*

» *What is your major? What are some of your hobbies / interests?*

» *What items are you planning on bringing when we move in (i.e. TV, VCR/ DVD player, Refrigerator, Microwave, etc.)?*

Some people prefer to study in the library with little noise while others listen to headphones. Discuss with your roommate when and where you prefer to study and in what type of atmosphere.

» *What time of day / night do you usually study? Where do you prefer to study?*

» *How much noise can you tolerate when studying? Can the radio / TV be on? (You may need to bring headphones.)*

» *Do you usually study alone or with groups?*

Be sure to discuss the cleanliness and orderliness of your room. This includes whether you leave clothes, towels, and possibly trash around the room.

» *Are you usually a little messy or super neat?*

> » *How will we divide chores, such as sweeping, mopping, dusting, taking out the trash?*

Depending on your school's visitation policy, students can usually entertain their friends in the residence hall. It is important that everyone be aware of the boundaries for bringing guests into the room, especially since you have a roommate.

> » *What hours are guests welcome in our room?*

> » *How many guests are reasonable to have over at a time?*

> » *Does it matter to you what gender they are?*

> » *How will we discuss when we want to have overnight guests?*

We all have different sleeping habits so be sure that you discuss your sleeping habits with your roommate.

> » *What time do you usually go to bed? Are you a morning person or a night owl?*

> » *Do you immediately wake up when the alarm sounds or do you push the snooze button 10 times?*

> » *What temperature to do you prefer when sleeping?*

> » *What about noise (TV/radio) and/or light?*

Here are a variety of additional questions that you may want to ask your roommate.

> » *What items may I borrow? Do I need to ask first? How do you feel about sharing food purchased for the room?*

> » *What are the rules of radio and TV/stereo usage? This includes times these*
> *electronics can be used and if they will be shared.*

> » *How will we deliver phone messages?*

> » *What are some of your pet peeves?*

> » *How do you try to handle disagreement or conflict?*

Chapter 74

How to Raise a Parent

 Reprinted with permission from the University of Texas at Dallas, Student Counseling Center

It is a little known fact that properly raising a parent requires attention and thought. Developing parents can be tough enough when you are with them on a day-to-day basis. Teaching them that you can take care of yourself and have a life is difficult. Acknowledging and working with their problem of letting go is challenging. When you are away at college and your days are filled with other activities, nurturing your parents may be, at best, an afterthought. Be proactive and invest time in your parents now. Doing so can make your life easier in the long run. Several tips and strategies can be helpful in this process.

You are not the only one learning and growing. Your parents are losing a bird from their nest. Whether or not you are the first in your family to go to college or the last, your family will change as a result of you leaving. The role you played in your family was important and will not easily be replaced. Try to understand life from your parents' perspective. A little empathy goes a long way. Know they have anxieties and fears about the shift in your life as well as their own.

Parents don't magically know how to relate to their grown children as adults. There is no secret formula to this process. They figure it out through interacting, effective communication, and conflict. Talk directly and openly with your parents about what you've learned. Know that they'll wish to contribute and allow them to.

Most parent-child relationships have a certain level of dependency. You count on your parents to be there in a time of need. Many adult children view being dependent as negative and strive toward independence. Your parents become accustomed to it. After all, you have been their child and were dependent on them for many years. Know that your parents may have difficulty immediately accepting that you are an adult. In fact, they may accept this idea only after considerable conflict occurs. Be patient with them. Tell them about your successes and failures. Reassure them that you are handling your mistakes responsibly.

The parental apple doesn't fall far from the grandparental tree. Your parents will likely approach your newfound adulthood similarly to how their parents approached them. Learn about the difficulties your mother or father had during this time. What did their parents do or say that was helpful or unhelpful? This history can be useful in understanding your parents' attitudes. Know that your parents are learning too, they need help relating to you as an adult, and they struggle with losing a child they care for deeply. Help your parents understand that they are gaining an adult who has learned much from their parenting.

When Conflict and Unexpected Changes Occur in Families

Change occurs constantly in families. Going to college, securing a career, getting married, having and raising children, and growing older are often expected events and inevitably change your relationship with parents and siblings. Divorce or separations are events that also can profoundly affect your relationship with family members.

Caught in the middle?

College students of divorcing parents often feel split between two worlds. Having two homes and two places to go during holidays can be confusing and upsetting. Adult children may feel as though they must side with one parent. They may react by becoming closer to one parent or distancing from both. They may feel guilt or responsibility for their parents' separation or divorce. At times, trust in romantic relationships may be difficult.

If you are experiencing any of this, talk to both of your parents together or individually about your concerns. Be open and honest. Understand that your parents are going through a difficult time, too. Keeping channels open between you and your parents will more than likely help maintain a good relationship amongst all three of you.

The following are some guidelines that may prove helpful during this time include:

☞ **Don't go through this period alone.** Support and acceptance by other people are absolutely essential during big changes.

☞ **Know your feelings will change.** At times you may have difficulty concentrating, may feel sad, angry or depressed. Reactions like these are normal and healing takes time. Sharing these feelings with others who have had similar experiences can be helpful.

☞ **Learn about what is going to happen.** Divorces and separations frequently are accompanied by an absence of accurate, open communication with the children. Focus on what you need to know for your plans, not on information that is more properly in the private domain of your parents.

☞ **Keep clear of unhealthy alliances.** Try to protect yourself by not being dragged into the middle.

☞ **Find out what works for you.** Reactions vary widely. Trust yourself. Learn what is effective and ineffective for you. Learn to use helping resources outside your family.

Chapter 75

Avoiding Burnout

Reprinted with permission from Texas A&M
University Student Counseling Service
College Station, Texas

☞ **Recognize the problem.**

Watch for signs of stress such as forget-
fulness, fatigue, sleeplessness, changes in
appetite, increased physical sickness like
colds and headaches, withdrawal from
social situations, increased mood swings,
or emotional outbursts.

☞ **Balance your lifestyle.**

People subject to negative stress are often perfectionists, idealists, and
workaholics, who can never really please themselves. Identify other
areas in you life you would like to develop besides your studies, then
get involved in some stress-relieving activities.

☞ **Build positive social supports, and control negativity in your environment.**

Seek out projects in which you'll work with people who have a positive attitude. If you have to work with a negative person, limit the
amount of time you must spend with the person, and stick to those
limits. Look for positive affiliations in your social relationships or club
memberships.

☞ **Gain control where you can.**

Ask to be involved in decisions that affect you. Seeking flexible hours
for work to accommodate your need to study, for example, may also

be an option. If you are not in control of your schedule, ask for help. Asserting yourself and expressing your needs help reduce the negative emotions of fear and anger.

☞ **Work smarter and not longer.**

Begin with staying and ending on time with all appointments. Schedule realistic breaks between working or studying. Allow yourself enough time to get to places. Pressuring yourself with tight deadlines increases stress and reduces you effectiveness.

☞ **Quit doing something.**

If you are overcommitted, say "no" and mean it the next time you are asked to do another favor that will greatly raise your stress level. If possible, cut activities out of your schedule that are causing you stress.

☞ **Control thoughts that you are indispensable.**

To control stress, you must learn to accept your mortality, your vulnerability, and your limits.

☞ **Employ personal strategies to avoid or cope with burnout.**

Do something for yourself each day. Eat well and get enough sleep. View mistakes and setbacks as learning experiences. Acknowledge your strengths and achievements, and reward yourself. Identify your life purpose, and pursue activities that are compatible with your mission.

☞ **Employ interpersonal strategies.**

Identify the people, places, and activities in your life that make you feel good. Stay away from relationships that drain you.

☞ **Use stress-management techniques.**

Fantasize a mini-vacation. Take a break during your day and close your eyes, imagining yourself in a favorite peaceful place. Go to the beach and feel the sand and warmth of the sun. Listen to the birds and the waves. See the calm beach scene. Five minutes there, and you will be mentally and physically relaxed.

☞ **Do what you love, or get career counseling.**

If we work too hard, even if it is at something we love, we get tired. The solution to that is rest. If you are not happy with what you are doing, you may need to look for something else.

Chapter 76

Dealing with Loneliness

Reprinted with permission from the University of Texas at Dallas, Student Counseling Center

Being lonely has been a frequent topic for popular songs and advice columns for years. Most people enjoy being with others, but may have periods of time where they feel disconnected and lonely. Also, many people may be alone for periods of time without feeling lonely at all.

What Is the Difference in Being Lonely vs. Being Alone?

Relaxation, creative thinking, and personal accomplishments are often achieved in a solitary environment. If you are accustomed to being in the constant company of others, the appreciation of being alone may take some time and effort to develop. Once you have told yourself it is okay, experiment with it and see if you can feel fulfilled on your own. Have fun indulging yourself in something you wouldn't do if others were with you.

Some people may find that they can't tolerate much time spent alone. If this is you, ask yourself "Do I just like being with others more or is there something I am afraid of when I am alone?"

If this is the case, it will help to identify the fear and then make a plan to overcome it. Some common fears are the fear of being bored and not being entertained; the fear of feeling sad or depressed; the fear of always being alone; and existential fears such as being alone in the universe.

How much time spent alone is normal?

There is no correct amount of time to spend with people vs. being alone. College students often experience many changes in personal contact levels that come with the other changes of being a student; a higher level of independence and choices in daily schedules, different living conditions, and expanded opportunities for jobs and extracurricular activities. With so many choices to make, some students find their days are filled with different people. Some may find that without the built-in contact of high school peers and family, their paths rarely cross with others in any meaningful way.

What Can I Do About Loneliness?

» *Recognize that loneliness is a common experience that can be changed and doesn't last forever.*

» *Identify what needs aren't being met in your life (e.g., meaningful friendships, being involved in social activities, feeling secure with being alone at times).*

» *Discover what might be going on in your life that may be contributing to your loneliness (e.g., living in a new place where you don't know anyone, a recent loss or major life transition, not feeling comfortable with the people you spend time with).*

» *Avoid things that could perpetuate loneliness such as isolating yourself from others and evaluating yourself in negative terms.*

How Can I Develop Friendships?

» *Remind yourself that meeting new people and building friendships requires some risk.*

» *Join clubs or groups in which you have a genuine interest.*

» *Find a study or exercise partner.*

» *Smile, make eye contact, be willing to listen, let people know you are avail-*

able, and be yourself.

» *Improve your ability to be genuine and trusting in relationships to bring you closer to others.*

» *Remember that not everyone has to like you and you don't have to be friends with everyone.*

» *Don't judge new friendships based on past experiences. Be open to new perspectives.*

» *Be patient. Remember that it takes time to feel comfortable and develop connections with new people.*

» *Seek counseling or other help to develop your social skills and deal with social anxiety and shyness that might be affecting your ability to make connections.*

» *Make efforts to re-connect with past friends (e.g., e-mail or call a friend you haven't spoken to in a while, send someone a card).*

» *It is important to remember that loneliness is a common experience that does not reflect any defect in your personality or character. Most people experience loneliness at some point in their lives. Learn to be comfortable with and even enjoy your time alone. Motivate yourself to take risks to develop new relationships and improve closeness in current relationships.*

Chapter 77

Coping with Homesickness

University of Kansas Counseling and Psychological
Services (CAPS), Lawrence, Kansas

Most of us, at one time or another, have missed home—the familiar, predictable atmosphere where we have generally spent the first eighteen years of our lives. Entering college is an exciting step—a passage to adulthood and independence. But what should you do when

that feeling of "Oh, I wish I were back at home—this is miserable" begins to set in?

☞ **First of all, realize that missing home is absolutely normal.** Missing home, the place (your house or apartment), the people (your family and friends), and the pets (the cat or dog) is absolutely normal. Learning how to cope in a new environment takes time to develop. Once you figure it out, that skill can provide you with coping tools that can be applied to moves or transitions later in life.

☞ **Look at this time as an exciting opportunity.** Developing an action plan and looking at this separation from home as an opportunity to develop new skills or interests can help you cope with challenges.

☞ **Schedule visits home.** Set a definite date for a visit home or to see your parents, but first allow yourself enough time to acclimate to this new environment. If you go home every weekend, you might deprive yourself of having a full college experience.

☞ **Stay in touch by phone and e-mail.** Daily phone calls can just reinforce a person's sense of homesickness or isolation. Calling less frequently, once or twice a week, may actually help to reduce feelings of homesickness. Encourage your parents to write or e-mail you on a regular basis; these can be saved and reread. A subscription to a favorite magazine or hometown newspaper can also help counter the vacant feeling of an empty mailbox.

☞ **Observe your own patterns.** At times, a little self-analysis is in order. Note if there is a special time of the day or week that is particularly difficult and try to figure out why. Try to develop a routine of your own for days that go slowly such as having a leisurely breakfast, reading the newspaper, or visiting with a friend.

☞ **Get out of your comfort zone.** Developing new friendships means taking risks. Sit with someone you don't know at lunch. Invite someone to have coffee with you. Start a conversation with someone you don't know at the bus stop or the elevator.

☞ **Plan time to feel homesick.** Missing familiar people and things from home is common. Plan some time to reflect on those feelings and to accept them. Taking charge of your feelings in this way often helps to work through them.

☞ **Notice your new patterns.** New patterns often develop gradually. Step back and mentally walk through your days, noting weekends particularly. Being aware of your new patterns and preferences will be helpful when you make your first visit home. Comparing the old routines you had at home with your new routines at college will help you realize how you are changing and becoming more independent.

Things to remember when coping with homesickness

☞ **Home will still be there.** Remember, your home will still be there when your return. However, try not to take it personally if your room gets transformed into a sewing room or den. Parents need something to keep them busy while you're away at college.

☞ **While it is difficult for them, your parents will manage to cope without you.** The crucial task is how you will learn to survive without them. This is a big step, but you will develop independent coping skills.

☞ **Try to keep your checkbook balanced.** When you call home, parents often ask about finances. It's nice to be prepared for these questions.

☞ **Develop healthy habits of coping such as talking, journaling, and exercising.** Spending Saturday recovering from a Friday night hangover does not help the problem.

☞ **Remember to eat healthy foods.** It is very easy with a busy college schedule to forget that you need good food to keep functioning at your best.

☞ **Don't be afraid to let other people know that you are having a hard time of it.** Feeling homesick, shy, lonely, and confused are very common for college students. Others may not look like they have had similar problems, but chances are they have; they just look more experienced and at ease now because they've been through it before and have survived.

☞ **Seek support if you are truly unhappy and are having difficulties coping.** Seek out counseling services at your school. They are there to assist you. They consult with many students every day and are there to help you adapt to your new home.

When things are too overwhelming

If you find that you are beginning to think pessimistically, develop marked changes in sleeping or eating habits, have prolonged crying spells, have concentration difficulties, or have suicidal thoughts, the problem may not be homesickness, but depression or anxiety. Depression and anxiety are the two most common complaints of college students when they visit counseling centers. These problems can be helped by professional treatment.

Chapter 78

E-mail Etiquette

Dennis H. Congos, M.S.Ed.,
University of Central Florida, Orlando, Florida

How to Communicate Effectively and Appropriately Using E-mail

College students need to make a good impression on their professors in the classroom, when completing homework assignments, in presenting class projects, and performing on exams. Impressions are also being formed by professors when receiving an e-mail message from a student in their class. College students must remember that this is not their high school friend from home they are sending a message to; it is the person who  will be recording a final grade at the end of the semester. Excellent grammar and sentence structure, appropriate word choice, and sensible organization of one's e-mail must be taken into consideration each and every time prior to hitting the send button.

Suggestions for sending a professional e-mail that will be read and responded to:

☞ **Appropriate Username**

» *Creativity can and should be appreciated, but what if one of your professors took attendance by reciting usernames and you had to raise your hand in front of other students in the class. Would you not acknowledge*

*your presence in class and take the absence or could you say with pride
"here".*

» *Would you feel comfortable saying your username out loud in front of
your mother, father, grandmother, etc. without being embarrassed or
ashamed?*

» *Don't be remembered for your username—be remembered for the message
you sent.*

» *Example— initials (jlw@) or something unique but tasteful like ucf-
grad2010@*

☞ **Subject Line—First and Last Name plus Course Name**

» *Identify yourself as a student in your professor's class: (Jake Allison -
SLS 1501)*

» *Identify the reason for the e-mail: course question, paper question, etc.*

☞ **Greetings/Acknowledgements—Start the E-mail with a Show of Respect**

» *Review the course syllabus to determine the prefix for the professor's
name. If his or her name is given on the syllabus as Dan Jones and you
unable to determine what prefix to use, to be safe, use Prof. Jones.*

☞ **The Message Itself—Be Specific and Present it in an Organized Manner**

» *Get to the point, the purpose of your e-mail. Avoid lengthy explanations.
Example "I need to clarify an aspect of the assignment due next week."*

» *If you must turn in a homework assignment via an actual e-mail message, present material in an organized manner using spacing and breaks
if necessary. You want your homework to be organized and presented in a
visually pleasing way for easy reading.*

» *Use good grammar and proper punctuation.*

☞ **Concluding the Message—End with Appreciation**

» *Examples:"Thank you for your time and I look forward to hearing from you soon." or "I appreciate your taking the time to consider my request."*

» *Sign and identify the e-mail: (Jake Allison, SLS 1501, Monday & Wednesday 11:00 am).*

☞ **Final Two Suggestions: Read the Message Out Loud & Hit Spell Check before Sending**

Chapter 79

The Value of Sleep

Susanna Barry, Program Manager,
Community Wellness at MIT Medical,
Massachusetts Institute of Technology, Cambridge, Massachusetts

Q. How long does it take a lab rat to die of sleep deprivation?

A. *About 5 days. "Sleep is as essential as food because [the rats] will die just about as quick from food deprivation as sleep deprivation,"*

—Matthew Walker, director of Sleep and Neuroimaging Lab at UC Berkeley told CBS's 60 Minutes in 2008. *"So it's that necessary."*

The Importance of Sleep

Sleep deprivation is one of the oldest forms of torture. And yet, humans are the only mammals that sleep deprive themselves. Some college students view being severely sleep deprived as a badge of honor, either academically or socially. Some have gotten used to "just getting by" on 6 hours of sleep or less each night, trying to get an edge.

Yet, ironically, it is sleeping that gives us the edge we seek. The human body really likes to get 7–9 hours of sleep per night on a regular basis, and more than 9 hours for adolescents. Sleep is such a primal need that our physical and emotional health starts to break down as a result of inadequate sleep. Sleep is crucial for memory and cognitive performance, tissue repair (like skin and hair) and muscle growth, and emotional processing.

Sleep Deficit

The body accumulates "sleep debt" if we don't get adequate sleep each night. If you are not getting your 8 or 9 hours each night, your body is going deeper and deeper into sleep deficit. After a week of missing an hour or two of your sleep requirement each night, you are functioning as though you've pulled an all-nighter.

One of the most famous voices in college sleep research, Dr. James B. Maas from Cornell University, shared his wisdom with the Cornell student newspaper in 2006: "It's interesting, because people are so concerned these days about nutrition and exercise in terms of the quality of their life. They watch so carefully what they eat, and everybody these days is conscious of exercise as being key to looking good and being healthy, but nobody really thinks very much about sleep. They all think sleep is a luxury."

Cognition Requires Sleep

Maas continues by saying, "Any cognitive effort after 16 hours of alertness is really wasted. If you look at the brain's ability to assimilate, organize, reorganize, and retain new information, it's almost zero after that amount of time."

College students who sleep less perform worse academically. Sleep not only helps to consolidate memory and learning, it helps to minimize the damage sleep deficit causes to one's cognitive and social intelligence.

Study Results

A study published in Occupational and Environmental Medicine indicated that more than 19 hours of sleeplessness has a larger impact on response speeds and accuracy measures than a blood alcohol concentration of 0.1 percent, which is legally drunk in all 50 states. Just as people who are drunk don't realize how drunk they are, people who have sleep deficit can't comprehend how compromised they are.

Sleep deprivation is read by the body as a severe form of stress which we are not biologically equipped to handle. It affects mood (especially in terms of depression and anxiety), heart health, immune system health, and is correlated with weight gain and pre-diabetes.

Sleep Advice

So, how can we minimize the damage? How can we get better quality sleep, even if we aren't getting optimal quantity? Try to improve your sleep with one or two of these wellness tips:

☞ **Your good night's sleep begins at the start of your day.** Try to wake and sleep at around the same time most days. Students who have a regular sleep schedule feel more alert from the same amount of sleep than students with a "yo-yo" schedule.

☞ **Sunlight and exercise in the early part of your day can help promote deep sleep later.** Try not to exercise within 3 hours of bedtime, since the body needs to be cool to sleep deeply.

☞ **A deep sleep environment: Keep your room dark, cool, quiet, and distraction-free.** Download free white noise or ocean wave sounds if you have loud neighbors. Use a sleep mask and cover up exposed lights from electronic equipment.

☞ **A deep sleep body: If mental or physical tension has you tossing and turning, or waking in the middle of the night, try relaxation practices like yoga or meditation during the day.** You can also do relaxation breathing right before you go to sleep. One form of relaxation is to simply lengthen your exhale. On your inhale, count to 3 or 4 (or whatever is comfortable for you), and allow the exhale to be a little longer, to a count of 6 or 8 (again, keep it comfortable).

☞ **Know what you're drinking: Caffeine stays in your system for many hours, so avoid caffeine after 2 p.m.** Caffeine is a stimulant, not a true source of energy for the body – and Caffeine Intoxication is a recognized clinical syndrome, which includes nervousness, anxiety, restlessness, insomnia, gastric upset, tremors, rapid heartbeat, and in some cases, death. Caffeine content in energy drinks varies wildly, from 50 to more than 500 milligrams per serving (500 milligrams is the equivalent of about 14 cans of Coke).

☞ **Know what you're ingesting: Avoid heavy meals, smoking, and alcohol for a few hours before bed.** Caffeine and extra food are common crutches used during sleep deficit, but as one student puts it, "Nothing tastes as good as sleep."

☞ **Have a pre-sleep ritual: Stop productive activity and do something light and relaxing for 15 minutes before sleeping.** Just like a stick-shift vehicle, the mind needs time to downshift from "doing" mode to "resting" mode.

☞ **Plan to spend some time over the weekend paying off your sleep debt.** Learn to say no. Take a power nap for 20–30 minutes in the early afternoon. If you have a huge sleep deficit, you might choose to take a 90-minute nap, which allows the body to go through deep sleep and come back up into a lighter stage of sleep, making it easier to wake up.

☞ **If dawn arrives and you haven't slept, clear your schedule as much as possible to get to bed extra early the next night.**

Part XVIII

Stress Management

Chapter 80

Managing Stress at College

Starting Out!® Research Group

Introduction

We all experience stress at different times, but for some people, stress can become a major health problem that interferes with our performance and quality of life. College presents new and challenging situations for students, heavier workloads than high school, more formal-

ized lectures, competitive pressures, totally new academic subjects, new people to get to know, new roommates from different places, social stress, high parental expectations, and the task of organizing a lot of activities into a limited amount of time. Any of these factors can produce stress and academic anxiety.

Signs and Signals of Stress

☞ **What happens when we become tense and feel stress?** There are many physiological changes that seem to happen when our stress level rises:

» *Our rate of breathing becomes more rapid and shallow.*

» *Our heart rate begins to speed up.*

» *Our muscles in the shoulders, back of the neck, and across the chest can feel tight.*

» *Our hands and feet can become cold and sweaty.*

» *We may feel effects in our gastrointestinal system, such as a butterfly stomach or diarrhea, possibly vomiting, and more frequent urination.*

» *Our mouth and lips may feel dry.*

» *Our hands and knees may tremble.*

» *Our voice may quiver.*

» *As stress and anxiety levels rise, we may have trouble sleeping.*

» *Our thought processes and clarity of thinking may also be affected.*

» *We may have difficulty concentrating.*

» *Our reaction might be to leave the stressful situation, such as walking out of a test because it is very difficult.*

» *We may begin to obsess about the situation.*

» *Our eating habits may change. Some eat more, while others cannot eat at all.*

» *For some people, excessive stress causes them to stay and fight back, and for others, the reaction is to turn away and avoid the situation (the fight or flight response).*

How Does Anxiety Affect Academic Performance?

We need a certain amount of anxiety and pressure to face new situations and challenges. Stress and anxiety can be a natural part of the motivation process when we are studying for an exam or writing a long term paper. They seems to push us along and give us extra energy to get the job done. In such situations, anxiety, such as the fear of failure, can produce positive results and help us meet difficult goals. However, too much stress or anxiety can negatively impact our ability to study, concentrate, and be successful in college.

The Wrong Response to Stress

Because of the "fight or flight response" that we may feel, some people try to reduce stress by sleeping, over-eating, drinking, or taking drugs, believing that they can forget about the stressful situation by changing the state of their mind. This is a dangerous way to deal with stress, because instead of learning constructive stress-reducing techniques, these temporary actions simply drown our stress or drug our minds, leaving the real roots of stress still in place.

The Key to Managing Stress

The overriding key to managing stress is to find a way to take greater control of the situation that is producing the stress. For example, if we feel a great deal of stress about an exam, it helps to put extra time into studying for it, since we will feel more confident about the material and be less apt to struggle with questions.

Another important stress management tool is to use different forms of relaxation to reduce the overall feeling of stress, such as by taking a yoga class. For others, the best way to deal with stress is to take some time out to exercise or play a sport, which can reduce the stress level and divert attention to another activity.

Attacking the Root Cause of the Stress

☞ **Consider modifying your course load if you feel you have too many academic demands.** Plan to make up a course during the summer so you have a lighter load during the semester. Modifying the pace of your education does not mean you are compromising your overall academic or career goals.

☞ **Learn to use your time more efficiently,** and eliminate unnecessary or extra activities or time demands that are competing with your academic goals. With more time you can pace yourself better, rebalance your life, and get more sleep

☞ **Be realistic about your abilities and performance.** If engineering turns out not to be your thing, change your major to something else, such as environmental science or economics. Deal with both success and failure realistically. We are not normally good at everything. Find the field that fits your abilities and talents and be willing to change your direction.

☞ **Don't "drift along" in troublesome or emotionally draining relationships or situations.** Take steps to resolve the problems, or consider ending the relationship or experience.

☞ **Make time to be with significant others** in relationships that are trusting and reciprocal, and that leave you feeling energized.

☞ **Find time every day for some form of relaxation or fun,** such as watching your favorite show, exercising, laughing with a friend, or spending needed time alone.

☞ **Get a sufficient amount of sleep so you can perform at your best.**

Techniques to Learn for Managing Stress

To get relief from stress, it is necessary to find ways to help let go of stress and simultaneously invigorate the mind and body. Here are some recommendations:

☞ **Do exercises to relax your neck and shoulders.**

☞ **Do stretching exercises.**

☞ **Get a massage.**

☞ **Go to the gym and exercise.** Physical exercise strengthens both mind and body.

☞ **Do aerobic exercises,** as they are an especially effective type of stress relief.

☞ **Try to direct your thoughts to subjects or places that give you comfort.** Take a mental vacation for a little while. Involve yourself in a favorite hobby like reading or playing music, or think about a forthcoming trip or getaway.

☞ **Learn to meditate.** There are many good sources to teach you how to do it on the Internet or in the library.

☞ **Just take a break, make a phone call, or watch a movie.**

☞ **Go for a walk and get your thoughts together.** Be inspired by the beauty of a park or another special place.

☞ **Seek comfort and reassurance from your friends and family.**

☞ **Try to laugh at yourself or at least find humor the world around you.**

☞ **Get a pet that gives you comfort and reduces your anxiety level.**

☞ **Pursue a hobby or sport that you especially enjoy.**

Be True to Yourself

☞ **Recognize your strengths and weaknesses,** and tailor your life to capitalize on those strengths, and avoid the areas you find difficult and stressful.

☞ **Determine a level of stress that you can deal with,** and get help from counselors and health professionals if your stress level gets out of bounds.

☞ **Realize that anxiety and stress, if left uncontrolled, can lead to more serious conditions,** such as insomnia or depression.

☞ **Don't try to be a hero.** Get help immediately if your stress level is too high, if you aren't getting enough quality sleep, or if you feel desperate.

☞ **Remember, college stress is a widespread problem.** You are not the first to feel it, and college counselors can help you deal with it.

Chapter 81

Brief Relaxation Exercises

Texas A&M Student Counseling Service,
College Station, Texas

On the following pages are descriptions of some brief relaxation exercises that you may wish to employ during your day: in between classes, before exams, while studying, before a presentation or speech, prior to a big date or an appointment.

General Directions

☞ **Gentle Beginning:** For all of these exercises, it is best to be seated, eyes closed, feet flat on the floor or crossed at the ankles, and hands resting comfortably in the lap. Begin each exercise with a deep breath that you let out gently. As you let it out, feel yourself beginning to relax already.

☞ **Gentle Arousal:** After the exercise, slowly and gently activate by breathing a little more deeply, wiggling your fingers and toes, and opening your eyes at your own rate.

Exercise 1: Tense-Relax

(Gentle Beginning first)

Clench your fists. While keeping them clenched, pull your forearms tightly up against your upper arms. While keeping those muscles tense, tense all the muscles in you legs. While keeping all those tense, clench your jaws and shut your eyes fairly tight…not too tightly. Now while holding all those tense positions, take a deep breath and hold it for 5 seconds…Then, let everything go all at once. Feel yourself letting go of all your tensions. Just enjoy that feeling for a minute as your muscles let go more and more. Actually, if we had a finely-tuned electromyograph hooked up to you measuring the level of tension in your muscles, it would show that you relax more and more and more as you repeat the activity for up to 20 minutes. Just enjoy focusing, gently, on letting go.

(End with Gentle Arousal)

Exercise 2: Heaviness and Warmth

(Gentle Beginning first)

Just imagine that your feet and legs are getting heavier and heavier and warmer and warmer. It's almost as if you are wearing some lead boots. Feet and legs heavy and warm, heavy and warm. Now, imagine your stomach and the whole central portion of your body getting warm… warm and relaxed. My forehead is cool…cool…relaxed and cool. And my breathing is regular…easy and regular. Just feel the warm and heaviness spread all over the body.

(End with Gentle Arousal)

Exercise 3: Breathing Your Body Away

(Gentle Beginning first)

Gently focus your attention on your feet and legs. Be aware of all the sensations from your feet and legs. Now, inhale a long, slow breath, and as you do, breathe in all the sensations from your feet and legs. In your mind's eye, imagine that you are erasing this part of your body. Now, as you exhale, breathe out all those sensations. Once again, breathe in your feet and legs, and exhale it from your body, so that, in your mind you can see only from your hips up. Now, with another long breath, breathe in all the parts of your body to your neck, and, as you exhale, breathe it away…Now, beginning with your fingers, breathe in your fingers, hands, wrists and arms, and exhale them away…Now, your neck and head… as you breathe in, imagine your neck and head being erased and, now, breathe them away. Go back over the whole body in one breath, beginning with the feet. A long slow breath in, and as you do, erase any little parts that still remain. Now, a long slow breath out, as you exhale all the remaining parts. Just sit quietly for a minute and enjoy feeling yourself relax deeper and deeper.

(End with Gentle Arousal)

Exercise 4: A Favorite Scene, Place, or Person

(Gentle Beginning first)

As you're sitting quietly, recall, in your mind, the most relaxing thought you can. Perhaps it's a favorite place, a vacation spot or favorite retreat of some sort; or it might be a person with whom you feel at peace, or some scene—a sunset, or whatever works for you. Take a few seconds to get that in mind…Now, see or imagine that in your mind. Be sure to feel those good feelings you have when you are in that place or with that person. Just let them take over your whole awareness…If your thoughts wander, just take them gently back to that peaceful, relaxing place.

(End with Gentle Arousal)

Exercise 5: Ideal Relaxation

(Gentle Beginning first)

With your eyes closed, take a moment to create, in your mind's eye, an ideal spot for relaxation. You can make it a real or an imagined place and furnish it any way you want. Wear the clothes you are most comfortable in. Enjoy, now, in your mind, going there. You'll want to feel at ease and mellow as you lounge in your ideal place for relaxation. Just enjoy it for a minute…

(End with Gentle Arousal)

Exercise 6: Cool Air In, Warm Air Out

(Gentle Beginning first)

With your eyes closed, and while relaxing quietly, gently focus on the end of your nose. As you breathe in, feel the air coming in the tip of your nose. As you breathe out, feel the air coming out the tip of your nose… Notice that the air coming in is cooler than the air going out…Gently focus on the cool air coming in, and the warm air going out. If your attention wanders, just gently bring it back to the tip of your nose…

(End with Gentle Arousal)

Exercise 7: Focus on a Word

(Gentle Beginning first)

Pick some word which has good associations for you—a word which you associate with relaxation, comfort, peace. It could be words such as "serenity, cool, peaceful, joy, free," etc…Now, just let that word hold the center of your thoughts…After a while, perhaps your mind will drift to other gentling, restful thoughts. If so, just let it wander…When it does drift to stressful thoughts, move back to your original word.

(End with Gentle Arousal)

Exercise 8: Something for Use Anywhere

(Gentle Beginning first)

With practice, you will become more adept at relaxing while awake, anywhere. As you do, here's a way to let yourself relax while going about your day. You can do it while walking, sitting in class, taking a test, on a date, etc. First, smile. Yes, smile to remind yourself that you don't actually have all the cares of the world on your shoulder—only a few of them. Then, take a long, deep breath, and let it out. Now, take a second long deep breath, and as you let it out, feel yourself releasing the tensions in your mind and in your body. Just let yourself relax more and more, as you continue whatever you were doing.

(End with Gentle Arousal)

Chapter 82

Dealing with Depression

University of Texas at Dallas
Student Counseling Center

Depression Facts

☞ **More than 13 million Americans** experience a depressive disorder each year.

☞ **Two out of three students** who suffer from depression never get help.

☞ **Treatments for depression are successful** more than 80 percent of the time.

☞ **Depression is known to weaken the immune system,** increasing susceptibility to physical illness.

☞ **Women are twice as likely** to be diagnosed with depression as men.

☞ **In men, irritability, anger, or discouragement** may be indicators of depression.

☞ **Suicide is the second leading cause of death** among college students.

All of us have felt "down" or discouraged at times when things were not going well. There are normal variations in moods over time and even day-to-day. However, depression is a disturbance in mood where you may feel particularly unhappy, discouraged, lonely, or negative toward yourself. Depression may range from mild to severe depending upon the associated symptoms and the extent the condition interferes with everyday functioning. In milder forms, depressed moods are usually brief and may have little effect on everyday activities. Moderate to severe depression includes symptoms that are more intense, last longer, and tend to interfere more with school, work, and social functioning.

Symptoms of Depression

There are a number of symptoms of depression. Below is a list of the most common.

> » *Feelings of sadness or emptiness*

> » *Inability to experience pleasure—even from activities that you used to enjoy*

> » *Feeling worthless, guilty, or hopeless*

> » *Isolating from others*

> » *Physical ailments*

> » *Fatigue*

> » *Lack of motivation*

> » *Irritability*

> » *Indecisiveness*

> » *Difficulty concentrating*

> » *Changes in sleeping and/or eating habits*

> » *Suicidal thoughts, feelings, or behaviors*

Why does someone become depressed?

Depression can be caused by biological, genetic, or psychological factors. Common triggers for depression (especially for college students) include transitioning to a new environment, academic difficulties, family conflict, the loss of a significant relationship, or concerns about the future. Depressive episodes can occur without identifiable causes. Depression is not the result of personal failure or lack of will power.

What should I do if I feel depressed?

Take time to assess why you are feeling down. In many cases, feeling sad is an expected and appropriate reaction to a situation; however, when these feelings last for an extended period of time or significantly interfere with your ability to function, it might be wise to change your situation.

☞ **Increase Social Support**

>> *Talk to friends or family.*

>> *Confide in others.*

☞ **Explore Thoughts, Feelings, and Problem Solving**

>> *Write about your situation in a journal.*

>> *Allow yourself to experience your feelings.*

>> *If you are angry, find a safe way to express it. Cry if you need to do so.*

>> *Replace negative thinking with realistic thinking.*

>> *Break large tasks into small ones, set manageable goals.*

☞ **Maintain Health/Exercise**

>> *Maintain healthy eating habits—junk food, caffeine, and alcohol can cause mood swings.*

>> *Workout.*

>> *Join an intramural team.*

>> *Attend yoga classes.*

» *Get enough sleep.*

» *Don't abuse alcohol/drugs.*

☞ **Practice Spirituality**

» *Participate in religious services.*

» *Talk to clergy.*

» *Read inspirational material.*

» *Meditate, pray.*

☞ **Engage in Fun and Rewarding Activities**

» *Do things you enjoy.*

» *Resume old hobbies or learn new ones.*

» *Volunteer in community service activities.*

Treatment of Depression

It is important to remember that depression is treatable. If symptoms of depression are interfering in you ability to perform daily functions or are causing significant distress, you should consider seeing a professional. There are a variety of very successful interventions in the treatment of depression. Psychotherapy or medication are effective interventions for treating the majority of depressive illnesses. Research studies have found a combination of the two to be the most effective treatment available. The type of treatment that is appropriate for you will depend on your specific symptoms, history, situational factors, and personal preference. A professional can answer any questions or concerns you may have about treatment.

Helping Someone who is Depressed

If someone you know is dealing with depression, the most important thing to remember as you help someone with depression is to remain supportive. Blaming the depression on the person, trying to "make them snap out of it," and other confrontational techniques can backfire and make the situation worse. It is important first to let the person know that you are concerned about her or him, want to help and are willing to be a resource. The way that you help may range from just listening to recommending that the person contact a mental health care provider for assistance.

Danger Signals of Suicide risk

☞ **Depression:** Most depressed people are not suicidal, but most suicidal people are depressed.

☞ **Talking about death or suicide:** People who commit suicide often talk about it directly or indirectly. Be alert to statements like, "My family would be better off without me." Sometimes those suicidal people talk as if they are saying goodbye

☞ **Planning for suicide:** Suicidal individuals often arrange to put their affairs in order. They give away articles they value and pay off debts.

Helping a Suicidal Friend

☞ **Take it seriously and don't ignore it:** Approach your friend and, without judgment, let him or her know your concern. "I'm worried about the changes I've seen in you lately. I hope you won't blow me off or think I'm putting you down. I want us to be able to talk."

☞ **Listen actively:** Sit facing your friend in a relaxed, open position. Keep eye contact and nod your head to show that you're paying attention. Paraphrase what you hear from your friend's perspective; "You felt hurt? or "It sounds like you were really disappointed."

☞ **Describe your observations:** "You've been missing class…isolating yourself…not eating … don't seem happy… drinking more…"

☞ **Offer your recommendations:** "I'm not sure, but I wonder if you're depressed. There's help available on campus. The Student Counseling Center offers confidential services ."

☞ **Don't minimize your concern:** If your friend says "Do you think I need help?" say "Yes, I do. That's a great idea. Can I stay with you while you call/walk to the school counseling center to make an appointment?"

Chapter 83

How Counseling Helps

 Reprinted with permission from the University of Kansas Counseling and Psychological Services (CAPS)

S ome people think counseling is only for people with depression or severe mental illness, but counseling can help anybody going through a tough time in many areas of life.

☞ **Counseling helps people to pinpoint problems and understand aspects of the problems that may be improved.**

> » *Identify negative or illogical thinking patterns that contribute to feelings of hopelessness and helplessness, to develop a more positive outlook.*

> » *Explore learned thoughts and behaviors that create or maintain problems.*

> » *Regain a sense of control and pleasure in life.*

> » *Encourage support from family and friends.*

> » *Find solutions to life's problems.*

> » *Discover personal strengths and how to use those strengths to grow stronger in other areas.*

Counseling offers people the opportunity to identify the factors that contribute to their difficulties and to deal effectively with the psychological, behavioral, interpersonal, and situational causes of those difficulties.

Myths About Counseling

☞ *Counseling is a sign of weakness.*

Nothing could be further from the truth. It takes courage to address problem areas and examine painful feelings. Entering counseling is taking the first step in resolving difficulties.

☞ *Counseling is only for people with serious emotional problems.*

Counseling is like seeing a doctor – you don't go to a doctor only if you have a heart attack. It can be helpful to see a doctor if you have the flu.

Students often seek and benefit from counseling for issues such as academic difficulty, relationship problems, adjustment concerns, managing stress, or choosing a major.

Suggestions for Referring a Friend to Your School's Counseling Center

» *Express your concern privately.*

» *Do not to use labels (e.g., "You have an eating disorder.")*

» *Talk about specific, observable behaviors that may suggest the need for counseling (e.g., "I am concerned because I noticed you have missed several classes.")*

» *Emphasize that counseling can be an effective tool for dealing with everyday problems.*

» *Offer to make the referral or to be with your friend while he or she calls the counseling center.*

» *Be ready to provide the phone number of your school's counseling center to your friend.*

» *If appropriate, go to the counseling center with your friend.*

» *Remember that you are not responsible for making the person ready to change, but you can provide him or her with the opportunity to get as-sistance.*

Counseling Center Services Increase College Success

» *Rummel et al. (1999) found that the majority of college students leaving their university were in academically good standing, and that nearly one in four left due to personal problems.*

» *Students who participate in counseling show positive changes in measured quality of life satisfaction, which is more predictive of student retention than overall GPA levels, high school grades, or SAT scores levels (Clark, Wettersen, & Mason, 1999; Osberg & Polland, 2002).*

» *Researchers at Iowa State University (Wilson et al, 1997) found that students who received 1–7 counseling sessions had a 14 percent higher retention rate than non-counseled peers. Retention rates showed similar gains (12 percent higher) among University of Wyoming students who participated in counseling (Turner & Berry, 2000).*

References

Osberg, T.M., & Polland, D.L. (2002). Comparative accuracy of the MMPI-2 and the MMPI-A in the diagnosis of psychopathology in 18 year olds. *Psychological Assessment,* 14, 164-169.

Rummel, A., Acton, D., Costello, S., & Pielow, G. (1999). Is all retention good? An empirical study. *College Student Journal,* 33, 241-246.

Turner, A.L., & Berry, T.R. (2000). Counseling center contributions to student retention and graduation: A longitudinal assessment. *Journal of College Student Development,* 41, 627-63.

Wilson, S.B., Mason, T.W., Ewing, M.J. (1997). Evaluating the impact of receiving university-based counseling services on student retention. *Journal of Counseling Psychology,* 44, 316-320.

Part XIX

Choosing a Major

Chapter 84

Assessing Your Interests and Skills

 Dr. Kay Grimnes, Professor of Biology, Alma College, Alma, Michigan

Identify Your Strengths!

☞ **A new focus.** The big buzz in personal, college, and management development right now is called the "Strengths Movement." All over the country, in colleges, in corporations, in bookstores, and on websites, it seems like it's the strategy that everyone is embracing. The general idea that you get further by focusing your effort on your strengths rather than on your weaknesses is hotly debated, but interesting because of its power to motivate and focus the effort of students and employees.

☞ **Strengths, not weaknesses.** We often focus on our weaknesses, as if spending all our time fixing what's weak is really going to help us achieve excellence. Bringing up a skill to functional competence is necessary; it's one reason colleges have placement exams and graduation competencies. And, like it or not, you need basic skills in a number of areas, especially math and communication (both speaking and writing) in order to interact with and be employed in the working world. By this point in your life, you may already know if you are "good" at math or science, or have a special gift for a specific area. The strengths movement is about pushing real and intentional energy into the areas of greatest ability.

Studies on people who love what they do and are successful in life (whatever their actual job might be) show that it is identifying and supporting our strengths that can make the biggest difference in our satisfaction with our lives. Living a life based on our strengths (what we love doing and are good at) can be an expected (but unacknowledged) goal of college students.

☞ **Not by accident.** It takes curiosity, courage and a sense of optimism in order to determine and acknowledge what you are good at! But when those strengths align with career goals… look out! It's rocket fuel for your future success!

Finding Your Strengths!

You can start to identify your talents and skills in a number of ways! Chip Anderson, an authority on assessing personal strengths, identified these general qualities as potential strengths indicators:

☞ **Your responses, and your feelings can hint at your strengths:**

» *Your hopes, dreams and longings*

» *Experiencing joy and delight when engaged in the activity*

» *Experiencing a sense of destiny or "rightness"*

» *Being passionate about something*

☞ **Ability/Acquisition of knowledge and skills can indicate strengths:**

» *A deep sense of satisfaction about learning*

» *Places where your learning seems rapid*

» *Any area with instant insights and understandings*

☞ **Actual performance parameters can indicate strengths:**

» *Where you perform at levels of excellence, even if for short periods*

» *Consistent patterns of success in a particular role, context or set of tasks*

> » *Doing something well and almost effortlessly*

☞ **Defining flow.** Mihaly Csikszentmihalyi (pronounced "cheeks-sent-me-high"), a noted Hungarian psychologist, is credited with using the word "flow" to describe moments of peak experience closely tied to our deepest self. He defined "flow" as the state in which we are so completely absorbed in a task that we barely notice the passage of time. Otherwise known as "being in the zone" or the Zen sense of "mindfulness," most of us are familiar with the concept of flow. It turns out that you can use moments of flow as landmarks of your strengths. You might want to read Csikszentmihalyi's book called "Flow: The Psychology of Optimal Experience" or search for more information on the web about his ideas.

☞ **Commercial website tests.** *The Clifton Strengths Finder 2.0, Strengths Quest,* (an older version of the same text) and *Now, Discover your Strengths* are a series of books and related websites built around the Gallup Poll Organization's work on positive psychology and research on the lives of thousands of energized, satisfied people. They code your responses into 34 Signature themes. The site must be accessed by a code (one use only) sold with one of these books. This movement has a lot of strength behind it (pun intended) and connects to both education and business applications.

☞ **Federal Government Assessment Tools/O*Net Career Exploration Tools** *(www.onetcenter.org / tools.html)* Valuable, free, and downloadable tests are available from the Occupational Information Network, a federal government service, including an Interest Profiler and an Ability Profiler, along with two assessment tests dealing with work preferences. These tools provide a useful starting point for understanding your range of interests side by side with your aptitudes and abilities. They will help you narrow down your career directions and lead you to specific types of employment.

☞ **State Government Assessment Tools.** Here are two examples of free state-provided assessment tools available;

» **ISEEK: Assessments (www.iseek.org)** ISEEK is a career, education, and job resource website provided by the state of Minnesota. You can examine your skills, interests, values, and traits with three different personal assessment tools to learn about future career directions.

» **North Carolina Career Resource Network (www.soicc. state.nc.us/soicc)** North Carolina's Career Resource Network website has several self-assessment tools and links to more. You can also find information on different careers.

☞ **Other possibilities:**

» *Visit your school's career center for additional resources or pointers.*

» *Talk to your advisor, instructors, parents, and peers to learn how they discovered their strengths.*

Chapter 85

Thinking About Your Major

Reprinted with permission from Dr. Patrice DiQuinzio, Associate Provost for Academic Services, Washington College, Chestertown, Maryland

A t most colleges, especially liberal arts colleges, first year students are not required to declare a major. By their second semester at college some first year students are ready to choose a major, but often students don't have to declare a major until the end of their sophomore year. Here are some thoughts and ideas to consider as you ponder this decision.

Follow your passion

Passionate interest or curiosity about a subject motivates you to do your best work and keeps you engaged when the course material and assignments get more difficult. Strong interest also helps you to connect your other experiences, including the work you do in required courses, to the subject matter you're passionate about.

Think creatively about how to follow your passion. If you're curious about why people do what they do, maybe you're thinking about majoring in psychology. But you can pursue that interest in a sociology or history major, too. If you're interested in the past, you'll probably consider a history major. But you can also pursue that interest in anthropology. If you're interested in human biology, you're probably thinking about majoring in biology. But you also learn a lot about human biology as a psychology major. And don't overlook interdisciplinary programs, such as environmental studies, gender studies, humanities, international studies and American studies, where you can pursue your interests from a variety of perspectives or pursue several related interests.

Play to your strengths

Assess your intellectual and personal strengths honestly and choose a major that requires your strengths. Maybe you have a knack for writing, or are particularly good at math, or you're good at research, or you're very creative. The staff at your college career center can help you assess your strengths and talents. They will have several interesting tools, such as books, quizzes, and online inventories that you can use to get a better sense of what you're good at.

Consider many different ways in which you can play to your strengths in choosing a major. For example, creativity is a plus in the arts, but it's also an advantage in the sciences, for instance, in designing good experiments. If you love to read and have a strong sense of narrative, you may be considering an English major. But those qualities are also strengths in the study of history. If you're good at math, you can consider a math major. But in majors like business management, economics, physics, or computer science, your math skills will also be an advantage. Maybe a double major is the best way for you to develop all of your strengths and talents.

Consider a minor

Most colleges' minors can complement any major. A minor gives you a different perspective on your major area, an opportunity to develop skills not emphasized in your major, and a chance to develop career-related skills. With a minor you can also pursue something you're interested in or truly love, but don't want to make a career focus.

Majoring in the humanities—English, philosophy, art, music, or a foreign language? Consider a minor in business. Majoring in business? Consider a minor in a foreign language, psychology, sociology, or history. Majoring in math? Consider a minor in physics, earth and planetary science, or music. Majoring in a natural science, such as biology, chemistry, or physics? Consider a minor in philosophy. Majoring in history or political science? Consider a minor in African American studies or gender studies. Majoring in economics? Consider a minor in psychology. You get the idea.

Prepare for a career

Choose your major and then consider careers that require the knowledge and skills you will develop in your major and find out how to prepare for those careers. Whether you major in anthropology, music, chemistry, communication, philosophy, or history, there are things you can do—even in your first year—to prepare for the job market. Plan now for internships where you can put your knowledge and skills to use, study abroad or gain other international experiences, and participation in extra-curricular activities where you can develop marketable skills, especially leadership skills. Talk to everyone you know in careers you're interested in and ask them about what they do and how they got there.

Prepare for further education

If you want to go to graduate or professional school right after college or you plan to go back to school after working for a couple of years, find out in your first year what you need to do to prepare. Meet with your college's pre-professional advisors. Talk to professors in the field you might pursue in grad school; ask them what are the best programs for your interests and what you should do as an undergraduate to prepare.

Also look into whether your college has dual degree programs or 3–2 programs, where you can get both your liberal arts degree and a degree in a field like nursing or other health care undergraduate degrees, pharmacy, or engineering, usually in five years. In most of these programs, you spend three years at your liberal arts college followed by two years at a university working on your professional degree. If you're interested in such a program, it's essential that you work with the program advisor from the beginning of your college career. That way you'll be sure to take the right courses in your first three years at college and be ready to move on to professional school.

But it's almost the end of freshman year and I'm still undecided!

No worries—think back over the courses you've taken so far and consider what you found most interesting in those courses. Ask your professors to suggest courses or other opportunities where you can pursue those interests. Continue taking courses to fulfill graduation requirements; they are further opportunities to discover your interests and talents.

And consider an independently designed major, based on your interests, if you feel that your college's majors don't address your interests in the way you want to pursue them. Check your college's website or ask your advisor or your college's registrar about the process for designing an independent major.

If you have another year before you must declare a major, take the time and make the most of it!

Chapter 86

Academic Risk-Taking

Starting Out!® Research Group

Introduction

Throughout school students are taught a pre-set curriculum of knowledge, from basic reading and writing and elementary arithmetic, to biology, chemistry, and world history. During  high school we read assigned books for our classes, usually write papers on assigned topics, and receive grades that reflect our performance relative to the required curriculum.

There are limited opportunities in high school to go outside these strict guidelines and take on new academic challenges and risks. But there are some. We can read any additional books we choose on our own time, on any subjects that interest us; we can pursue out-of-school volunteer projects from which we can learn; we can take courses at local community colleges, especially during the summer; and we can do independent research and compete in science fairs and academic competitions that increase the breadth of our knowledge in a specific field.

But it is the transition to college that opens up the real opportunities for independent learning and academic risk taking, and these are some of the most important aspects of higher learning. As with some forms of investing, a greater risk may produce a greater personal reward.

What it Means to Take Academic Risks in College

Students have extensive choices in college, since they can select their own courses beyond those that may be required, perform original research and independent work, choose their own major, and even pre-test their career interests with internships with local organizations during the summer. College is all about academic risk-taking.

Here are some of the benefits of academic risk taking:

1. **New Opportunities for Personal Growth**: By venturing into uncharted waters, with courses available on almost every subject, students become exposed to a whole world of knowledge, to global problems, to government policy, to social issues, and to the forefront of technological change.

2. **Academic Risk-Taking Builds Leadership Skills**: When you venture beyond your known world into the unknown, you become an explorer, surprising yourself with your newly-acquired knowledge. As your knowledge in new areas grows, you often take leadership positions in courses and discussions, building upon your growing knowledge of a new subject. As a result, you may select a college major and become a leader in your department, or discover a powerful skill, that opens up entirely new opportunities for the future.

3. **Leaders Are Risk-Takers**: Just as academic risk-taking may lead to leadership opportunities, successful leaders learn that they must take risks to move ahead and be successful. Whether in the classroom or at work, a good leader is willing to take calculated risks to perform original work, create original ideas, and find new solutions to old problems.

4. **Academic Risk-Takers Learn to Accept Disappointment or Failure**: The student who is willing to try a course in physics or economics only to find out that these subjects are too difficult is still ahead of the game. Learning what you do best requires taking risks,

and sometimes we win and sometimes we lose, but it is always a valuable experience.

5. **Discoveries**: Research is inherently a risk-taking process. We delve into new areas, test hypotheses, see relationships and causes and effects, and especially demonstrate a willingness to try the untried. This type of independent, adventurous spirit leads to solutions to complex problems, new inventions, and greater understanding.

Academic Risk-Taking Builds Goal-Setting and Analytical Skills

☞ When you move into uncharted waters, you often have a goal in mind, or create a goal once you have begun your exploration. This is the way research often works. You set out to understand a particular problem (your preliminary goal) but may uncover new and unexpected directions, and ultimately may establish a different or more ambitious goal, or just a more focused goal.

☞ Academic Risk-Taking leads to evaluating alternative paths and directions. You need to examine the potential directions you could take, and make a decision about where you want to start.

☞ Academic Risk-Taking requires an assessment of risks and rewards: Some academic choices seem to be riskier than others, and may pose or create new problems. Consider what you have to gain (and lose) and whether you are taking a worthwhile risk from an academic point of view. For example, selecting a major without real thought and preliminary exposure to the field may not be sensible. Take a few course in your proposed major before you make your final choice. Conversely, don't abruptly abandon your direction just because it is more difficult than you expected. Usually hard work pays off. No pain, no gain.

Academic Exploration and Risk-Taking is Exciting and Pays Off

College is expensive, time-consuming, and academically challenging, but at the same time it offers an exciting launching pad for our working lives. With so many choices and opportunities in college, it is well worth adding a dose of adventurous spirit to your academic life. Take chances, and above all, take advantage of the opportunities before you.

Finding a new talent, ability, or field for a career is exciting and personally enriching. When you discover what you like and where your talents lie, you feel good about yourself, and know that you have accomplished the basic mission of college.

Academic risk-taking pays off. Whenever you try something new you begin to build the tools to take on other opportunities and risks, and soon you learn that life itself offers a constant menu of risks and rewards, not just academically, but in our social, family, and working lives as well.

Part XX

Looking Ahead

Chapter 87

Staying on Track: A 4-Year Career Plan

 Colorado State University-Pueblo Career Center, Pueblo, Colorado

Below is a checklist of activities if you are planning on attending a four-year college. Use this checklist to keep your career planning on track.

First Year

☞ **Enroll in a career planning class** within your academic department, if available.

☞ **Begin to identify your interests, skills, and values.** Visit your school's Career Center or Student Academic Services.

☞ **Explore all majors and develop a tentative curriculum.** Meet with your academic advisor.

☞ **Become familiar with the resources available in the Career Center, you school's library, other university libraries, and your community library.** Research careers to determine the skills and requirements needed, projected supply and demand, and entry-level salaries.

☞ **Become familiar with the programs and services** offered by the Career Center.

Sophomore Year

☞ **Continue to explore career possibilities** related to your academic major, and to your interests, skills, and values.

☞ **Confirm your choice of an academic major** by the end of your sophomore year. Meet with an academic advisor.

☞ **Learn about programs offered by companies and organizations** that provide career-related work experiences including internships, cooperative education (co-op) programs, and summer employment.

☞ **Use the resources in the library, your community library, or other university libraries** to research companies and organizations of interest to you for possible internships, co-op programs, and summer employment.

☞ **Attend special programs or workshops** sponsored by the Career Center.

☞ **Improve your interpersonal communication, leadership, and social skills** through involvement in campus or community organizations, student activities, and residence life.

☞ **Begin developing a personal portfolio** by collecting writing samples, awards, certificates, news clippings, thank you cards, letters of appreciation, photographs, and even videos. The purpose of the portfolio will be to document your skills and accomplishments to prospective employers.

Junior Year

☞ **Attend a Career Fair or Educator's Fair at your school.** Attend fairs at other universities or citywide job fairs in other locations.

☞ **Continue to research your career options** and decide which are most appealing to you.

☞ **Focus on selecting classes and a major field of study** which will help achieve your career and life goals.

☞ **Arrange informational interviews** with people in the career fields that interest you.

☞ **Take leadership roles** in campus or community organizations, student activities, or residence life.

☞ **Pick up copies of free literature** from the Career Center discussing careers, job hunting, and graduate schools.

☞ **Attend graduate school fairs** to learn more about attending graduate school, if interested. Use library resources and the Internet to research schools. Request application materials.

☞ **If planning to go on to graduate school, purchase appropriate test materials and practice taking the test.** Take the test(s) during the spring/summer semesters.

☞ **Research sources of financial aid** for graduate school.

Senior Year

☞ **Participate in an internship even though it might delay graduation.** In today's competitive job market, the valuable work experience you will gain IS worth the delay.

☞ **Gain valuable experience and improve your transferable skills** by continuing to actively participate in campus or community organizations by serving in leadership positions.

☞ **Attend workshops or other special programs** sponsored by the Career Center.

☞ **Become familiar with job posting services** available on the Internet.

☞ **Attend a career fair or educator's fair.** Attend fairs at other universities or city-wide job fairs in other locations.

☞ **Begin contacting employers** by using a targeted, self-directed job search.

☞ **Purchase a professional presentation portfolio from an office supply store.**

Organize your portfolio so the materials effectively present you to a prospective employer in a professional manner.

☞ **Interview with companies.** Be sure to check with the Career Center to see if any companies interview on campus.

☞ **If interested in graduate or professional school, meet all application deadlines** and requirements during the fall term.

☞ **If applying to graduate school, make contact with potential reference writers.** Confirm letters have been sent.

Chapter 88

Choosing a Career and Lifestyle

Upon graduating from college, you will not only have to determine what career interests you, but your life goals, such as how you would like to live, where you would like to work, and whether or not you would like to have a family. The following information can help you start thinking about these questions.

Part 1: Choosing a Career

Reprinted with permission from Texas A&M University, Student Counseling Center, College Station, Texas

Here is a basic outline of steps to take in choosing a career.

☞ **Identify your interests, values, abilities, and personality.**

☞ **Generate a list of occupations** that best fit these interests, values, abilities, and personality.

☞ **Narrow your list to those occupations** that you feel are worth further investigation.

☞ **Talk with people actually employed in the occupations** in which you are interested. Ask if it is possible to spend some work hours with those persons for an agreed-upon period of time. This will give you an idea of the day-to-day tasks of the occupations. Also try to find materials to read or videos to watch about the occupations you are interested in to give you an idea of the daily working life of someone in a particular occupation.

☞ **Attempt to gain first-hand experience** in work settings of interest through volunteer work, part-time or summer employment, internships, or cooperative education.

☞ **Decide which career to pursue.**

☞ **Develop your academic degree plan** with your advisor so that you are prepared to find a job in your chosen profession.

Part 2: Understanding Your Life Goals
Reprinted with Permission from the University of Texas at Dallas Student Counseling Center Dallas, Texas

Finding your life goals can be daunting; however, if you examine the following six areas of investigation and answer the questions, you will be well on your way to recognizing those goals.

➤ **Increased Energy**

» What gives you a sense of being alive, energetic, having possibilities?

» At what activities do you feel energized, even though you had to work hard at them?

➤ **Attention/fascination**

» What captures your attention and holds you "spellbound"?

» What do you continue to return to when you have some time?

» What do you make time to do even when you are busy?

» About what do you daydream?

➤ **Righteous Indignation**

» What would you talk about if given an hour of prime time television to influence the nation or the world?

» What makes you mad that you would like to correct in other people or the world?

➤ Admiration of Others

» What do other people have or do that you would like for yourself?

➤ Recognizing "this" is your place

» What have you done that feels "just right"?

» Where did it take place?

» What do you feel like you were born to do?

➤ Role Models

» Whose work or life do you admire?

» Who inspires or moves you?

Accomplishing your goals

Now that you have a sense of how to identify life goals, use the following five steps to accomplish them:

1. **Make as specific a description of the goal as possible.**
   If you were to see and hear yourself on video doing it, what would it look and sound like?

2. **Find any interior barriers** (fears and negative beliefs) that stand in the way of your goals.

3. **Identify external barriers** (in the outside world) that might obstruct the path to your goal.

4. **Make a plan** to overcome or reduce the barriers.

5. **Take action** and adjust as needed.

Chapter 89

Where and How to Look for Career Information

 U.S. Department of Labor, Bureau of Labor Statistics

L ike any major decision, selecting a career involves a lot of fact
finding. Fortunately, some of the best
informational resources are easily
accessible. You should assess career
guidance materials carefully. Information that seems out of date or glamor-

izes an occupation—overstates its earnings or exaggerates the demand for
workers, for example—should be evaluated with skepticism. Gathering as
much information as possible will help you make a more informed decision.

People You Know

☞ **One of the best resources can be those you know, such as friends and family.** They may answer some questions about a particular occupation
or put you in touch with someone who has some experience in the
field. This personal networking can be invaluable in evaluating an occupation or an employer. These people will be able to tell you about
their specific duties and training, as well as what they did or did not
like about a job. People who have worked in an occupation locally
also may be able to recommend and get you in touch with specific
employers.

Local Libraries

☞ **Libraries can be an invaluable source of information.**

Since most areas have libraries, they can be a convenient place to look for information. Also, for those who do not otherwise have access to the Internet or e-mail, many libraries provide this access.

Libraries may have information on job openings, locally and nationally; potential contacts within occupations or industries; colleges and financial aid; vocational training; individual businesses or careers; and writing résumés. Libraries frequently have subscriptions to various trade magazines that can provide information on occupations and industries. These sources often have references to organizations which can provide additional information about training and employment opportunities. Your local library also may have video materials.

If you need help getting started or finding a resource, ask your librarian for assistance.

Professional Societies, Trade Groups, and Labor Unions

☞ **These groups have information on an occupation or various related occupations with which they are associated or which they actively represent.**

This information may cover training requirements, earnings, and listings of local employers. These groups may train members or potential members themselves, or may be able to put you in contact with organizations or individuals who perform such training.

Another valuable source for finding organizations associated with occupations is *The Encyclopedia of Associations,* an annual publication that lists trade associations, professional societies, labor unions, and fraternal and patriotic organizations.

Employers

☞ **This is the primary source of information on specific jobs.**

Employers may post lists of job openings and application requirements, including the exact training and experience required, starting
wages and benefits, and advancement opportunities and career paths.

Postsecondary Institutions

☞ **Colleges, universities, and other postsecondary institutions may put a lot of
effort into helping place their graduates in good jobs** because the success
of their graduates may indicate the quality of their institution and
affect their ability to attract new students. Postsecondary institutions frequently have career centers with libraries of information
on different careers, listings of related jobs, and alumni contacts in
various professions. Career centers frequently employ career counselors who generally provide their services only to their students and
alumni. Career centers can help you build your résumé, find internships and co-ops which can lead to full-time positions, and tailor your
course selection or program to make you a more attractive job appli-
cant.

Guidance and Career Counselors

☞ **Counselors can help you make choices about which careers might suit you best.**

Counselors can help you determine what occupations suit your skills
by testing your aptitude for various types of work, and determining
your strengths and interests. Counselors can help you evaluate your
options and search for a job in your field or help you select a new field
altogether. They can also help you determine which educational or
training institutions best fit your goals, and find ways to get financial
assistance. Some counselors offer other services such as interview
coaching, résumé building, and help in filling out various forms.

Counselors in secondary schools and postsecondary institutions may arrange guest speakers, field trips, or job fairs.

➤ **Common places where guidance and career counselors can be found are:**

» High school guidance offices

» College career planning and placement offices

» Placement offices in private vocational or technical schools and institutions

» Vocational rehabilitation agencies

» Counseling services offered by community organizations

» Private counseling agencies and private practices

» State employment service offices

When using a private counselor, check to see if the counselor is experienced. One way to do so is to ask people who have used his or her services in the past. The National Board of Certified Counselors and Affiliates is an institution which accredits career counselors.

To verify the credentials of a career counselor and to find a career counselor in your area, contact:

☞ **National Board for Certified Counselor and Affiliates**
3 Terrace Way, Suite D, Greensboro, NC 27403-3660.
Internet: *www.nbcc.org/cfind*

Internet Resources

☞ **With the growing popularity of the Internet, a wide variety of career information has become easily accessible.** Many online resources include job listings, résumé posting services, and information on job fairs, training, and local wages. Many of the resources listed elsewhere in this section have Internet sites that include valuable information on potential careers. Since no single source contains all information on an occupation, field, or employer, you will likely need to use a variety of sources.

When using Internet resources, be sure that the organization is a credible, established source of information on the particular occupation. Individual companies may include job listings on their websites, and may include information about required credentials, wages and benefits, and the job's location. Contact information, such as whom to call or where to send a résumé, is typically included.

Some sources exist primarily as a web service. These services often have information on specific jobs, and can greatly aid in the job hunting process. Some commercial sites offer these services, as do federal, state, and some local governments.

CareerOneStop, a joint program by the Department of Labor and the states as well as local agencies, provides these services free of charge.

Online Sources from the Department of Labor

A major portion of the U.S. Department of Labor's Labor Market Information System is within the **CareerOneStop** site. This site includes the following sections.

✓ *America's Job Bank* allows you to search over a million job openings listed with state employment agencies.

✓ *America's Career InfoNet* provides data on employment growth and wages by occupation; the knowledge, skills, and abilities required by an occupation; and links to employers.

✓ *America's Service Locator* is a comprehensive database of career centers and information on unemployment benefits, job training, youth programs, seminars, educational opportunities, and disabled or older worker programs.

☞ **Career OneStop,** along with the National Toll-free Helpline (877-USA-JOBS) and the local One-Stop Career Centers in each state, combine to provide a wide range of workforce assistance and resources:

> **Career OneStop**
>
> *www.careeronestop.org*

☞ **Use O*NET** to find more information on specific occupations:

> **O*NET Online**
>
> *www.onetcenter.org*

☞ **Career Voyages,** in collaboration with the U.S. Department of Education, provides information on certain high-demand occupations:

> **Career Voyages**
>
> *www.careervoyages.org*

☞ **The Department of Labor's Bureau of Labor Statistics** publishes a wide range of labor market information, from regional wages for specific occupations to statistics on national, state, and area employment.

> **Bureau of Labor Statistics**
>
> *www.bls.gov*

☞ The **Career Guide to Industries** discusses careers from an industry perspective. The Career Guide is also available at your local career center and library.

> **Career Guide to Industries**
>
> *www.bls.gov / oco / cg / home.htm*

☞ **For information on occupational wages:**

> **Wage Data**
>
> *www.bls.gov / bls / blswage.htm*

☞ **For information on training, workers' rights, and job listings:**

> **Education and Training Administration**
>
> *www.doleta.gov / jobseekers*

Disabled Workers

☞ State counseling, training, and placement services for those with disabilities are available from:

State Vocational Rehabilitation Agency

www.ed.gov / Programs / EROD

☞ Information on employment opportunities, transportation, and other considerations for people with all types of disabilities is available from:

National Organization on Disability

www.nod.org / economic

910 Sixteenth St. NW., Suite 600, Washington, DC 20006.
Telephone: 202-293-5960. TTY: 202-293-5968.

☞ For information on making accommodations in the work place for people with disabilities:

Job Accommodation Network (JAN)

www.jan.wvu.edu PO Box 6080, Morgantown, WV 26506.

☞ A comprehensive federal website of disability-related resources is accessible at: *www.disabilityinfo.gov*

Blind Workers

☞ Information on the free national reference and referral service for the blind can be obtained by contacting:

National Federation of the Blind, Job Opportunities for the Blind (JOB):

www.nfb.org

1800 Johnson St., Baltimore, MD 21230.
Telephone: 410-659-9314.

Veterans

☞ Contact the nearest regional office of the U.S. Department of Labor's Veterans Employment and Training Service or **Credentialing Opportunities Online COOL** (*www.cool.army.mil/index.htm*), which explains how Army soldiers can meet civilian certification and license requirements related to their Military Occupational Specialty (MOS).

Women

For work issues affecting women:
☞ **Department of Labor, Women's Bureau**
   www.dol.gov/wb
   200 Constitution Avenue NW, Washington, DC 20210.
   Telephone: 800-827-5335.

Office of Personnel Management

Information on obtaining civilian positions within the federal government is available from the U.S. Office of Personnel Management through USA Jobs, the Federal Government's official employment information system.

This resource for locating and applying for job opportunities can be accessed through the Internet or through an interactive voice response telephone system at 703-724-1850 or TDD 978-461-8404. These numbers are not toll-free, so charges may result.

☞ **USA Jobs**
   www.usajobs.opm.gov

Military

The military employs and has information on hundreds of occupations. Information is available on the Montgomery G.I. Bill, which provides money for school and educational debt repayments. Information on military service can be provided by your local recruiting office. For more information on careers in the military:

☞ **Today's Military**
www.todaysmilitary.com

State Sources

Most states have career information delivery systems (CIDS), which may be found in secondary and postsecondary institutions, as well as libraries, job training sites, vocational-technical schools, and employment offices. A wide range of information is provided, from employment opportunities to unemployment insurance claims.

Each state has detailed information on occupations and labor markets within their respective jurisdictions. State occupational projections are available at: *www.projectionscentral.com*.

Chapter 90

An Internship Search Timeline

 University of Washington-Whitewater,
Career and Leadership Development,
Whitewater, Wisconsin

A successful internship search requires you to invest time and effort, because an internship is not and should not be a "regular" job. The following plan is designed to assist you in preparing for and conducting your search for an internship. Remember that all of the following tasks are important for finding the best internship for you.

One Year BEFORE You Want to Start an Internship

☞ **Determine your career goal by talking with a career counselor** about your interests and your professors about the learning outcomes expected in your major. Follow up with your own research. Think about your responses to the following items:

» The work I have imagined doing is…

» What really interests me is…

» The lifestyle that I would like to live is…

» The kinds of skills I have and would like to use are…

» The kind of environment in which I'd like to work is…

» The kinds of people with which I'd like to work are…

» My work values which must be met are…

» Some careers that interest me include…

☞ **Decide what you want in an internship.**

» What are three things that you want to learn/gain from an internship experience?

» Identify what you are looking for in an internship, and then prioritize your preferences:

Rank	Criteria	Your Preferences
	Geographic Location	
	Pay	
	Academic Credit	
	Time Commitment	
	Semester	Fall Spring Summer
	Industry	
	Types of Projects	
	Other	

☞ **Begin to network!**

» Networking is not just about who you know, but who knows you. It is about creating and cultivating trusting, supportive, give-and-take relationships.

» Your network begins with your family, friends, neighbors, supervisors, and instructors.

» Connect with relevant professional associations or with student organizations that have ties to these groups.

» Let your contacts know that you're looking for an internship.

9 Months or 2 Semesters BEFORE You Want to Start an Internship

☞ **Be aware of when most employers recruit for interns.**

» For a Summer Internship – January through May

» For a Fall Internship – April through August

» For a Spring Internship – September through January

☞ **IMPORTANT: Summer internships, in particular, are in high demand** which means there is more competition for these positions. Don't wait until the last minute to apply. Additionally, some summer internships may have application deadlines in November or December of the preceding year. Be alert for these deadlines.

☞ **Prepare a rough draft of your resume,** using your school's career center or online resources for assistance, and have it reviewed by a career counselor.

☞ **If you wish to earn academic credit for your internship,** talk with the faculty internship supervisor for your major on how to proceed.

☞ **Understand the criteria of a quality internship:**

» Work assignment is at a pre-professional level and clearly relates to your career goal and/or major.

» The organization acknowledges and supports your learning goals and provides an opportunity for you to develop the skills you need.

» Proper supervision is given by a professional in the field.

» The length of the assignment is clearly defined and is not listed as "on-going."

» Systems are in place for proper evaluation of and feedback on your performance at the end of the assignment.

☞ **Begin identifying potential internship opportunities** using a variety of resources and strategies.

» Search employers' websites for employment opportunities. To find employers in the geographic region of your search, explore local Chamber of Commerce websites.

» Attend job fairs.

» Network by connecting with relevant professional associations and/or career-related student organizations.

» Design your own internship! The process of developing an internship proposal does take time and effort. Schedule an appointment with your school's career center for assistance.

4 Months or 1 Semester BEFORE You Want to Start an Internship

☞ **Finalize your resume.**

☞ **Write individualized cover letters** for each opportunity you wish to apply for.

☞ **Send your application materials,** typically your resume and a cover letter, to potential sites.

☞ **Schedule a mock interview** with a career counselor.

☞ **Continue to practice your answers** to potential interview questions on your own.

☞ **Do your research** on employers before you interview with them.

☞ **Begin interviewing!**

2 Months BEFORE You Want to Start an Internship

☞ **Continue to interview.**

☞ **After each interview, write a thank you note** to the interviewer(s) and send it within 24 hours after your interview.

☞ **Continue to apply for opportunities.**

☞ **If you will be earning academic credit,** check in with your faculty internship supervisor regarding the registration process.

Once You Secure an Internship

☞ **When you accept an offer,** get all of the important details: start date, work hours, etc.

☞ **Contact other employers** you submitted application materials to and withdraw your application.

☞ **Write thank you notes** to the people in your network who helped you and let them know that you got an internship.

☞ **Start your internship and be successful!**